THE DARKNESS LIFTS

On April 15, 1942, His Majesty King George VI made the following announcement: "To honor her brave people I award the George Cross to the island fortress of Malta, to bear witness to a heroism and devotion that will long be famous in history."

Exactly a week after the ceremony in the Palace Square, the Maltese were given an omen that the long night of devastation had passed its darkest hour.

Early on the morning of April 22 the air was filled with a great roaring. Yet the sirens were silent. Uncertainly, the Maltese looked up. They saw that overhead the sky was filled with unfamiliar planes, planes with strange elliptical wings.

The Spitfires had come at last. . . .

THE BANTAM WAR BOOK SERIES

This series of books is about a world on fire.

The carefully chosen volumes in the Bantam War Book Series cover the full dramatic sweep of World War II. Many are eyewitness accounts by the men who fought in a global conflict as the world's future hung in the balance. Fighter pilots, tank commanders and infantry captains, among many others, recount exploits of individual courage. They present vivid portraits of brave men, true stories of gallantry, moving sagas of survival and stark tragedies of untimely death.

In 1933 Nazi Germany marched to become an empire that was to last a thousand years. In only twelve years that empire was destroyed, and ever since, the country has been bisected by her conquerors. Italy relinquished her colonial lands, as did Japan. These were the losers. The winners also lost the empires they had so painfully seized over the centuries. And one, Russia, lost over twenty million dead.

Those wartime 1940s were a simple, even a hopeful time. Hats came in only two colors, white and black, and after an initial battering the Allied nations started on a long and laborious march toward victory. It was a time when sane men believed the world would evolve into a decent place, but, as with all futures, there was no one then who could really forecast the world that we know now.

There are many ways to think about that war. It has always been hard to understand the motivations and braveries of Axis soldiers fighting to enslave and dominate their neighbors. Yet it is impossible to know the hammer without the anvil, and to comprehend ourselves we must know the people we once fought against.

Through these books we can discover what it was like to take part in the war that was a final experience for nearly fifty million human beings. In so doing we may discover the strength to make a world as good as the one contained in those dreams and aspirations once believed by heroic men. We must understand our past as an honor to those dead who can no longer choose. They exchanged their lives in a hope for this future that we now inhabit. Though the fight took place many years ago, each of us remains as a living part of it.

Red Duster, White Ensign

The Story of Malta and the Malta Convoys

Ian Cameron

BANTAM BOOKS
TORONTO · NEW YORK · LONDON · SYDNEY

◪

RED DUSTER, WHITE ENSIGN
*A Bantam Book / published by arrangement with
The Author*

PRINTING HISTORY
*Doubleday edition published 1960
Bantam Edition / September 1983*

*Drawings by Greg Beecham and Tom Beecham.
Maps by Alan McKnight and William McKnight.*

*All rights reserved.
Copyright © 1959, 1960 by Donald Payne.
Cover art copyright © 1983 by Chris Mayger,
courtesy of Peacock Press.
This book may not be reproduced in whole or in part, by
mimeograph or any other means, without permission.
For information address: Doubleday & Company, Inc.,
245 Park Avenue, New York, N.Y. 10167.*

ISBN 0-553-23491-9

Published simultaneously in the United States and Canada

In the name of the people of the United States of America I salute the island of Malta, its people and defenders, who, in the cause of freedom and justice and decency throughout the world, have rendered valorous service far and beyond the call of duty.

Under repeated fire from the skies, Malta stood alone but unafraid in the center of the sea, one tiny bright flame in the darkness—a beacon of hope for the clearer days which have come.

Malta's bright story of human fortitude and courage will be read by posterity with wonder and gratitude through all the ages. What was done in this island maintains the highest traditions of gallant men and women who from the beginning of time have lived and died to preserve civilization for all mankind.

FRANKLIN D. ROOSEVELT

December 1943

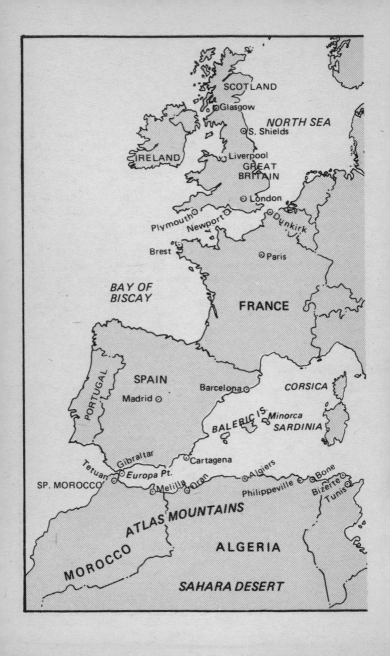

EUROPE & NORTH AFRICA
Scale of Miles

0   100   200   300   400

Acknowledgments

Without the co-operation of the Admiralty this book could not have been written, and the author would like to thank all those members of the Navy (both serving and retired) who so often went out of their way to help him in his researches: especially Commander Titterton, Lieutenant Commander Kemp, Mr. Hurford, and Mr. Gardner.

The assistance given by the shipping companies, who without exception made their records available, is also gratefully acknowledged; and the author particularly thanks for their help all those participants in the siege and convoys whom he personally interviewed: especially Captain Mason, Captain Horn, Captain Riley, Captain Thomas, and Flight Lieutenant Barnham.

The author also wishes to thank the controller of Her Britannic Majesty's Stationery Office for permission to reproduce extracts from Admiralty files, which are British Crown copyright.

Foreword

By Captain S. W. Roskill, D.S.C., R.N.

The story of the Malta convoys will live for as long as the spirit of man is stirred by tales of high endeavor and unflinching sacrifice; and Mr. Cameron here not only sets down the facts with clarity and accuracy but re-creates the spirit in which those desperate undertakings were carried out. His researches, especially into the memories of the Merchant Navy crews who took part, have enabled him to record some delightful and characteristic anecdotes, and have preserved for posterity many details which would otherwise probably have been lost; and he has closely investigated the reasons why, on some occasions, things went wrong, stating his conclusions fearlessly yet fairly.

Many different factors contributed to the happy outcome of Malta's long ordeal. First among them I would place the fortitude of the islanders themselves; and in the present days of difficulty and misunderstanding it is timely and heart-warming to recall how they welcomed every British man-of-war and merchantman which broke through the blockade to bring them sustenance and reinforcements. "Then," wrote Captain Friedberger of H.M.S. *Welshman* in May 1942, "there came a ring of cheers which seemed to come from the bastions of Valletta and Senglea...[which] expressed the spirit of Malta." But, alas, many ships did not arrive; and the fact that the Merchant Navy men, who were not trained for war like their Royal Navy comrades, imperturbably faced what was probably the most hazardous journey of all time must surely be given second pride of place. When Admiral Syfret commented on "the steadfast manner in which these vessels pressed on their way to Malta through all attacks," he summed up what was perhaps the most outstanding feature of every single convoy. What of the airmen and soldiers forming the garrison of the beleaguered island? A recently arrived

Spitfire pilot answered the question best. "The tempo of life here is just indescribable," he recorded. "The morale of all is magnificent... but life is certainly tough.... It all makes the Battle of Britain and fighter sweeps over France seem like child's play... but it is certainly history in the making." Mr. Cameron brings out very well the truth of that unnamed airman's concluding remark; for there is no doubt at all that, had we lost Malta, our tenuous hold on the Mediterranean and Middle East would also have been lost. If that is so, the reader may well ask, why is it that the story of the Malta convoys has received so little attention? Partly, it may be, because the British habit is always to forget what we have quite recently paid a terrible price to relearn; partly perhaps because the convoy battles have no names that ring in the memory like Matapan. They are even today only remembered by the often quite inappropriate code names given to them at the time—"Excess," "Halberd," "White," "Pedestal," "Harpoon," and so on; and such names are unlikely to recall great deeds to posterity. Yet each and every one of those operations was a major undertaking, into which both sides threw all their available strength; and most of them produced as much sea and air fighting as any fleet action in any theater of the war.

It may seem invidious to single out, from such a galaxy of high endeavor, the contribution of any particular ships. But Mr. Cameron suggests that, if that be done, he would name the *Welshman*, *Wasp*, *Breconshire*, and *Ohio*; and I fully agree with him. Quite apart from their individual accomplishments, their wide variety of type, country of origin, and service epitomizes the whole series of Malta convoys; for the *Welshman* was a Royal Navy ship, the *Wasp* belonged to the United States Navy, the *Breconshire* was a British merchantman converted to naval auxiliary, and the *Ohio* was an American-built tanker on charter to Britain, whose Merchant Navy men manned her. But the whole long catalogue of ships' names, and of their captains and masters, is recorded here; and Mr. Cameron's gripping account of what they endured and accomplished will surely help to perpetuate their memories. "The Royal and Merchant Navies," he finally concludes, "alone possessed the resources, both physical and spiritual, to endure so much, so frequently, and for so long"; and we may let that fine tribute stand as the epitaph of all who fought and died in the Malta convoys of 1940–42.

Contents

GOZO

Cominotto I.

COMINO

Comino Channel

MEDITERRANEAN SEA

Paul's Bay

MALTA

Takali

Notabile

Rabat

Valletta

Grand Harbor

Zonker Point

Luqa

Safi
Strip

Hal Far

Marsaxlokk Bay

Delimara Point

Kalafrana

MALTESE ISLANDS

Scale of Miles

0   2   4   6

1

Malta was the rock on which our hopes in the Mediterranean foundered.

—ITALIAN N.I.D. PAPERS

Like random leaves, green in summer, yellow and brown in autumn, the Maltese islands lie scattered across the eastern end of the narrow reach of water which runs between Sicily and Tunis. There are five islands: Malta, Gozo, Comino, Filfla, and Cominotto: five fragments of thrust-up tertiary limestone whose single magnificent harbor had for centuries dominated the central Mediterranean.

But all that, the experts said, was in the past.

In 1939, at the outbreak of the Second World War, it was generally agreed that Malta would quickly become "untenable." The island was considered too vulnerable to Italian bombers, too dependent on sea-borne supplies. "Nothing can be done," reads a minute of the Chiefs of Staff, "to defend Malta."

This view was based on a number of indisputable facts. Malta was the most densely populated fragment of Europe—over 300,000 people packed into 112 square miles. The islands produced only 30 per cent of their food and only 5 per cent of their other essential requirements (such as clothes, iron, and coal). And they lay within 60 miles of the Sicilian shore: within a few minutes' flying time of the Italian bombers. It was this last fact which caused the experts to shake their heads. A few heavy raids, they said, and Malta would be reduced to a heap of useless rubble. The islands were not worth bothering over, not worth the trouble of defending.

Because this view was widely accepted, the outbreak of war found Malta virtually defenseless: stripped of troops, guns, planes, and stocks of food.

It was fortunate that one man had enough strategic acumen

1

and enough faith in human nature to disagree with the
experts. Sir Winston Churchill, from the moment he took
office, made it abundantly clear that he regarded Malta as the
key to the Middle East; and in spite of bitter opposition from
high-ranking officers of both Army and Air Force—opposition which continued right through to the summer of 1942—
he never ceased to champion the island's cause. In this he
was supported by the Navy, who, to quote Admiral Cunningham, had "always considered that Malta should be held at
all costs."

E-Boat

Thus, there were two battles of Malta; Churchill and the
Navy had to fight not only the Axis dive bombers, submarines,
and E-boats but also a block of prejudiced and ill-advised
opinion, which never ceased to hold that Malta was "a
millstone round our necks and a wasteful drain on our
resources." It is interesting to note that as late as May 1942
those in charge of the land campaigns in Africa were recom-
mending the abandonment of Malta and the concentration of
all resources in the desert.

Looking back, it is easy to judge which viewpoint was right. Had Malta been allowed to fall, Allied warships and planes would have been unable to operate in the Central Mediterranean; the German and Italian armies in North Africa would have been reinforced, quickly and easily, across the Narrows; Cairo and Alexandria would certainly have fallen, and the whole of the Middle East (with its vital supplies of oil) might well have been brought under Axis control. The importance of Malta can also be judged by another and more tangible yardstick. For two and a half years Allied fortunes in North Africa fluctuated in direct and immediate sympathy with Allied fortunes in Malta. When the island was strong, and able to take an appreciable toll of Axis supplies, our campaigns in Africa prospered. When the island was weak, and unable to harry the Axis supply routes, our campaigns in Africa invariably failed. In confirmation of this, both German and Italian historians have since admitted that "Malta was the rock upon which our hopes in the Mediterranean foundered."

The task of defending these tiny "untenable" islands, in other words, eventually developed into one of the most vital commitments of the war.

To understand just what the task involved, two things are needed: an analysis of the island's resources and a map of the Mediterranean.

Malta's resources on the eve of war were, to say the least, pitiably inadequate. Thanks to the parsimony of successive governments and the lack of vision of successive Chiefs of Staff, Malta in 1939 had a garrison of less than four thousand troops, food stocks for a bare five weeks, fourteen coastal-defense guns, one operational airfield, and only four crated and obsolescent planes.

The garrison consisted of five battalions of infantry, inexperienced, under strength, and poorly equipped; their rifles (about the only weapons they had) dated back to the *First* World War!

The food stocks, stored in underground vaults in Valletta and Notabile, consisted of only a few hundred tons of flour, grain, frozen meat, sugar, coffee, and tea. There was practically no reserve of the fresh vegetables and edible oil which were the Maltese staple diet.

Most of the fourteen coastal-defense guns, which between

them had to cover over a hundred miles of shore, were sited at the approaches to Grand Harbour: and the exposed beaches in the north of the island were virtually undefended.

There were three airfields—Hal Far, Takali and Luqa—but only the last mentioned was fully operational. For Hal Far consisted of a single and very narrow strip of grass, bordered by cliffs on one side and a ravine on the other; it flooded easily. Takali was hemmed in by hills; like Hal Far, it had no runways, and—being built on the bed of a dried-up lake—it, too, degenerated after each shower into a morass of mud. Luqa alone measured up to the conventional idea of an airdrome, with intersecting runways, taxi tracks, and dispersal points. But it was only half built; and the difficulties of completing it appeared to be insuperable. For the whole site had to be leveled out of hills, quarries, and nullahs overlooking Grand Harbour, and the airfield-construction unit which had started this work in 1938 had, on the eve of war, been posted to France (where its need was considered more urgent). So Luqa was left unfinished, its runways three-quarter length, its dispersal points still on the drawing board, and its control tower no more than a pipe dream. Its completion was left to improvisation and manual labor.

As for fighters to operate from the airfields, they were nonexistent. For the powers that be, having written Malta off as "undefendable," were unwilling to sacrifice aircraft (which were in desperately short supply) in a cause they considered already lost.

This was the extent of Malta's unpreparedness when France fell, Italy entered the war, and the island, overnight, was shifted from a peaceful backwater to the front of the firing line.

In spite of the pessimism in official circles, Churchill insisted that an attempt be made to hold Malta, and plans to reinforce the island were, somewhat tardily, set in train. The first need obviously was to rush in food, at the same time evacuating *"les bouches inutiles."** The second was to build up the island's defenses, especially in AA guns and fighters. And the third—assuming the first two needs were successfully met—was to transform Malta from a defensive link to an offensive springboard.

---

*Useless mouths.

The onus of bringing in these much needed supplies fell on the shoulders of the Royal and Merchant Navies—supply by air was never considered practicable—and onus is none too strong a word. For Admiral Cunningham, Commander in Chief, Mediterranean Fleet, reckoned that to fulfill Malta's needs he would need to run two 40,000-ton convoys to the island each month; a task which, in view of his other commitments, bordered on the impossible. For each convoy to Malta would, he knew, involve a complete fleet operation; each convoy would be the potential tinder to touch off a major naval engagement; and each convoy would—almost inevitably—come under heavy attack and suffer heavy losses. A glance at the map will explain why.

Malta, it will be seen, lies over a thousand miles from either Alexandria or Gibraltar, the only two Mediterranean ports at which Allied merchantmen could assemble in large numbers and reasonable safety. Thus, the physical distance each convoy had to cover was in itself something of a problem, calling for careful conservation of ammunition and careful arrangements for refueling. But the length of the routes to be followed was less of a problem than their direction. For the first part of each voyage, it is true, the ships would be passing through waters that were more or less under Allied control; but as they progressed toward Malta they would come to waters increasingly under enemy control, until at last they arrived at the Narrows: a four-hundred-mile stretch of shallows and sand bars dominated by Axis planes, U-boats, and E-boats, heavily guarded by enemy mine fields, and within a few hours' steaming of the great Italian naval bases of Naples and Taranto. And there was no way of avoiding the Narrows; they were a danger that had to be faced; a gantlet that had to be run. And—to quote the prosaic but authoritative words of the R.N. Battle Summary—"the passage of a convoy through such waters is inevitably one of the most hazardous and arduous operations of the war at sea."

And so, when Italy entered the conflict, most people didn't give Malta a dog's chance of lasting long. Mussolini had boasted he would review his battle fleet in Grand Harbour within a month of declaring war: and it seemed all too likely that he would. For over and above the dangers and difficulties of keeping the island supplied, there loomed another and equally cogent problem: that of the Maltese people.

How would they measure up to the demands of war?

Malta had been part of the British Empire for only just over a hundred years; her ties of loyalty, in other words, didn't stretch far into the past. The creation, in 1869, of a naval base in Grand Harbour had done something to create a bond between British and Maltese; but whether this bond was one of affection or convenience was, on the eve of war, none too easy to determine. For the Maltese and the British had, on the surface, little in common. Insofar as any people conform to generalizations, the Maltese are happy-go-lucky extroverts: volatile, excitable, and temperamental; and they are Catholics. They would seem, in other words, to have more in common with the Italians than with the British— indeed, for years Mussolini had been assuring them that the Italians were their "blood brothers," who would soon be coming to free them from "the 70 per cent of British Imperialism." So, not unnaturally, the reaction of the island-ers to war was awaited with some anxiety. Few people expected them to show any open pro-Italian sympathy. But whether they would be willing to face the horror and heart-break of a prolonged siege, for the sake of a cause which wasn't really theirs, was another matter.

Malta's survival, in other words, depended on two things. Could the British, in the face of continual and heavy losses, continue running in supplies? And could the Maltese, in the face of continual and heavy bombing, summon up the will and the fortitude to hold out?

In the event, both questions were answered—and answered gloriously—in the affirmative. But it was a near thing. And the annals of war can boast of few finer or more exciting achievements than the fighting through of the epic convoys of Malta; while few tales of fortitude can equal that of the Maltese, who endured so much and for so long in a battle against such overwhelming odds.

2

*I wish to report that every member of the Ship's
Company did their best, under trying conditions.*
> —CAPTAIN PRETTY, S.S. "CORNWALL"

The S.S. *Cornwall* was a typical merchant ship: built in 1920,
dead-weight tonnage 10,600, maximum speed 13 knots. In
July 1940 she left Bombay carrying a general and refrigerated
cargo—mostly coal and grain, together with a little cottonseed and five hundred tons of frozen Australian beef.

Her orders routed her to Liverpool via the Cape; but
halfway across the Indian Ocean an emergency signal diverted
her to Port Said. On her way she put in to Mombasa,
discharged part of her cargo, and reloaded with ack-ack
shells, five hundred tons of edible oil, and several thousand
boxes of matches. This odd consignment led to a good deal of
speculation among her crew, who ran a sweepstake on the
ship's destination. The stoker who drew "Malta" wasn't thought
to have much of a chance—for war had only recently come to
the Mediterranean and the island had not yet achieved any
sort of fame.

The *Cornwall* spent a week at Port Said, then stood
westward, hugging the delta of the Nile. On August 20 she
entered the fleet anchorage at Alexandria.

She was in good company now; for dispersed around the
sundrenched harbor was the greater part of Admiral
Cunningham's Mediterranean Fleet: the battleships *Warspite*,
Malaya, and *Royal Sovereign*, the aircraft carrier *Eagle*, some
half dozen cruisers, and twelve to fifteen destroyers. And it
was clear from the plethora of signals and the frequent
comings and goings between ship and ship that a large-scale
operation was being planned.

For several days there was no official intimation of what

7

H.M.S. Warspite

this operation would be—though both Egyptian bumboats and Italian radio provided a spate of surprisingly accurate rumor. Then, on August 27, the *Cornwall*'s master, Captain F. S. Pretty, was summoned to a conference aboard the *Warspite*.

There were two other masters at the conference—the masters of the merchantmen *Plumleaf* and *Volo*—and that evening in Admiral Cunningham's flagship, the plans for Operation "Hats" were explained to them with a meticulous attention to detail.

It was to be a complex operation with three interrelated objectives: to pass fleet reinforcements from Gibraltar to Alexandria, to tempt the Italian fleet to a surface action, and to pass a convoy to Malta. Captain Pretty was concerned only with the last two objectives.

The Malta convoy was to be a fast one, for the merchantmen had to work in with the plans for the battle fleet, and the three ships chosen—*Cornwall*, *Volo*, and *Plumleaf*—were all officially capable of thirteen knots. It was explained to the masters that the convoy would have a light escort only—just the destroyers *Jervis*, *Juno*, *Dainty*, and *Diamond*—for its immediate protection. Its real safety would lie in the presence of the battle fleet, which would stand some hundred miles to the northeast, ready to close as soon as the trap had been sprung and the Italian fleet was at sea and making for the supposedly lightly guarded convoy. This, to the masters, seemed a highly dangerous scheme; for they knew that the Italian battleships were several knots faster than the British, and it appeared quite likely that they would be able to gobble the bait and escape before Admiral Cunningham could catch them. But they kept their fears to themselves, and after a couple of hours the conference broke up.

Next morning the merchantmen were ordered to get up steam and remain at two hours' readiness to sail.

One of the things which had been discussed at the conference was the need for secrecy. It was therefore especially galling for Captain Pretty, when he returned to his ship, to hear the Italian radio smugly broadcasting details of the convoy's assembly and destination. And next day an Egyptian garbage boat, on its diurnal visit to *Cornwall*, passed on the news that their convoy was scheduled to sail next evening an hour before midnight. Everybody, it seemed, knew exactly what was happening—except those sailing on the ships themselves. The role of bait—unattractive in the most favorable circumstances—began to look positively suicidal.

The operation began early on August 29. That morning, two thousand five hundred miles to the west of Alexandria, four warships entered the Strait of Gibraltar. They were the battleship *Valiant*, the aircraft carrier *Illustrious*, and the ack-ack cruisers *Calcutta* and *Coventry*: reinforcements from home waters for Admiral Cunningham's Mediterranean Fleet. The ships refueled; then early next morning, while folds of sea mist still clung to the foot of the Rock, they headed westward, escorted by units from Gibraltar. And as they took up their cruising disposition, far away at the opposite end of the Mediterranean the warships and merchantmen in Alexandria harbor prepared to put to sea. The rendezvous of the two groups—a pin point of rock a thousand miles from either— was Malta.

The Egyptian garbage boat had been right. A few minutes after eleven o'clock on the night of August 29–30, the *Cornwall*, together with the *Volo* and *Plumleaf*, crept out of Alexandria harbor. By midnight they were well into the open sea: eighteen miles due north of Great Pass Beacon. Here they were met by their destroyer escort: *Jervis, Juno, Dainty, and Diamond*. Quietly the ships moved into cruising disposition; the destroyers forming the four corners of a square inside which the merchantmen kept station in the shape of a triangle, *Cornwall* in the van, *Plumleaf* on her starboard quarter, *Volo* on her port. Captain Mack, senior officer of the escort, signaled their course and speed: 325 degrees, 12 knots. And the convoy was under way.

The night was fine, the sea calm, the wind light from the east. Conditions were perfect; but the start of the convoy was not auspicious, for almost as soon as the ships were under way, *Jervis* obtained an asdic contact: doubtful but persistent. Italian submarines, it seemed, knew of their departure: were lying in wait for them.

Jervis attacked the contact with a single depth charge but obtained no result. She dropped astern of the convoy, hunting the echo among the offshore shoals and currents. But even a second attack with full charges produced no tangible result, and at 3:45 A.M. the destroyer gave up and rejoined the merchantmen.

And that—surprisingly—was all the excitement the convoy had for the next thirty-six hours. For the first day and a half nothing happened. Operation "Hats," at least for the *Cornwall*, soon bid fair to turn into an anticlimax.

And it was the same for *Illustrious* and her escort coming east from Gibraltar; and for *Warspite* and her fellow battleships moving west from Alexandria. Over the whole of the Central Mediterranean the Italians were conspicuous by their absence.

This, it is now known, was because two diversionary feints had proved unexpectedly successful. In the west, Admiral Somerville had sent a pair of destroyers—*Velox* and *Wishart*—to circle Minorca; and from here, well within range of the Italian listening posts, they broadcast a stream of spurious signals preparing for a quite imaginary bombardment of Genoa, and this caused Italian warships and planes to be rushed to the "threatened" port. While, in the east, Admiral Cunningham stood the aircraft carrier *Eagle* toward the Aegean, and this again caused Italian forces to mass in the wrong area.

All this, of course, wasn't known at the time—at least not on board the *Cornwall*, whose crew quickly found an explanation of their own to account for the lack of incident. "Bloody Eye-ties are scared stiff" was the general opinion. "They daren't come near us."

That was why, when, a few minutes after noon on the second day out, the planes were spotted and identified as Italian, nobody took much notice.

Not until, quite suddenly, the bombs were falling all around them.

There were five bombers, Savoia 79s; they came in high, at about 13,000 feet, and out of the sun. They had carefully skirted the battle fleet to northward, thus avoiding the *Eagle*'s fighters; and their attack was skillfully conceived and executed with great accuracy.

And this perhaps is a good time to say something about the Italians' capabilities as fighters. It has been customary for wartime writers to pooh-pooh them, to treat them as a sort of comic-opera joke. But their reputation for cowardice is not altogether deserved. For every now and then one came

across Italians who really knew their stuff and who fought like
the very devil. The Gurkhas who did battle with them at
Keren said they were the most courageous and stubborn
enemy they had ever met (and courage is something a
Gurkha knows about). The Italian midget-submariners performed
acts as brave and audacious as the men of any navy; while
certain squadrons of the Aeronautico Italiano invariably pressed
home their attacks far more bravely and skillfully than any
German squadron (with the exception of Fliegerkorps X).
Certainly no one who served with Admiral Cunningham's
fleet during 1940–41 regarded Italian bombing as a joke.
Based on Sardinia, Sicily, and Calabria were several squadrons
specially trained for sea reconnaissance and shipping strikes;
and the British fleet soon developed a very wholesome
respect for them.

It was a wing of one such squadron that now pattern-
bombed the convoy. They came in out of the heat-hazed
midday sun, unseen until they were almost over the ships.
Before a gun had been fired the first bombs came screaming
down: a sighting stick: three 250-pounders that fell midway
between *Cornwall* and *Dainty*. Then the bombers turned;
dropped lower; started their second run.

The vessels increased speed: and zigzagged. Ack-ack patterned
the sky. But accurate firing into the sun-bright haze wasn't
easy. The bombers came steadily on.

"Oh! Oh! Antonio..." whistled one of the *Cornwall* lookouts.
But his whistling was drowned by the shriller whine of falling
bombs; and the ships of the convoy disappeared in steeple-
high fountains of spray.

Several vessels were near-missed. *Dainty* was straddled.
And *Cornwall* was hit three times: was turned in a handful of
seconds into a blazing, drifting wreck.

The first bomb hit her aft. Ricocheting off her poop, it
burst on the flat between the 4-inch-gun mounting and the
12-pounder. The gun crews, less than a dozen feet away, were
sprayed with shrapnel, picked up bodily by the force of the
explosion, and flung through the awning onto the deck below.
All were injured; but none, miraculously, was killed. This
bomb destroyed the Cornwall's steering; jammed her rudder;
knocked her after lifeboats off their davits; and started a fire
close to the 4-inch-ammunition locker. The fire spread.

The second bomb fell amidships; flush on the wireless

room. Here both the *Cornwall*'s radio operators were on duty; one transmitting, one sitting on his bunk reading signals. The junior operator, Mr. Chamberlain, a young Londoner on his first voyage, was killed instantly. The senior, Mr. McNeill, had an incredible escape. Everything around him disintegrated: the equipment, the furniture, the bulkheads, the decks. In the confined space the force of the explosion was so great that the rescue workers, quickly on the scene, found few pieces of wreckage larger than fingerlength splinters. Yet Mr. McNeill was only stunned! By some freak of fortune his only injuries were a small cut on the forehead and a strained back. This second bomb wrecked the crew's quarters amidships, especially the engineers' mess deck, which simply ceased to exist. It also caused about a dozen below-decks casualties; riddled the superstructure with splinters; colandered the *Cornwall*'s funnel; pitted her bridge; wrecked two more of her ship's boats; and started several minor fires.

But it was the third bomb that did the most serious damage. It sheared through the port deck rail and exploded at water level immediately next to the engine room. The ejection valves were blown off the side of the ship; the hull plating was split; and through a gaping five-foot rent in the bulkheads sea water flooded into the *Cornwall*'s engines.

Listing drunkenly to port, the ship lost way. Smoke from the fires on her deck mingled with steam from the damaged boilers and cordite fumes from the convoy's ack-ack, which now blazed angrily but ineffectively at the retiring bombers.

Captain Pretty's first impression was that the *Cornwall* was lost. From the bridge her superstructure looked like a smoldering breaker's yard of scrap: guns knocked cockeyed, boats dangling at fantastic angles, the deck plates buckled, the cargo and ammunition in flames. A lesser man would have abandoned ship. But when Pretty started to assess the damage more closely, he saw that though spectacular it was in some ways superficial. Because the Italian bombs had been light (approximately 250-pounders), they hadn't penetrated the deck, but had exploded on impact. They had therefore expended most of their violence on the ship's superstructure without damaging her vital innards. It seemed to Captain Pretty that, if only the fires could be brought under control and the engines restarted, they had a chance of saving the ship.

What happened next was no epic of the sea. There were no heroics, no outstanding feats of bravery, no inspired touches of technical ingenuity. There was simply a group of men, many of whom were badly wounded, fighting to save their ship. And fighting under conditions which Captain Pretty described, with typical understatement, as "trying."

Within sixty seconds of being hit, the captain had given his orders, and the fight to save the *Cornwall* was on.

His orders were simple. To Mr. Thomas, the chief officer: "Put out the fires." To Mr. Drummond, the chief engineer: "Restart the engines." It says much for the good humor and common sense of these two officers that they did not come to blows. For their orders called for lines of action that were diametrically opposed.

Mr. Thomas had only one way of putting out the fires—with water: with water sprayed from above onto the burning holds. This water, of course, quickly found its natural level: in the bottom of the ship, in the already flooded engine room, where water was Mr. Drummond's most dangerous adversary. For here, in the bowels of the *Cornwall*, the engineers were struggling to dam back the steadily rising flood; and no sooner had they shored up the rent in their hull and were starting to pipe the water away than a new deluge cascaded into their engine room from Mr. Thomas's hoses. There was the question of pressure, too; there was very little, and what there was, both chief officer and engineer wanted: Mr. Thomas for his hoses, Mr. Drummond for his engines.

Mr. Thomas went into action first. Collecting his fire party, he started to spray the most dangerous area—the burning deck beside the ammunition locker. But the hoses were riddled with splinters; punctured, fractured, blown into fantastic loops; and the water came through reluctantly, in weak, spasmodic jerks. They stopped spraying, and set to to mend the hoses, wrapping canvas around the rents, plugging the holes, waiting for the pressure to build up. And while some mended, others formed a bucket chain, hand-tipping water onto the flames. But they couldn't work fast enough. The flames spread, fanned by a steady fifteen-knot wind, and they were soon licking at the ammunition locker.

The gun crews wrapped canvas over their heads, crawled through the flames, and started to toss the red-hot shells over the side. Able Seaman Dabner had been injured by the original bomb blast, which fractured his ankle; now he was badly burned, but—like the rest of the crew—he wouldn't give up; he went on crawling in and out of the flames, salvaging burning ammunition. They got about half of it out of the locker; then the heat of the fire drove them back.

Exactly ten minutes after they had first been hit the ammunition locker blew up.

The effect was spectacular. To Captain Pretty, as he looked down from the bridge, it was as if the *Cornwall* had been hit by another, and heavier, bomb. A great sheet of flame leaped out of the ship's stern; exploding shells were tossed like squibs about her deck; and, even more serious, the flames spread downward: down into No. 5 hold. Soon the bales of cottonseed started to smolder.

The *Cornwall* drifted on, wreathed in smoke, shaken at intervals by the shells exploding on her deck. The rest of the convoy, zigzagging west, passed her by. There was nothing they could do to help; though a destroyer—*Juno*—temporarily dropped back and circled her twice.

> From our bridge [one of the destroyer officers wrote] the *Cornwall* looked an utter shambles. She was listing, her deck was buckled and ablaze, and she was giving off great quantities of steam and smoke. Yet to our astonishment she suddenly got under way, and after a couple of erratic circles came lurching after the convoy at a quite surprising pace.

For Mr. Drummond had got his engines going.

The starboard engine picked up first; and with the steering jammed, the ship yawed around in two complete circles before the port engine also began to pull; then the swing was partially corrected. By experiment Captain Pretty found that the rudder had jammed in a fortunate position: almost exactly amidships. He was therefore able, by keeping the starboard engine at half speed and the port engine at nearly full, to steer at least an approximate course.

At an erratic, yawing eight and a half knots the *Cornwall* went lurching after the convoy.

They waited for her, steering in a wide zigzagging circle until she had caught up with them. Within half an hour of being hit she was again in convoy.

But her troubles were far from over.

To start with, she couldn't make more than eight and a half knots. The convoy, however, had to keep to schedule, and a lengthy reduction in their speed would have jeopardized the whole operation. Yet Captain Mack was loath to leave the *Cornwall* behind. He therefore did three things. He ordered her to keep as straight and steady a course as possible while the rest of the ships zigzagged either side of her. He ordered an alteration of course which would take them by a more direct (if slightly more dangerous) route to Malta. And he continually urged Captain Pretty to work up his speed.

And the *Cornwall* responded nobly. Within a couple of hours of being hit she was making nine and a half knots; within four hours she was making twelve: only one knot less than her maximum speed. It was a fantastic sight to see the burning ship, her superstructure almost nonexistent, steaming away, apparently quite happily, in the center of the convoy. But only those who were actually on board the *Cornwall* knew quite how difficult the job was proving: how much the effort was costing them: how close they were to failure and disaster.

Down in the engine room the rent in the hull had been shored up—with tarpaulins, collision mats, bales of cotton, blocks of timber. But a certain amount of water still seeped in, augmented every now and then by an unwelcome cascade from above, from Mr. Thomas's fire hoses. Steadily, on the engine-room deck, the water level rose. By one o'clock it was within eighteen inches of the boiler fires; by two o'clock, within six inches; by three o'clock within two and a half inches. If it rose any higher the *Cornwall* would grind to a halt and would almost certainly be lost. The engineers worked frantically to pump and pipe the water away. It was dark, wet, exhausting work. But they kept at it, hour after hour. The engines overheated, giving off hissing clouds of steam; the air became foul, lacking in oxygen; and success or failure was measured by the fraction of an inch. All that afternoon it was touch and go.

But if the engine-room battle hung for many hours in the balance, the fire battle swung, slowly but surely, in favor of Mr. Thomas. By two o'clock all the fires on deck were out—though patches of blackened superstructure still smoldered fitfully—and the scene of operations shifted to the deck below. Here the crew's quarters were still ablaze, while dark spirals of smoke were seeping out of the cotton bales in hold No. 5.

The fire parties now ran into difficulties. Access to both the burning hold and the engineers' mess deck—the apparent heart of the fire—was blocked by exploding ammunition. For when the locker blew up, many shells toppled through the holed deck; and it was these, still exploding at intervals, which now drove the fire fighters back. They managed to get to the cotton bales by dangling men over the ship's side (in bosun's chairs) to spray the hold through shell holes and portholes, and in this way the cotton was thoroughly saturated. By four o'clock all danger of cargo fire had passed. A new danger, however, now took its place. The cottonseed started to swell; it increased in weight; many bales burst and shifted. The *Cornwall's* list increased: suddenly and sharply.

It was becoming quite difficult to stand on the canted deck as Mr. Thomas, together with Mr. Frater, the carpenter, made their assault on the last stronghold of the fire. Rushing through the area of exploding ammunition, they brought their hoses to bear on the shattered mess deck; and within half an hour the last of the *Cornwall's* fires died to ash beneath the spray of the pressurized hoses. Quite suddenly everything seemed strangely quiet.

The ship by now had been steaming for some time at twelve knots. Neither the 10-degree list nor the thousand-odd tons of water pumped below deck seemed seriously to incapacitate her. Only Captain Pretty realized that she was slowly becoming more difficult to steer: more wayward, slower to answer her helm, harder to bring back each time she began to yaw. He wondered how much longer she would manage to stay with the convoy.

Late that afternoon wind and sea—which for the last twenty-four hours had been moderate to strong—slackened off; and by five o'clock the ship was out of immediate danger. Her list remained constant; in her engine room the water gradually subsided; on her deck the fires smoldered and died.

Now, for almost the first time, the *Cornwall's* crew stopped thinking of their ship and thought of themselves.

Several were badly wounded. The worst cases had already been taken to the saloon; and here, Mr. Jesse, the chief steward, had saved the life of at least one man by his practical first aid. Now, others came to Mr. Jesse: men with shrapnel

wounds, fractures, and burns. The chief steward had plenty
of bandages and plenty of common sense, but not much else.
He was short of tourniquets, antiburn jelly, and, above all,
morphine. And he badly needed medical help: the sort of
help that couldn't come from textbooks, but only from a
qualified doctor. They signaled *Jervis*, but the destroyer's
reply was not encouraging.

"Regret we cannot transfer you doctor until dark. Report
symptoms of those most seriously injured."

So all that afternoon signals flashed from ship to ship and
in *Cornwall*'s saloon tourniquets were tightened, splints set,
and wounds swabbed according to the advice of a doctor who
couldn't see his patients and could only hope that the treat-
ment he prescribed was doing more good than harm.

At about seven o'clock things in the saloon didn't look too
hopeful. The steward's boy was growing weaker—an artery
high in his leg had been cut, and a lump of shrapnel the size
of a tablespoon was lodged beside his elbow. Next to him a
seaman felt the numbness of a crushed foot spread upward;
first into his leg, then into his thigh. And opposite them an
engine-room greaser found he could blow smoke rings through
a couple of shrapnel holes in his chest. Time, for those who
were wounded, passed slowly: and painfully. They knew they
would get no morphine until dark—it was too risky to heave
to and transfer a doctor in daylight, for Italian bombers were
still about and the Italian battle fleet had been reported only
a hundred miles to the north. So they lay there waiting;
uncomplaining; hour after hour; until, at last, a few minutes
after eight o'clock *Juno* came alongside and Surgeon Lieutenant Adnams (and his morphine) was hoisted aboard.

All that night the life of the steward's boy hung in the
balance, but in the end—like the *Cornwall* herself—he survived.
And Adnams was able to write in his official report: "Considering
the merchantman's deck was such a shambles, it was amazing
there were so few casualties and only one fatality."

But when Adnams came to analyze how the casualties had
occurred, something even more incredible came to light. He
found that in nearly every case those on the exposed and
devastated deck had escaped unhurt, while those sheltering
below, in apparently safe positions, had been injured. Out of
the ten members of the gun crews, for example, only one
(Able Seaman Dabner) was badly hurt; yet a bomb had burst

within a few feet of them. Whereas two decks down, far from any of the explosions, all twelve members of a fire party sheltering between the refrigerating engines had been injured—although they were taking cover in the very center of the ship, in a place specially chosen for its safety. At first nobody could discover how these men had been injured: where the shrapnel had sprayed them had come from. Then a series of deeply etched furrows in the refrigerator's air vent provided a clue. When the bomb had hit the wireless room, a shower of splinters had flown straight into the air ventilator, ricocheted along the piping, and emerged out of an air hole beside the refrigerator, two decks below and thirty feet forward from where the bomb had landed!

Another example of the capricious effects of bomb blast was the fate of Ordinary Seaman Dawnay. Dawnay, of all the *Cornwall*'s crew, had been farthest away from the bombing; when the attack developed he was on duty in the crow's-nest, some two hundred feet above the deck. Yet a few minutes after the bombs burst he came scrambling down, very white and clutching the seat of his pants. Where the shrapnel had hit him was considered a great joke—by everyone except Ordinary Seaman Dawnay.

All that night the convoy stood westward. Hour after hour they kept to their twelve to twelve and a half knots. They had to. For in the darkness, somewhere to the northeast, the Italian battle fleet was hunting for them. Delay would have been fatal, would have jeopardized the whole operation. And that is the sum of Captain Pretty's achievement: that he not only saved his ship but—by keeping up his speed—saved the convoy as well.

For by next morning the Italians had missed their opportunity; and Captain Mack and his convoy were able to keep their various rendezvous on time. At sunrise they met the 3rd Cruiser Squadron; and a couple of hours later the main battle fleet, augmented now by the Gibraltar reinforcements, appeared over the northern horizon.

During September 1 the sea slowly continued to moderate; and this was just as well, for on board the *Cornwall* conditions were gradually worsening. It was only in little ways that the changes were noticeable; and the deterioration was mercifully slow. But that morning the engines again started to overheat and to run roughly; the steering became ever more erratic; and the crew began to realize that their clothing and personal effects had been lost, that they were thoroughly exhausted, and that their food was lukewarm and inadequate (for both mess decks and galleys were gutted). At noon the cargo shifted again, and the list fractionally increased.

All this Captain Pretty noticed. He had been on the bridge a long time now: thirty-six hours. He was tired; as tired, battered, and exhausted as his ship. But luckily for both, the passage to Malta was now a matter of hours rather than days. And late that evening the *Cornwall* was at last able to slacken speed.

A little after sunset, with the danger of bombing past and the Italian fleet running for harbor, the convoy split up. At seven o'clock, when Malta was only twelve hours' steaming to the west, the *Plumleaf* and *Volo*, escorted by *Dainty* and *Diamond*, increased speed to their maximum and headed straight for Malta, running the most dangerous area, the Narrows, by night; the following morning at 7 A.M. they arrived safely at the entrance to Grand Harbour. Meanwhile, *Cornwall*, escorted by *Jervis* and *Juno*, kept steadily on at nine knots, the merchantman holding as straight a course as she could, the destroyers zigzagging on either side. For her, too, the night was uneventful; and at 9 A.M. next morning she was met off St. Elmo's Light by two tugs: *Jaunty* and *Ancient*. An hour later she was towed and nudged through the narrow entrance to Grand Harbour.

The S.S. *Cornwall* was the first merchantman to be damaged while bringing supplies to Malta. Her passage was not especially vital to the island, nor was it especially bitterly contested—many vessels in months to come were to suffer far greater ordeals, and many crews were to show far greater ingenuity and courage. But of all the ships which ran the gantlet to Malta, the *Cornwall* was the first to have to fight her way through. She set a good example; and her story displays, in a minor key, all those virtues and qualities which were to raise later convoys to the rank of epics. Qualities such as courage, endurance, good seamanship, and the spirit of co-operation between the Royal and Merchant Navies.

These qualities, Captain Pretty took, quite simply, for

Sliema
Lazaretto Manoel
Marsamuscetto Harbor
Fort St. Elmo
Ricasoli Pt.
Misida VALLETTA
Pieta Rinella
Floriana Fort St. Angelo
Grand Harbor
Hamrun Senglea Vittoriosa
Cospicua
Zabbar
Pawla

GRAND HARBOR

Scale of Miles

0 ½ 1

granted. All he had to say about the voyage was one short sentence: "I wish to report that every member of the Ship's Company did their best, under trying conditions."

But Captain Mack, the senior officer of the escort, was a little more articulate.

I consider [he wrote] that great credit is due to Captain Pretty, for the seamanship he displayed in handling his ship and in dealing so efficiently and rapidly with the damage he sustained. . . . The maintenance of a speed only one knot less than his maximum and the keeping of an accurate course with no steering at all constitutes, in my opinion, a most seamanlike performance. It also, I submit, contributed very largely to the safe arrival of the convoy at Malta.

Cornwall took only a couple of days to unload. But she didn't leave Malta for six months. She was so heavily damaged that her superstructure had to be almost entirely rebuilt.

Captain Pretty left the *Cornwall* a week after she berthed —masters of his quality couldn't be spared to sit in idleness while their ships were repaired. He took command of the *Nottingham,* a brand-new motor vessel of 8000 tons. Six days out of her maiden voyage the *Nottingham* was torpedoed off Greenland and lost with all hands: a sad end to a man who initiated a tradition.

Gloster Gladiator

3

The three Gloster Gladiator aircraft known as FAITH,
HOPE, and CHARITY fought alone against the
Italian Regia Aeronautica between June and October
1940.

—R.A.F. INSCRIPTION

Sixty miles from Malta lay the island of Sicily, its shore line
dotted with a series of large modern airdromes—Catania,
Augusta, Siracusa, and Pandrino to the east; Comiso, Biscari,
Bo Rizzo, Marsala, and Trapani to the south; and inland the
airstrips of Gela and Gerbini and the great civil airport of
Castelvetrano. Based on three dozen airdromes, all of them

within fifteen minutes' flying time of Malta, were the cream
of the Italian Air Force: some three hundred and fifty bombers (Cants, Savoias, and B.R.20s) and some two hundred
fighters (C.R.42s, Reggiane 2001s, and Macchis); fast modern
planes, based on first-class airfields and manned by skilled
pilots, many of whom had gained operational experience in
the campaigns in Abyssinia and Spain. Only one target was
within range of this great armada of aircraft—Malta. Seldom,
if ever, had so much strength been ranged against so small
and defenseless a target.

Nor was there any doubt about the manner in which, in
the event of war, this strength would be used. Giulio Douhet,
the high priest of strategic pattern bombing, the man whose
theories had been proved in the holocaust of Barcelona, was
quite specific on this point. "The guiding principle of bombing,"
he wrote, "is that the target should be obliterated in one raid.
If, however, this is not possible, the target should be 'saturated'
by unremitting waves of attackers. A people who are bombed
today as they were bombed yesterday, and who know they
will be bombed again tomorrow and can see no end to their
martyrdom, are bound to call for peace in the end."

Sixty miles away Malta watched and waited. And every day,
during the last uneasy weeks of peace, an Italian civil airliner
flew openly over the island taking photographs, noting the
absence of defending aircraft, pinpointing the dozen or so AA
batteries which alone stood between the Maltese people and
the acolytes of Giulio Douhet.

Early on the morning of June 11 the expected happened:
the sirens started their high-pitched wail; Mussolini had
declared war and within a few minutes—to be precise, at
6:57 A.M.—the first wave of Italian bombers were approaching
the island.

There were only ten of them in this first wave: ten Savoia
79s, which approached the island at 14,000 feet in two
V-shaped formations. The AA that greeted them was spasmodic
and ragged, and the Italians, in perfect formation, came
steadily on. They dropped their bombs with undisturbed
precision; half on Hal Far, half on the dockyard. Then they
turned for home.

It had, for the men of the Regia Aeronautica, been as easy
as they had expected. They knew Malta hadn't a single
defending aircraft; they knew her defenses were pitiably thin.

They knew Mussolini had boasted he would be in Grand Harbour within a matter of weeks—and it seemed there was nothing to stop him. In the hindmost Savoia the rear gunner sang to himself contentedly. 'Vido mare quante bello . . .' He smiled; for the sea, as they set course for Sicily, really did look beautiful: hushed and very still in the pale half light of dawn.

> Vido mare quante bello,
> Spira tantu sentimente . . .

And that was as far as he got. For his serenade was cut short by the clatter of machine guns. A neat little row of bullet holes perforated the fuselage not a foot from his head. He looked back. And—unbelievably—there on his tail was a fighter.

The Air Officer Commanding, Malta—Air Commodore Maynard—had been told that the island's official quota of aircraft, in the event of war, was four squadrons of fighters (Hurricane Mk.IIs) and two squadrons of bombers and reconnaissance planes (Wellingtons and Blenheims). But he knew that this was a pipe dream: that there wasn't a chance of the aircraft arriving, for they were needed too desperately elsewhere. In time the authorities admitted this. "There is no immediate prospect," reads an Air Ministry signal of May 14, "of any aircraft being available for Malta."

Many British commanders, on the eve of war, were faced with the job of making a little go a long way. Maynard's task was more difficult than that. He was faced with the job of making something out of nothing. His efforts to beg, borrow, or steal aircraft from neighboring commands were thwarted. His attempts to convert the island's few civil or nonoperational aircraft were unsuccessful. And it began to look as if the outbreak of war would find Malta without even a single makeshift fighter. Then, at last, Maynard had a stroke of luck.

One day he got to hear that a series of mysterious packing crates were standing on the slipway at Kalafrana. On opening these he found they contained the component parts of eight naval Sea Gladiators, aircraft which should have been embarked on H.M.S. *Glorious* when the carrier sailed for Norway, but which had, in the rush to get her to sea, been overlooked.

The aircraft were old, dismantled, and the property of another service. There were no pilots qualified to fly them and no maintenance crews trained to service them. But—of a sort—they were fighters. Maynard went to his opposite number, Rear Admiral Willis, and asked if he could have them.

This request put Willis in a difficult position, for the Admiralty knew all about the Sea Gladiators and had earmarked them for another carrier, H.M.S. *Eagle*. But, fortunately for Malta and the Maltese, Willis was a man who could recognize an emergency. Like Nelson, he turned a blind eye to Admiralty orders, and gave half the Sea Gladiators to Maynard.

Such was the birth of a fighter defense force whose deeds will be honored for as long as the spirit of man is stirred by tales of high endeavor and unflinching sacrifice.

The Gladiators were sturdy little machines, but they were sadly outdated by the planes of the Regia Aeronautica. They were single-bay biplanes, descendants of the Pups, Camels, and S.E.5s that had fought in the First World War. With their fixed undercarriage and one-pitch propellers, their maximum speed was no more than 250 m.p.h. But, on the other hand, they were tough—their compressed-steel lattice ribs making for great internal strength— and they were highly maneuverable—they, if any plane could, could turn on the proverbial sixpence, and in the Air Display of 1938 three of them had looped the loop, *chained together*. The Gladiators, in fact, though something of transition machines between ancient and modern, were not mongrels, but no thoroughbreds either. What they lacked in speed and firepower they made up for in airworthiness. They were the final flower of the sturdy old dogfighting biplanes.

Having got his fighters, Maynard set about finding pilots to fly them and ground crews to maintain them.

There were, on the eve of war, about a dozen pilots in Malta, most of them either in administrative jobs or flying the nonoperational aircraft of Station Flight, Hal Far. Not one of them had been trained as a fighter pilot, but they all volunteered, without exception, to fly the newly acquired Sea Gladiators. In the end seven were chosen and formed into a Fighter Flight. The names of the seven deserve to be remembered: they were Squadron Leader Martin, Flight Lieutenant Burges, Flight Lieutenant Keeble, Flying Officers Hartley, Waters, and Woods, and Pilot Officer Alexander.

As for the men to service the Gladiators, the Aircraft Repair Section at Kalafrana could boast an experienced and highly efficient team: Maltese ex-dockyard apprentices, Maltese Auxiliary Air Force mechanics, and a nucleus of R.A.F. riggers and fitters. Under the leadership of Flying Officer Collins, an ex-warrant officer, who had been on the island since 1936, these men had been welded together into a competent, hard-working unit. The fact that they had no experience in handling Gladiators and no spares didn't unduly perturb them. They had faith in their ability to improvise.

So the Sea Gladiators were taken to Hal Far, assembled, stripped of arrestor hooks and other evidence of their naval ancestry, tested, and flown—though not when the Italian civil airliner was over the island.

The pilots were unanimous about their new machines. They may have been archaic-looking and long in the tooth (officially all operational squadrons had been re-equipped with Hurricanes in 1938), but they were first-class aircraft. As John Waters said, "They could turn on a sixpence and climb like a bat out of hell. Other aircraft all had their nasty little ways, but the Gladiator had no vices at all."

And so, day after day, the seven pilots practiced formation flying, emergency take-offs, interception tactics, and air-to-air firing. They couldn't, of course, help wondering what chance of survival they would have if Italy did enter the war: four planes matched against five hundred and fifty: four obsolescent biplanes facing the cream of a modern air force. But—perhaps luckily—there wasn't much time for thinking. For, a few weeks after their aircraft had been uncrated, the sirens were wailing, Hal Far tannoy was blaring "Scramble the fighters," and the Gladiators were roaring down the take-off strip—and into history.

That first day the Italians, true to the principles of Giulio Douhet, mounted eight raids against Malta. They used well over a hundred and fifty bombers, and in the later raids—as a tribute to the Gladiators—they brought over a fighter screen of Macchis and C.R.42s. When the Italians had a clear run their bombing was unpleasantly accurate. But they didn't like the Gladiators. And the ancient biplanes, whose top speed was actually less than that of the bombers they were trying to intercept, managed again and again to break them up or turn them aside. And they gave the Italian fighters something to

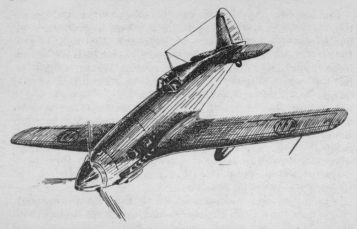

Macchi C. 202 "Folgore"

think about, too. Here is Timber Woods' report of one of the evening engagements.

We sighted a formation of Savoia 79s approaching Valletta at approximately 15,000 feet. We climbed until we were slightly above them, then delivered an attack from astern. The enemy turned out to sea. I closed from astern and got in a good burst at a range of about 200 yards. My fire was returned. I broke away and returned to the island.

While climbing to gain more height, I heard machine-gun fire behind me. I immediately went into a steep left-hand turn and saw a single-engine fighter (a Macchi) diving and firing at me. For quite three minutes we circled each other tightly, than I got him in my sights. I got in a good burst, full deflection, and he went down in a steep dive with black smoke pouring from his tail. He fell into the sea a little to the south of Grand Harbour.

Beneath the bare facts of this report can be seen a story of coolness, resolution, and superior skill. Woods had proved that, contrary to all expectations, the antiquated Gladiators could outfly and outfight their more modern opponents. That, in itself, was heartening.

But more heartening still was the effect on the Maltese of the destruction of an enemy aircraft within full view of hundreds—if not thousands—of onlookers. The sight of the Italian falling like Icarus out of the sky, over which he had so insolently claimed dominion, gave civilian morale a boost at just the right psychological moment. Malta, it seemed, wasn't defenseless, after all. She could hit back.

And from that moment the Gladiators took on, in the eyes of hundreds of thousands of Maltese, a special sort of significance. They became a symbol of the island's spirit of defiance. As long as they stayed in the air, Malta, it was felt, would stay unconquered.

But how long *could* they stay in the air?

That first day all four planes miraculously escaped damage. But such luck was clearly too good to last; and it was decided on the evening of June 11 that from then on one plane (No. N.5524) must be kept permanently in the Aircraft Repair Section at Kalafrana as a source of spare parts: a skeleton which could be stripped to keep the other planes serviceable.

It was decided, too, that new interception tactics were called for. George Burges put the case very clearly here. In a talk with the A.O.C after the first day's fighting he said, "The Italian bombers are faster than we are. So our only chance is to scramble and climb as quickly as we can, and hope to get four or five thousand feet above them by the time they reach the island. Then we must dive on them; but not from astern: from the beam."

And that, in the engagements to come, was just what they did. Day after day. Week after week. Month after month.

The Regia Aeronautica, of course, tried everything they knew to destroy the three little planes which, alone, stood between them and a complete control of the air. They came over in massed formations: fifty to sixty bombers escorted by stepped-up tiers of Macchis and C.R.42s. They sent over decoy planes, with packs of fighters shadowing them, up in the sun. And they deliberately straggled out of formation to try and tempt the Gladiators into dogfights. But somehow the little biplanes, slippery and elusive as eels, always managed to outtwist or outmaneuver them.

But they didn't, of course, escape undamaged. Time and again, in those early days of June and July, a Gladiator landed back on Hal Far so appallingly damaged that it seemed as if nothing short of a miracle would get it back into the air. Three times a plane touched down with its entire tail unit dangling by a single strut and a strand of cable; twice a wing tip was shredded entirely away; often the cockpits were ringed with bullet holes, the mainplanes colandered, the landing wheels shot off, the instrument panels shattered. Yet somehow, thanks to the planes' basic toughness and the skill and hard work of the Aircraft Repair Section, the damage was always patched up. Somehow, no matter how often the sirens wailed (and there were, that first month, a total of over a hundred raids), either two or three of the Gladiators always managed to struggle into the air.

And they gave the Italians plenty to think about. Although they scored comparatively few kills, they broke up countless formations, forcing the bombers off their targets, making them bomb quickly, inaccurately, or (in quite a lot of cases) jettison their bombs harmlessly into the sea. Gradually, in their efforts to avoid the Gladiators, the Savoias and Cants were forced higher and higher: to twenty; twenty-five, and finally to thirty-thousand feet; and from these heights their bombing, of course, was far less accurate. The bombing formations shrank in size, too; to start with, the Italians had sent over, say, thirty Savoias and a dozen Macchis; but soon the ratio was reversed. But the end of June, in an effort to scotch the Gladiators, the Italians were sending over a handful of bombers, escorted by stepped-up tiers of Macchis and C.R.42s. But somehow the little biplanes, against all the odds, still managed to stay in the air.

And so, week after week, the fantastic struggle went on. Three obsolete planes against the might of a modern air force. With the unbelievable happening. The three planes seeming to bear a charmed life, and the air force being reduced to angry impotence.

By the end of June the Gladiators and their pilots had won a niche in history. They had won, too, a unique place in the affections of the Maltese. People showered the pilots with St. Christophers, pasted photographs of them beside their beds, and prayed for them nightly at the shrines in their rock shelters. When the pilots went into the streets, they were followed by admiring crowds; when they took to the air, thousands of people disdained the safety of their shelters and, forgetful of the danger of bomb and shrapnel, stood watching

Fiat C.R.42

the fantastic dogfights that took place daily over the island. It was history in the making.

One quiet evening in early July, when there hadn't been a raid for several hours, the pilots were sitting on the grass at Hal Far, watching the three Gladiators being refueled.

"You know," Jock Martin said reflectively, "we ought to give them a name."

Someone suggested Pip, Squeak, and Wilfred; but this wasn't received with much enthusiasm. It was John Waters—quiet, good-looking, and technically the most brilliant pilot of the seven—who made the inspired suggestion.

"How about Faith, Hope, and Charity?" he said.

The names caught on. They spread beyond Hal Far, beyond Valletta and the Three Cities, beyond the shore of Malta itself. Soon, every time the Gladiators took to the air, people would stop, point skyward, and cry:

"Look! There they go. *Faith, Hope, and Charity!*"

To most Britishers on the island the names brought no more than a wry, appreciative smile; but to the Maltese they brought something more. For the people of Malta are intensely religious, and it meant a great deal to them that the men and machines which were defending them so valiantly had been christened with the words of St. Paul. Now, more than ever before, the three Gladiators came to epitomize the island's spirit of defiance; they became symbols of a cause which began to take on something of the sanctity of a crusade. As, four centuries earlier, the people of Malta had helped the Knights of St. John to defend their island against the hordes of the Ottoman Empire, so the twentieth-century Maltese now rallied around the British garrison in defense of their island against the forces of another and even greater menace to Christendom. If the British, in spite of the fantastic odds, were willing to make a fight for it, so were the Maltese.

Exactly how many aircraft *Faith*, *Hope*, and *Charity* shot down will never be known. By the end of a month each of the pilots could claim at least one kill, and Burges ("*Il Ferocio*," the Maltese called him) could claim as many as six. And it is now known that many aircraft claimed only as possible did, in fact, fail to make the return journey to their Sicilian bases. In all, in June and July, the Italians probably lost upward of sixty or seventy aircraft in their assault on Malta—about half to the AA and half to the Gladiators. And the island still stood firm. Mussolini wasn't in Grand Harbour yet. Or anywhere near it.

All through June and the first half of July, *Faith*, *Hope*, and *Charity* kept up their fantastic battle. Then the inevitable happened.

July 16 was a day of heavy raids, and late in the afternoon Burges and Keeble got involved in a dogfight with a mixed formation of Macchis and C.R.42s. One of the AA gunnery officers has described the combat that followed:

> I watched them twisting and diving and trying to get on each other's tail. Keeble dived onto a Macchi, but two C.R.42s followed him down. He managed to shake one of them off, but the other was good—one of the rare ones—and he clung to Keeble's tail. In a desperate effort to elude him, Keeble came down to ground level and flew under the wireless aerials to Pinella, hoping his pursuer would hit one of the cables. But the trap failed. As Keeble dipped under the aerials the Italian followed and shot him down; but he himself was so close to the ground that he hadn't time to pull out of his firing dive. The two aircraft crashed in the same field and exploded within a few yards of each other. Both men were brave pilots, and very young.

Peter Keeble's death was felt as a personal loss throughout the island. Normally the death of a pilot in action, though mourned by his friends at the time, is regarded as part of the inevitable price of war. But the outstanding immunity of the little squadron through six weeks of bitter fighting and in the face of outrageous odds had lulled everyone into a sense of false security. The Gladiator pilots had seemed to bear a charmed life: to be near immortal. Now it was suddenly brought home how pitiably mortal they were.

But the struggle, of course, still went on. The strain on the pilots was terrific; but the strain on the ground crews (many of whom worked twenty hours out of twenty-four) was even greater. For soon the Gladiators began to crack up.

It was only to be expected, really. They had been flown flat out for a couple of months, and there hadn't been either time or spares for the routine overhauls without which no aircraft can stay airworthy for long. Now, quite suddenly, the engines lost power and began to seep oil; one afternoon when the fitters stripped down *Faith*'s engine they found holes, big as florins, in the cylinder heads. They patched the engine up as best they could, working in the open with bombs falling all around them and low-flying Macchis machine-gunning the airstrip, and by the evening *Faith* was air-borne again. But everyone knew that the repair was only temporary: that unless something drastic was done the aircraft would soon be grounded for good.

Then Flying Officer Collins had an idea. In the Aircraft Repair Section at Kalafrana were a number of crated Mercury 8 and Mercury 15 engines. These had been intended as spares for the Blenheims; but perhaps, with adaptations, they could be fitted into the Gladiators? At any rate, it was worth a try.

The miracle that followed can be fully appreciated only by those with a knowledge of air engineering. For to fit the engine of one aircraft into the fuselage of another is a stupendous undertaking. In this particular case the Blenheim engines were designed to operate a host of ancillary controls which didn't exist in the Gladiators, and each of these devices had to be laboriously sealed off. Then a number of major components had to be radically adapted—oil sumps, petrol pumps, carburetors, and oil throwers, to mention only a few—and all this the mechanics had to do with improvised tools, *and* in double-quick time and in the midst of near-continuous air raids. Somehow they achieved the impossible:

and after forty-eight hours' nonstop work the change-over was made, and the surviving Gladiators took on a new lease of life.

A few days later Collins was responsible for another masterpiece of improvisation. It had been decided to use one Gladiator as a high-level interceptor to break up the Italian bombers and the other as a low-level patrol plane to deal with fighter strafing attacks on the air-dromes. In the latter plane maneuverability was less important than firepower, and it was decided to increase the Gladiator's armament. This was easier said than done. But in the end Collins hit on the scheme of mounting a pair of .303s, Great War fashion, on top of the upper mainplane. The result was that the silhouette of the low-level Gladiator took on an even more archaic outline than ever. With its biplane wings, outsized engine, makeshift propeller, and upper-mainplane guns, it looked, in the uncertain twilight, like the silhouette of a ghost plane flown straight from the Western Front. Somebody, catching sight of it for the first time, aptly christened it the "Bloodiator." It was certainly a bizarre-looking machine. But at least it could fly. And one afternoon it shot down a Macchi *and* a C.R.42.

So the days passed: days of raid after raid, with the pair of patchwork biplanes continually taking on odds of anything up to fifty to one. It was the sort of hopelessly heroic struggle that caught at the imagination of the Maltese; and the debt that is owned to *Faith, Hope,* and *Charity* lies not only in the thirty to forty planes they shot down, not only in the thousands of tons of bombs they caused to miss their target, but also in the inspiration they afforded the people of Malta. For the Maltese never forgot the gladiator pilots' example of fortitude and self-sacrifice. It was an example they themselves were to follow, with equal heroism, in the months to come.

By late August the end seemed very near. The Gladiators and their pilots had flown themselves to exhaustion. They were reeling about the sky like a pair of punch-drunk boxers, fighting instinctively in a haze of tiredness, sleeplessness, and pain. Then the miracle happened. One morning there was a louder-than-usual roar over the airstrip at Hal Far. The AA guns were silent as four sleek monoplanes came hurtling over the airfield. Burges and Waters, who were standing by, dived instinctively for shelter. Then they looked up.

"By God!" Both spoke as one. "Hurricanes!"

4

The range of a Hurricane Mk. II (tropicalized) in still air, at 130 knots, at 10,000 feet is 521 miles.
—PILOTS' HANDLING NOTES

The problem of flying fighter reinforcements to Malta was twofold. In the first place, every available plane was needed, in the summer of 1940, in the Battle of Britain. In the second, there was no Allied airfield within flying range of the island—even with extra fuel tanks and a following wind neither Spitfires nor Hurricanes had the slightest hope of reaching the island without refueling.

Eventually, a system of embarking fighters on an aircraft carrier, convoying them to within range of the island, and then flying them off was perfected; with the result that in two years some three hundred and fifty fighter aircraft were flown to Malta with no more than a dozen casualties. These air-ferry operations, being primarily a Navy commitment, were planned and controlled by Admiral Somerville from his head-quarters at Gibraltar; and generally speaking, their history is one of effective co-operation between Navy and Air Force.

The smooth running of the later trips, however, was achieved only at a price—the price of men's lives: lives that were lost in the early star-crossed Operation "White," one of the most poignant tragedies of the war

The first air-ferry operation had taken place in August, when twelve Hurricanes had flown in to relieve *Faith, Hope,* and *Charity.* This operation had been an unqualified success. But from the moment the planes touched down, the Italians stepped up the tempo of their attacks in an effort to prevent the R.A.F. from gaining a permanent foothold: and by October only four Hurricanes and one Gladiator were left. It was therefore decided to repeat the operation, and toward the end of the month twelve tropicalized Hurricanes and twelve specially chosen pilots were embarked on the ancient aircraft carrier *Argus* and taken at short notice to Gibraltar. Here they waited, until the warships of Force H were ready to guard them on their way to a flying-off position somewhere south of Sardinia.

The basic plan of Operation "White" was simple. Admiral Somerville would escort the *Argus* and her Hurricanes to within flying range of Malta; the aircraft would then take off in two subflights of six, each subflight being led by a Fleet Air Arm Skua (in which an observer would plot their best course for the island). It was found that the route followed would take the planes very close to Galita Island (off the Tunisian coast); and as an additional safeguard, Air Officer Commanding Malta agreed to have two of his long-range bombers waiting over the island to meet the Hurricanes and guide them back along the last stage of their journey. As soon as the planes had left *Argus*, Admiral Somerville was to retire to Gibraltar. Nothing, it seemed, could be simpler.

There were, however, two outside factors which had to be taken into account: the weather and the Italian fleet. Bad

Blackburn Skua

weather could, of course, jeopardize the whole operation; while if the Italian fleet put to sea it could, all too easily, interfere decisively, annihilating both the *Argus* and her comparatively light escort. It was, in the end, an unhappy combination of these two factors which was to prove disastrous.

At 4 A.M. on November 15, 1940, Force H pulled out of Gibraltar. The night was fine, with bright moonlight silhouetting the ships as they moved past the back cloth of the Rock.

Admiral Somerville had managed to muster quite an impressive-looking escort. The *Renown* was there, flying the admiral's flag; so was the *Ark Royal*, together with three cruisers and seven destroyers. The Hurricane pilots, as they watched the massive warships positioning themselves around their carrier, must have reckoned that they were in good hands. Yet in many respects Force H was more impressive in appearance than in fact. The *Renown*, for example, was something of a white elephant, being slow, lightly armored, and no match for a modern Italian battleship; the *Ark Royal*, with her unarmored flight deck, was peculiarly vulnerable; while the *Argus* (she was *pre*-First World War!) was unbelievably snail-like. Small wonder that Admiral Somerville, as he surveyed his ships, hoped the Italian fleet would remain in harbor.

And within a few hours of sailing, something happened that added to his already considerable anxiety. At 11:30 that morning a Spanish civil airliner, bound from Tetuán to Melilla, passed almost directly over the fleet; and it was well known that Spanish radio operators were prone to forget international law and broadcast on Italian frequencies.

That evening Somerville's suspicions were confirmed, and his anxiety deepened. For at sunset came news of Italian naval forces concentrating in the Gulf of Sorrento.

A couple of hours later the barometer began to fall.

November 16 dawned dull and overcast, with a blustering westerly wind, low cloud, and poor visibility. By noon the weather was too bad for flying, and *Ark Royal*'s antisubmarine patrols had to be withdrawn. Withdrawn, too, were Malta's reconnaissance planes from the Gulf of Sorrento; though not before one of them had reported a battleship, seven cruisers, and an unspecified number of destroyers standing south out of Naples.

Admiral Somerville was now in a difficult position. If he

kept on, he might well, in the bad weather, run slap into the Italian fleet. If he turned back, Malta would fail to get her badly needed planes. His own words (in the official report written after the operation) explain his dilemma exactly—and his solution to it.

It seemed to me [he wrote]

1. The Italians were probably aware of our departure from Gibraltar.
2. They might well consider engaging Force H with their superior forces in the hope of balancing their recent losses at Taranto.

In view of this I deemed it advisable to fly off the Hurricanes from a position as far to the west as weather would permit. In reply to an enquiry, *Argus* informed me that with the wind as at present the Hurricanes could be flown off from Latitude 37° 40′ N, Longitude 6° 40′ E. Since all available meteorological information indicated a continuation of the westerly winds . . . I decided to accept this as the flying-off position.

Position 37° 40′ N, 6° 40′ E was some forty miles to the west of the flying-off area originally agreed on. But it seemed to Admiral Somerville, and to Captain Rushbrooke of the *Argus*, that this new position still gave the Hurricanes a reasonable margin of safety. For the amended position was rather less than 420 miles from Malta, and the range of the Hurricanes, in still air, was—according to the Air Ministry Handling Notes—521 miles. Bearing in mind the following wind, there seemed not the slightest doubt that the Hurricanes could reach the island without difficulty.

So the new position was unanimously agreed upon.

During the night of November 16–17 the weather started to clear, but the latest "met." report from Malta (timed 11:30 A.M. on the sixteenth) indicated that the wind in the Malta Channel was still west-southwesterly. And there seemed no reason to believe it would change. On board the *Argus* the first subflight was ranged on deck, ready to take off at dawn.

Force H arrived in position 37° 40′ N, 6° 40′ E at 5:45 A.M. It was still dark. Loath to proceed farther east, Admiral Somerville waited impatiently for dawn. At six o'clock the eastern sky paled imperceptibly; the Hurricanes and the Skua started their engines, and at 6:15 A.M. the first planes roared safely off *Argus'* narrow deck. They circled the carrier several times, climbing to 2000 feet. In the gray uncertain light it took them the better part of fifteen minutes to get into formation and take departure over the center of the fleet. As they left the deck, *Argus'* meteorological officer checked the wind. It was 220°/20 knots. An hour later the second subflight followed the first; and again the meteorological officer checked the wind. It was 250°/16 knots. Veering and falling.

Before the planes were out of sight, Admiral Somerville had reversed course and was heading at top speed for Gibraltar. He thought at first that Operation "White" had been an unqualified success; but toward midday a spate of disturbing signals came streaming in. By sunset he knew the worst. Of the fourteen planes to take off from *Argus*, only five had arrived. Somewhere, in the sea lanes leading to Malta, nine of the aircraft had run out of petrol and crashed.

The leader of the first subflight of Hurricanes was Flying Officer J.A.F. Maclachlan, D.F.C. Though only twenty-one, Maclachlan was an experienced pilot; he had served with 88 Bomber Squadron in France (earning his D.F.C. by blowing up the last bridge over the Marne) and had later transferred to a Hurricane squadron and taken part in the Battle of Britain. Now, he formed up beside the Skua and soon saw the rest of his subflight strung out beside him in loose echelon starboard.

And so, at 150 m.p.h., they headed for Malta. Their height was 2000 feet.

After a while the observer of the Skua noticed something strange. On the surface of the sea, cloud shadows were moving increasingly slowly; and the sea itself was changing its pattern. He dropped smoke floats and found a wind. To his amazement it was east-southeasterly, eleven knots: almost an exact reciprocal of when they had left the carrier. He realized that with the wind now almost dead ahead, they would be hard pressed to reach Malta before they ran out of fuel. Making a slight alteration of course to allow for the new direction of the wind, he kept steadily on. There was nothing more he could do. (All pilots had been briefed to fly at a certain height and speed: the most economic, he assumed, for the Hurricanes.) Soon, to add to their difficulties, visibility worsened; patches of thickening sea mist drifting over the

Tunisian shore. By seven o'clock they were flying blind through a baffling patchwork of mist and cloud. But the Skua observer kept his head; he concentrated on his dead-reckoning plot and made an exact landfall—albeit twenty-five minutes late—over the northern tip of Galita Island. Here, much to the pilots' relief, a Malta-based Sunderland was waiting for them, to lead them back on the second stage of their journey.

But this second stage proved even more nerve-racking than the first. For the Hurricane pilots realized now what was happening: realized that with every revolution of their propellers, with the combustion of every drop of their petrol, their expectation of life was draining inexorably away.

Maclachlan—who had recently taken a course on Hurricanes—adjusted his mixture control and his constant-speed airscrew to squeeze the last fraction of a mile out of his dwindling supply of fuel; but several of the other pilots, accustomed to flying older Hurricanes with variable-pitch propellers, were uncertain how to adjust their pitch, mixture, and throttle controls to the most economic setting. They were forty-five miles short of Malta when the engine of the Hurricane next to Maclachlan started to run roughly. For several minutes it spluttered and coughed uneasily. Then it cut. Stone-dead. The Hurricane broke formation. Like a slowly falling leaf she spiraled down: down into the sea. Maclachlan watched her. For a moment he hesitated; then he, too, broke formation. Losing height, he began to circle the spot where the Hurricane had ditched. He could see the pilot struggling in the sea. He called up the Sunderland, and soon the big unwieldy flying boat came down to join him. Maclachlan flew low over the pilot, rocking his wings; and the Sunderland landed on the sea, taxied across to the pilot, and hauled him aboard. Then Sunderland and Hurricane again headed for Malta.

Soon they saw the other planes, away ahead of them: five Hurricanes trailing the single Skua. They disappeared into a veil of cloud. When they emerged there were only four Hurricanes. Another of the fighters had run out of fuel: had fallen helplessly into the sea. The pilot was never found.

Visibility in the Malta Channel was very bad, with a light southeasterly wind drifting a mixture of fog, mist, and cloud over the sea. But both Sunderland and Skua were in radio contact with Luqa, and D.F. bearings enabled the planes to home directly on to the island. Without the radio they would hardly have stood a chance; for Malta lay wreathed in cloud: invisible until they were actually over the land. Then, sudden and unexpected, out of the mist rose the plateau of Mdina Rabat, and two minutes later the dusty runways of Luqa. The Hurricanes hadn't sufficient fuel for a circuit; they plummeted down, higgledy-piggledy, as quickly as they could. The engine of one cut dead before the plane had taxied clear of the runway; the second plane to touch down had three gallons left in her tank; the third had less than four; and in Maclachlan's tank there wasn't sufficient petrol to cover an upended sixpence! Another five minutes and all four of them would have crashed.

The first subflight had been lucky; it was otherwise with the second.

Exactly what happened to them will never be known, and it is perhaps kinder not to probe too searchingly. But the basic facts are these.

The second subflight missed Galita Island; they never kept their rendezvous with the bomber from Malta. As soon as he realized they were lost, the Skua observer called up Malta for help. But his radio receiver was faulty, and he couldn't pick up the island's reply. Desperately he cast around the Sicilian Channel, hoping every minute to see the longed-for shore. But no shore came. One by one the Hurricanes that were with him ran out of fuel and fell helplessly into the sea. At last only the Skua was left. Soon she, too, was very close to the limit of her endurance. Then suddenly, through the curtain of mist, the pilot sighted land: a low, green shore line sweeping the width of the northern horizon. He turned toward it. Crossing the coast, he was still trying to identify his landfall when ack-ack guns barked angrily; and the Skua— seventy-five miles off course—fell blazing off the Sicilian shore.

Of the fourteen aircraft that had that morning taken off from *Argus*, only five were left. It was a tragic loss of vitally needed planes and brave men's lives.

Like every other wartime disaster, Operation "White" was followed by boards of inquiry, top-secret reports, and a spate of official findings. After twenty years the ashes are too cold to be raked over again. Yet it is perhaps easier to assess responsibility now than it was at the time, and certainly today the official findings strike an unbiased observer as being more than a little unjust.

For the board of inquiry ascribed the catastrophe as being "mainly due to a lack of knowledge on the part of the Hurricane pilots as to how to fly their aircraft when fitted with constant speed airscrews"; while a contributory cause was stated to be "bad navigation on the part of the observer of the second Skua." It is easy to blame air crew; especially when they are dead. A more balanced judgment, made today, would seem to indicate that the tragedy was brought about by four contributory factors.

(1) Inadequate weather forecasting. The significant point here is that when the Hurricanes took off at dawn on November 17 the latest meteorological report they had received from the area they were flying into was timed 11:30 A.M. on the day before: was, in other words, nineteen hours out of date. In subsequent operations far greater attention was paid to obtaining accurate, last-minute weather reports.

(2) Lack of liaison between Navy and Air Force. The Naval Air Operations officers aboard *Argus* and *Ark Royal* were unaccustomed to dealing with Hurricanes; all their information about them had to be gleaned from the Air Ministry Handling Notes. These Handling Notes state specifically that "the range of a Hurricane Mk. II (tropicalized) in still air, at 130 knots, at 10,000 feet is 521 miles." Yet the pilots were briefed to fly at 2000 feet. Naturally their range in the "heavier" lower air was considerably less than if they had flown at the correct height. An R.A.F. liaison officer, to assist in briefing the pilots, would have prevented such a mistake. In every subsequent air-ferry operation, one was carried.

(3) Excessive caution on the part of Admiral Somerville. Bearing in mind that the safe arrival of the Hurricanes was the sole objective of Operation "White," it is reasonable to argue that greater risk to the fleet ought to have been accepted in order to penetrate far enough east to make the success of the operation beyond doubt. Certainly in subsequent trips the carriers concerned nearly always stood well to the east of 6° 40′ E, and as Sir Winston Churchill put it, "Never again were the margins cut so fine, and though

many similar operations took place in the future never did such a catastrophe recur."

(4) Pilots' and observers' errors. That some of the pilots and one of the observers made errors of judgment is undeniable. But, looking back, it would seem that these errors were among the lesser rather than the greater of the factors which contributed to the disaster. For even if no air-crew errors had been made, the fate of the Hurricanes would still have hung precariously in the balance. What happened to Maclachlan proves that. It is interesting to note that when planning subsequent air ferries an attempt was generally made to give the pilots concerned a certain amount of practice in long-distance sea flying.

And this underlines the heartening factor which goes far toward relieving the tragedy of Operation "White." Its lessons were well learned, were never forgotten; and subsequent air ferries were conducted with a degree of concentrated efficiency which enabled consignment after consignment of fighters to be flown without loss to the island which had such desperate need of them.

5

Illustrious *müssen sinken*.*
—HITLER'S INSTRUCTIONS TO GENERAL GEISSLER

It was April in Barrow-in-Furness—April 1937: and the ship-yards were steaming gently in the warmth of sun after rain. Down in Vickers' No. 1 slipway a historic little ceremony was taking place. Watched by a knot of workmen and the vulture silhouettes of the cranes, the keel of a new warship was being laid: the keel of Job No. 732. Mr. Nicholson, the shipyard manager, was there; so was his foreman, Mr. Parnell, together with a couple of dozen shipbuilding technicians; and in the middle of them stood a gray-haired rather diffident man, whom none of the others knew with any degree of intimacy— Mr. Forbes, the Admiralty architect: the creator of Job No. 732.

Early in 1936 Mr. Forbes had been commissioned to design an aircraft carrier for the Navy's air arm—only recently taken over from the R.A.F. The result, after nine months' sweat and toil and tears, was Job No. 732: a ship of beautiful but revolutionary proportions.

The difference between Mr. Forbes' design and the host of other designs concurrently being accepted in Washington, Paris, and Tokyo lay in the position of the carrier's main deck. Now, a ship's main deck is her center of gravity: her strongest, heaviest point; all the superstructure above it has to be comparatively light. In other carriers the main deck was always the hangar floor; which meant that everything on top of the floor, including the hangar itself and the flight deck, were of necessity flimsy structures: highly vulnerable. But in

---

*Illustrious must be sunk.

Mr. Forbes' design the main deck was the hangar roof and flight deck combined, where a mass of interlaced 100-ton girders gave the ship her strength. And on top of these girders was laid the armor plating: strong 3½-inch riveted sheets of steel, designed to withstand the heaviest bomb envisaged in 1937—the 500-pounder. Thus, the heart of the carrier, the hangar, was turned into a bombproof box.

It says much for the foresight of the Admiralty that they accepted this revolutionary design with no quibbles, no reservations, and a deal of enthusiasm.

Two years after the laying down of her keel, Job No. 732 was completed, and Mr. Forbes came up to Barrow for another ceremony: her commissioning. She was christened H.M.S. *Illustrious:* the first aircraft carrier in the world with an armor-plated flight deck.

She entered the Eastern Mediterranean in September 1940—at the same time that Captain Pretty was coaxing the *Cornwall* into Grand Harbour. And if ever a single ship helped to shape the course of the war, it was the great steel-shod carrier which now arrived in Alexandria as if in answer to Admiral Cunningham's prayers.

For up to now the Mediterranean Fleet had been forced to endure Italian shadowing and bombing without hope of retaliation; they had had no radar, no effective fighter protection, and no force capable of striking at the Italians (whose vessels were superior to the Britsh in almost every respect except the morale and efficiency of their crews). But when *Illustrious* joined them things were different: very different. Within four months the carrier had crippled half the Italian battle

CRDA Cant. Z. 506B

fleet and had established Admiral Cunningham in complete
control of Mussolini's *"mare nostrum."* A hint of things to
come had occurred within a few hours of her joining her new
command. Her radar had picked up a couple of shadowers;
her Fulmars had roared off the flight deck; and in a matter of
minutes the surprised Cants had been toppled into the sea
within full view of the Commander in Chief. The effect on
Admiral Cunningham was, to use his own word, "indescribable."
For the next four months he took *Illustrious* with him wherev-
er he went: from Malta to Beirut, from the Gulf of Sidra to
the Ionian Sea. She was the most overworked—and the
happiest—ship in the fleet.

In October she escorted a small convoy to Malta: three
ships that got through unopposed under cover of a week of
storms. Early in November she achieved her most famous
victory—at Taranto—when twenty-one of her aircraft put out
of action three battleships, two cruisers, and two fleet auxilia-
ries (doing more damage in a couple of hours than 151
warships of the Grand Fleet had achieved at Jutland in two
days!).* After that her aircraft ranged the length and breadth
of the Eastern Mediterranean, sinking supply ships off Tunisia,
blasting airdromes in the Dodecanese, and blowing up Rommel's
supply dumps in the Libyan Desert. Toward the end of
November she met and escorted yet another convoy, which
had come right through the Mediterranean from west to east,
having dropped three merchantmen at Malta en route. And
this last operation demonstrated beyond all dispute how
firmly Admiral Cunningham now had the Eastern Mediterranean under his control. For, throughout the whole of the
seven days his fleet was at sea, not a single gun had to be
fired. The Italians gave him a wide berth; allowed him a clear
passage. Once bitten by *Illustrious*, they now fought shy of
her with a prudence carried to almost ludicrous extremes.

Thus, thanks very largely to the great armor-decked carrier,
the autumn of 1940 was, in the Mediterranean, a season of
almost uninterrupted success, culminating in the C. in C.'s
visit to Malta three or four days before Christmas. To some,
the situation at the end of the year appeared to be roses, roses

---

*For the full story of the Italian Fleet's disastrous defeat, read *To War
In a Stringbag* by Commander Charles Lamb. Another volume in THE
BANTAM WAR BOOK SERIES.

all the way. Various offensive projects, including the capture
of Pantelleria and the invasion of Sicily, were planned for the
immediate future. But before these could be carried out,
certain far-reaching events ended all hope of a large-scale
offensive.

For Mussolini, seeing his fleet shattered, his armies in
retreat, and his air force rendered impotent, called to Hitler
for help. And so, at the turn of the year, the Luftwaffe came
to the Mediterranean: three hundred and fifty Heinkels,
Junkers, and Messerschmitts, spearheaded by Fliegerkorps
X, the antishipping dive bombers, cream of the German Air
Force.

It was a case of cause and effect. *Illustrious'* Swordfish had
gone to Taranto. Now, in retaliation, the Luftwaffe's Stukas
had come to Sicily. And they had come for one overriding
purpose. General Geissler, commanding officer of Fliegerkorps
X, had been given a list of priorities; and the first of these
read simply and briefly: "Illustrious *müssen sinken.*"

As soon as they had settled into the Catania and Comiso
airstrips, Fliegerkorps X began their preparations. Day after
day, screened by protecting fighters, they dive-bombed a
mock-up model of *Illustrious* floating off the Sicilian shore.

General Geissler had estimated that no more than four
direct hits would be needed to sink the carrier; and this
number would certainly have finished off any ordinary flattop.
(Looking through a list of aircraft carriers sunk during the
war, it is interesting to note how easily the unwieldy vessels
were usually sent to the bottom. *Ark Royal,* one torpedo;
Soryu, three bombs; *Akagi,* two bombs; *Lexington,* one bomb
and one torpedo.) As, day after day, General Geissler watched
the practice bombing, he felt confident that his highly trained
Fliegerkorps X would achieve at least four hits.

The *Illustrious* meanwhile, unaware of the wrath to come,
was about to join another convoy, or rather a series of
convoys, known by the code name of Operation "Excess."

Operation "Excess" consisted of another through convoy
from west to east. It was planned that the bulk of the
merchantmen (some bound for the Piraeus, some for Malta)
should leave Gibraltar escorted by Admiral Somerville's Force
H; they would be met south of Pantelleria by Admiral
Cunningham and the heavy units of the Eastern Mediterra-

nean Fleet. Opportunity would also be taken, while the fleets were at sea, to pass two storeships into Malta from the east and to escort eight empty merchantmen back to Alexandria.

This somewhat cumbersome plan came into being principally through Admiral Somerville's fear of an attack by the Italian fleet while the convoy was still in the Narrows; this fear led him to press for the presence of heavy units in the area between Pantelleria and Malta. Admiral Cunningham took the view that the superior numbers of the Italian fleet "did not greatly matter"; nevertheless, he was persuaded to take *Warspite*, *Valiant*, and *Illustrious* some hundred miles to the west of Malta in order to meet and protect the convoy.

Nothing could have suited Fliegerkorps X more perfectly. From their Sicilian bases it was less than an hour's flight to the sea lanes west of Malta.

Convoy "Excess" left Gibraltar a little before dark on the evening of January 6. Openly, without pretense of secrecy, the merchantmen and their escort stood westward, out into the broad Atlantic. The Axis spies, who kept a check on Allied shipping movements, were deceived. They didn't know that late in the night the ships turned, retraced their steps, and a little after moonset passed back into the Mediterranean. Dawn found them standing east-northeastward, hugging the Spanish shore: ostensibly a random gaggle of merchantmen bound for Cartagena. Again they were unobserved. On the night of January 7, as soon as it was dark, they increased speed and cut due south, straight for the African coast. They made a good landfall; then again they headed east-northeast, keeping some thirty miles offshore. All through the night of January 8–9 they followed the African coast, undetected, while Admiral Somerville and the warships of Force H patrolled far to seaward. The wind was light, the sea calm, the sky flecked with cloud, the Italians conspicuous by their absence.

Meanwhile Admiral Cunningham had left Alexandria with the Eastern Mediterranean Fleet. His passage, for the first few days, was as uneventful as Admiral Somerville's (though he was persistently shadowed from the moment he left harbor). On January 8 two of his cruisers, *Gloucester* and *Southampton*, arrived in Grand Harbour; they disembarked a number of troops, then proceeded west through the Skerki Channel to join Admiral Somerville. They met him at dawn the following morning—January 9—and a few minutes later came the first intimation that the Italians knew a convoy was at sea: a formation of ten Savoias delivered a co-ordinated, well-rehearsed attack.

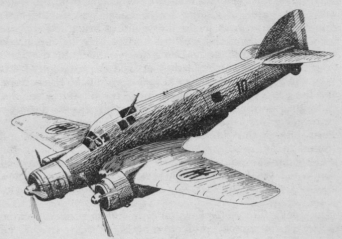

Savoia-Marchetti S.M. 79

It wasn't so much the attack itself that was disturbing, as the manner in which it was made. The convoy, it was clear, was no longer a secret; it had been discovered; it was being observed. There was nothing Admiral Somerville could do about it. They beat off the Savoias and pushed on. At midday they passed Galita Bank. At sunset they reached the start of the Skerki Channel.

Everything was very quiet. *Ark Royal* had seven aircraft up, searching for the Italian fleet; but when the pilots landed at dusk their reports were all the same: "Nothing sighted." So the convoy and its reduced escort moved quietly into the Narrows, while Admiral Somerville returned to Gibraltar.

The first stage of Operation "Excess" had been successfully accomplished.

By dawn next morning the second stage—the passage of the Skerki Channel—had also been completed with no great difficulty. All through the night of January 9–10, the convoy had headed east-southeast, undisturbed. The only excitement came at dawn, when two Italian torpedo boats were encountered at the eastern end of the channel. One of these—the *Vega*— was sunk after a brisk exchange of fire.

It was a still, near-windless morning, and over the quiet water the sound of gunfire traveled far. Away in the east, Admiral Cunningham heard the sound of firing and saw the flash of guns along the western horizon. He led his battle fleet—*Warspite, Valiant*, and *Illustrious*—straight for the scene of action. But by the time they arrived the excitement was over; the *Vega*, fighting bravely, had been sent to the bottom; and the convoy had debouched out of the Skerki Channel.

As, that morning, the ships moved quietly eastward it must have seemed that the worst of their troubles were over. They were through the Narrows; they were past Pantelleria; and around them lay a screen of heavy warships, including the great armor-decked carrier whose aircraft for four months had dominated the Levant. By ten o'clock Malta lay less than a hundred miles to the east. The sun shone pleasantly out of an azure sky.

At 10:06 *Illustrious* flew off five Fulmars on a routine fighter patrol: convoy protection at 14,000 feet. At first all was quiet. But a little after eleven o'clock a succession of single Italian aircraft tried to approach the convoy. The Fulmars drove them off; shot two of them down. But the persistent teasing and feinting approaches depleted the Fulmars' fuel. And their ammunition. By 12:15 one of them had been damaged and had landed back on *Illustrious;* two were completely out of ammunition, and two had used 50 per cent.

At 12:20 came yet another feint. A pair of Savoia torpedo bombers approached the convoy from the south. They came in low, almost feathering the sea. They headed straight for *Illustrious*. They forced her to turn out of line in order to avoid their torpedoes. They also drew the last pair of Fulmars down in pursuit; zigzagging back toward Sicily, they decoyed them away from the fleet.

Above the convoy the sky was suddenly empty: devoid of fighters. The time was 12:28.

On the bridge of *Illustrious* Captain Boyd looked first at the empty sky, then at this watch. He wasn't especially worried, for he knew that in seven minutes another group of Fulmars was due to take off—already the planes were ranged on the flight deck, warming their engines. He wondered for a moment if he ought to try and get them air-borne early; but it seemed hardly worth it, just for the sake of seven minutes.

He hadn't reckoned with General Geissler's timing. For, in those seven minutes that the fleet lay unprotected, Fliegerkorps X made its attack.

At exactly 12:30 radar picked up a large group of aircraft coming in from the north. Captain Boyd felt a sudden stab of fear: a premonition of disaster. He gave two orders (the only possible orders): recalling the Fulmars that were air-borne and ordering those on the flight deck to take off.

There now occurred one of those tragic delays that lose battles if not wars.

Before the Fulmars could take off from the flight deck, it was necessary for *Illustrious* to swing into the wind. But Captain Boyd's standing orders expressly forbade his turning into wind *without prior permission from the C. in C.* It was four minutes before the necessary permission was flashed from the flagship. And in those four minutes the Stukas arrived overhead.

Captain Boyd's battle summary describes the events that followed with dispassionate brevity:

12:30	Radar detects large formation of enemy aircraft.
12:34	C. in C. orders alteration of course to fly off Fulmars.
12:34½	First Fulmar leaves flight deck.
12:35	Large formation of enemy aircraft sighted on starboard quarter.
12:36	Last Fulmar leaves flight deck. Carrier opens fire.
12:37	Ordered alteration of course and adopted loose formation.
12:38	Attack begins. First hits on *Illustrious*.

Fliegerkorps X's bombing of the *Illustrious* ranks as one of the great flying achievements of the war (comparable with the crippling of the Italian fleet at Taranto; Guy Gibson's breaking of the Möhne Dam;* the Mosquito bombing of Amsterdam Jail; and the Air Arm's Barracuda attack on the *Tirpitz*). It

---

*For the full account of this action read *The Dam Busters* by Paul Brickhill another volume in the Bantam War Book Series.

was carried out by forty Stukas; and it lasted no more than six and a half minutes.

The Stukas came in at 12,000 feet. They were almost unopposed by fighters (the Fulmars which had just taken off couldn't climb fast enough to intercept them before they'd released their bombs), but they were heavily engaged by ack-ack from the combined convoy and fleet. They avoided the ack-ack by breaking into two formations; one of thirty aircraft, which concentrated on *Illustrious*, and one of ten aircraft, which carried out diversionary attacks on other ships—mostly on *Warspite* and *Valiant*.

The formation attacking *Illustrious* split into three subflights; three cloverleaves, in which the Stukas adopted a loose, flexible formation, constantly changing their height, speed, and relative position, to prevent the ack-ack getting their range. They timed their attack to a split second, peeling off first from one subflight then from another; screaming down nearly simultaneously from different bearings so as to divide the carrier's fire. Some planes dived straight in from 12,000 feet; others dived to 7000 feet, checked with a twisting spiral turn, then plummeted into the aiming dive. Their angle varied from 65 to 80 degrees; their height to release, from 1200 to 800 feet—though most of them, after bombing, came screaming down to deck level, machife-gunning the carrier as they flattened out. Their attack was so perfectly co-ordinated that no two aircraft got in each other's way by bombing simultaneously; yet at no time were there ever less than six aircraft actually in their dive, drawing the carrier's fire. Captain Boyd—who was used to an extremely high standard of flying—described that attack as "severe, brilliantly executed, and pressed home with the utmost skill and determination." At the end of six and a half minutes the last of the Stukas was zigzagging away at sea level; and *Illustrious* lay disabled, a crippled, blazing shell, smothered by no fewer than six direct hits and three fractional misses.

Fliegerkorps X had lived up to its reputation. The *Illustrious* ought to have sunk.

On board the carrier conditions were so cataclysmic that the usual adjectives of disaster fail to give any sort of accurate picture. But the facts speak for themselves.

The first bomb hit the *Illustrious* at 12:38. It was the only one which did no serious damage. It passed through the loading platform of No. 1 port pom-pom, wounding two of the gun crew. But it didn't explode on impact; it passed clean through the ship's side, burst on hitting the water, and colandered the hull with splinters of shrapnel. *Illustrious* lurched uneasily but passed through the bomb splash virtually undamaged.

A few seconds later she was hit again: hit right for'ard, close to her bow, where her armor plating was weakest. This bomb penetrated the flight deck and burst in the paint store. Sheets of multicolored flame gushed out of the fractured deck. Clouds of rainbow-tinted smoke streamed away downwind; and a stench of burning oil made the for'ard gun crews choke and retch. The damage-control parties rushed into action. The paint locker was sealed off and flooded; and though for several hours spirals of smoke kept eddying out of the buckled deck, the damage was quickly localized and brought under control.

The third bomb missed the island by less then eighteen inches and burst flush on No. 2 starboard pom-pom. The pom-pom was wrenched off its mounting, twisted into a blackened laminated wreck, and flung against the base of the island. Every man of its gun crew was killed. This bomb, a 500-pounder, was fitted with a direct-action fuse; was specially designed to burst on impact; to wipe out personnel. Its fragments swept the flight deck, killing four men in the gun crew from No. 1 starboard pom-pom and toppling the ammunition-supply parties into the catwalk like a line of string-jerked marionettes. Within a minute of the start of the attack, 20 per cent of *Illustrious'* for'ard gun crews had been killed or seriously wounded.

But it was the fourth hit which started the real damage. Having disrupted the carrier's ack-ack with antipersonnel bombs, the second wave of Stukas used bombs of a different kind: armor-piercing 1000-pounders. And at 12:40 the first of these fell flush on the after lift.

The lift, at the time, was halfway between hangar and flight deck, and on it was a Fulmar, the young midshipman pilot strapped into his cockpit. In one terrible moment Fulmar and pilot were obliterated; and the great 300-ton lift platform was unended like a matchbox. For a second it hung poised at a fantastic angle; then it came crashing down into the hangar. Bomb fragments scythed through the after gun bays, knocking out 70 per cent of the 4.5-inch turrets. And down in the hangar, the parked aircraft—nine Swordfish loaded with depth charges and torpedoes and four Fulmars recently refueled—started to burn.

But once again the fire- and damage-control parties tackled the flames. They lowered the fire screens; isolated the burning aircraft; and within a couple of minutes the fires were coming under control.

Then *Illustrious* was hit again: was hit twice within ten seconds: and in her most vulnerable parts.

At exactly 12:42 a 1000-pound bomb struck the after lift within ten feet of where the previous bomb had landed; and struck the lift at such a point and at such an angle that it didn't burst on impact but skidded along the slope of the upended lift platform, shot into the hangar, and burst in the very heart of the ship. Showers of white-hot metal ricocheted among the planes. The fire-screens disintegrated, their steel walls shattered into a myriad scythe-sharp splinters, which joined the bomb fragments to sweep like a flurry of cosmic hail through the crowded hangar. The fires were restarted. Ammunition and fuel tanks exploded. Casualties were heavy.

Ten seconds later another 1000-pounder burst almost beneath the carrier's bow, level with the for'ard lift. This lift, already damaged by the second and third bombs, was now punched up into the shape of an arch. And through this arch a great draft of wind swept into the stricken hangar. The fires were fanned to a blazing inferno. Great torrents of smoke and fifty-foot tongues of flame poured out of the after-lift well. The heart of *Illustrious* became one white-hot laminated furnace.

To the rest of the fleet it seemed impossible that the carrier would survive. She yawed out of line, smothered in bomb splashes, belching smoke and flames. Above her circled the last subflight of Stukas: ten planes which now dived screaming onto the stricken ship.

There was little in the way of ack-ack to stop them now; for half *Illustrious'* guns lay shattered and twisted, while those still capable of firing couldn't see their targets for the torrents of smoke. But the last few Stukas ran up against another, and more effective, deterrent than ack-ack: *Illustrious'* Fulmars.

The Fulmars had taken off through the spray of the first near misses. They were heavy, near-obsolescent planes:

notoriously slow climbers. Desperately their pilots clawed skyward; but no power on earth could give them sufficient height to intercept the first few attacks. But with the last attacks it was different. Though the Fulmars were still in a most unfavorable position—below the planes they were trying to intercept—they could at least do something: could divert the final stages of the Stukas' dives. They flung themselves at the German planes: twisting, near ramming, their machine guns a-clatter, they fought desperately to save their ship. Those with no ammunition carried out dummy attacks. And they disrupted the Stukas, shooting five of them down and forcing the others to bomb quickly, inaccurately. Out of the last ten planes only one got through to deliver an undisturbed attack.

But this last plane struck a virtual deathblow.

It dropped its bomb—the sixth to score a direct hit—flush on the center line of the flight deck, about twenty feet for'ard of the lift. The flight deck, fractured and buckled by previous hits, collapsed. The bomb tore through the armor plating, plunged through the blazing hangar, and burst in the deck below. It exploded flush on the after ammunition conveyor. The ship was plunged into darkness. Everywhere aft of the wardroom the fires took hold and raged through the shattered compartments, where upward of a hundred men lay trapped by fallen debris. A broken petrol pipe sprayed streams of liquid fire through the dark, smoke-filled passageways. The decks became laminated with the heat. Water sprayed from the fire hoses, evaporated into hissing clouds of steam: steam which mingled with the smoke and flames now pouring out of the whole of the after part of the ship.

The Stukas zigzagged north to Catania. The Fulmars, unable to return to their ship, headed east for Malta. And *Illustrious* pulled out of line. Listing, wreathed in smoke, her engines pulsating unevenly, she lurched into a series of erratic tightening circles. From her halyards fluttered a single pennant: "Not under control."

The time was 12:55. It wouldn't be dark for another seven hours. Malta was eighty-five miles to the east. And Captain Boyd knew that Fliegerkorps X would—if necessary—be back.

As the damage-control reports came pouring into the bridge, the captain realized that he had one ray of hope: one chance of saving his ship. The engines seemed virtually undamaged. *Illustrious* was still steaming at well over twenty knots. If only he could get her to steer in the right direction—eastward: to Malta.

During the next half hour the engineers fought a desperate battle to bring the carrier under control. Twice the senior engineer improvised electric circuits to establish some sort of relationship between the position of indicators, rudder, and wheel, but each time the current failed. Three times he rigged up emergency systems of steam steering; but after a few minutes each of them broke down. Eventually he managed to jam the rudder at midships (by using the steam-steering engine), and from that moment Captain Boyd was able to steer an approximate course on engines alone.

Within half an hour of the attack, *Illustrious*, still blazing almost from stem to stern, was running for Malta at a speed of twenty-one knots. If only she could reach the repair yards and ack-ack guns of Grand Harbour, there would be a chance of saving her.

Then came another attack.

At 1:20 *Valiant* picked up the aircraft on her radar: height 14,000, range twenty miles. No fighters were available; but the fleet clustered around *Illustrious*, protecting her as best they could with a curtain of gunfire. Luckily the bombers this time were Italian: seven Savoias which made a very halfhearted attack. They stayed at 14,000 feet, refusing to face the ack-ack, and all their bombs fell wide.

But *Illustrious* chose this inopportune moment to run amuck. Once again her steering broke down, and for several minutes she cavorted in erratic circles in the center of the fleet. But by two o'clock she was again under control and heading east, though at a slightly reduced speed—fifteen knots.

In and around her hangar the fires raged with unabated fury.

Gradually the fight to save her developed into a life-or-death battle in two compartments: the boiler rooms and the hangar.

Down in the boiler rooms conditions were appalling. The senior engineer had ordered: "Boilers must keep going, *whatever the cost*." But by two o'clock the task looked hopeless. The stokers were fainting every few minutes, the temperature was steadily rising—120°, 130°, 140°—and great volumes of smoke and chemical fumes were pouring in through ventilators and fans. Sprayer flaps and speed fans couldn't disperse the asphyxiating clouds, and soon the bulk-heads started to glow red hot. But the stokers didn't give up. The fumes were too thick for them to see the water-level and steam-pressure gauges from where they worked; so they organized a lookout watch on the dials through a shattered vent in the deck above. They used wet rags to breathe through. They drank and sluiced themselves with feed water from the auxiliary pumps. And they stayed by the boilers. As Captain Boyd afterward wrote: "The courage and devotion to duty of the boiler-room crew was quite magnificent."

In the hangar, too, it was touch and go. The prompt action of three men—Commander Tuck, Lieutenant Commander Jago, and Lieutenant Gregory—had got the sprayers working. But even the torrents of water which came pouring out of the overhead sprays couldn't quench the flames. And soon the sprayers became buckled and welded together in the all-consuming heat. All over the hangar ammunition was exploding; fuel tanks were bursting; pools of blazing petrol were sluicing across the deck; and the aircraft were burning like funeral pyres.

Hour after hour the fire parties fought the flames; and at last the fires in the for'ard part of the hangar began to slacken off and were brought more or less under control. But around the after-lift well—where three 1000-pound bombs had land-ed within a dozen square yards—the fires spread: gaining in intensity, they became utterly out of control. Neither water, foamite, nor asbestos sheeting had any noticeable effect. Hour after hour the fifty-foot banners of blue-tipped flame poured out of the after lift.

By three o'clock it seemed that the fire was certain to spread to magazines and fuel tanks. Then the senior engineer discovered that the oil pipeline pressurizing the steam steering was leaking and was pouring oil straight into the flames. Steam steering was discontinued; and almost at once the fire fighters found themselves making headway. Inch by inch the flames were beaten back.

By four o'clock *Illustrious* was within forty miles of Malta. She was still belching volumes of smoke, she was still listing drunkenly to starboard; 40 per cent of her guns were out of

action, and most of her flight deck was too hot to walk on.
But she was making eighteen knots and steering reasonably
straight.

Then Fliegerkorps X struck again.

There weren't so many planes this time: fifteen Stukas and
five Messerschmitts. They dived on the carrier in three
consecutive waves, coming in from astern, half hidden by the
pall of smoke. And this time they were met by the Fulmars,
which had flown to Malta after the first attack and had now
come back, refueled and rearmed, to protect their ship. And
protect her they did. Though outnumbered four to one, they
broke up the attacks. Five Stukas were shot flaming into the
sea. Only a single plane, the last but one to attack, got
through in an accurate dive. But this plane, once again,
struck what ought to have been a deathblow.

It seemed that *Illustrious'* after lift was a magnet to the
Stukas' bombs. For once again a 1000-pounder fell flush on
the carrier's stern, within a dozen feet of the lift.

This bomb penetrated the armor plating and burst on the
quarter-deck, where a temporary sick bay had been rigged
up. In the flash of the explosion between twenty and thirty of
the ship's company died instantaneously.

And down in the hangar the fires were rekindled.

The damage-control and fire-fighting parties were utterly
exhausted by now. For two and a half hours they had been
battling with the flames; spraying water and foamite; salvaging
ammunition; dragging out injured men; shoring up damaged
compartments; working all the while in a haze of noise and
smoke and heat. They had had no food and no rest. Now—
just when they had come to the limit of their endurance—
their enemy had been revived, and the fires in the lift well,
fanned to white heat by the latest bomb blast, again started to
spread. The reports passed up to the bridge became increasingly grave.

16:30   Fire aft still burning.
17:00   Fire aft appears to be gaining.
17:30   Fire aft out of control. Pump motors burned out.

Soon the flames were dangerously close to the magazines.
Captain Boyd was urged to flood them. He thought of air
attacks still to come, and refused.

All that evening the battle to save the carrier ebbed and flowed; the fires sometimes gaining, sometimes receding, but never coming wholly under control.

Then, an hour before sunset, within twenty-five miles of Malta, another threat developed. Suddenly and sharply the carrier began to list.

The reason wasn't hard to find. For the last five hours the overhead sprays had been discharging into the hangar, so that by evening several thousand tons of water was swirling about in the heart of the ship. And this water couldn't escape. For the scuppers and soakaways out of the hangar were blocked with fallen debris. Two things were essential: to stop the sprays and to channel away the water. Neither proved easy. But at last it was found that a shell splinter had lodged in the electric circuit controlling the sprayers, jamming them at "full on"; and once this was dislodged, the flow of water was cut off. As for the water already there, a working party crawled into the smoldering hangar and knocked the flaps out of the base of the ventilators, allowing the water to flood away through the vents of the air-conditioning system. Within an hour the list had been partially rectified.

Daylight was fading now as *Illustrious*, shrouded in steam and smoke, entered the swept channel. Ahead, a dark indeterminate mass rose out of the eastern sea: Malta. Only another fifteen miles to go. Soon the sun set, and the moon rose; colors faded and softened; even the glow in the after-lift well became less lurid, more diffused. Then came a radio message from Malta. Torpedo planes were approaching the island: were searching for *Illustrious* in the silver light of the moon.

They found her five miles from the entrance to Grand Harbour. There weren't many of them—probably only six—and they were Savoias, not Stukas. *Illustrious* and her destroyer escort fired a blind two-minute barrage, and when the smoke cleared, the torpedo bombers had vanished. Two minutes later the destroyer *Hasty* picked up a U-boat contact, fine on her port bow. The roar of depth charges echoed back from the shore; but no U-boat was seen. Slowly, steaming on engines only, the great carrier slid quietly through the swept channel. Quite suddenly everyone on board realized they were going to make it.

At exactly 10:15 that evening H.M.S. *Illustrious* secured to Parlatorio Wharf. From the dockyard rose a great wave of

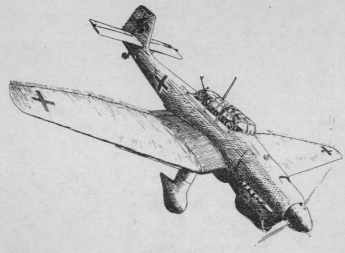

Ju 87 "Stuka"

cheering, and—incongruous but strangely moving—the strains
of "Roll Out the Barrel."

She lay like an embryo cocoon, festooned with repair
stages, dockyard pumps, fire hoses, Jacob's ladders, and
tubular scaffolding. The dockyard repair parties pumped out
her hangar, hoisted up her laminated lift platform, and plugged
her hull with wooden pegs. They rigged up temporary lighting and temporary steering. They patched up her flight deck.
All this took thirteen days. Thirteen days and thirteen nights
of unceasing, flat-out work: a desperate race to get the carrier
seaworthy before Fliegerkorps X struck again.

For they knew where she was. Within a couple of hours of
her securing to Parlatorio Wharf, a reconnaissance plane had
spotted her. And there followed raid after raid, as the Stukas
came screaming down to finish off in harbor what they had
begun at sea. *Illustrious* found her ordeal hadn't ended, it
had only just begun. And as, through day after day of vicious
concentrated bombing, the carrier suffered, so the neighboring dockyard suffered with her: became reduced to a strip of
devastated rubble.

As repairs neared completion, the German attacks rose to a furious crescendo. Malta's defenses were hard pressed. On Thursday, January 16, *Illustrious* was hit again—almost inevitably beside her after-lift well. On Sunday, the nineteenth, two near misses to port lifted her out of the water and flung her against the wharf. She was holed below the water line, her port turbine was fractured, and her boiler room flooded. But an all-night shift of a hundred special technicians patched the damage up.

The Hurricanes and Fulmars, meanwhile, had been taking their toll. In one day alone—Sunday, the 19th—they accounted for fifteen bombers and two fighters; while ack-ack averaged a score of five a day. The Luftwaffe couldn't stand such crippling losses: not day after day. They withdrew, gathering themselves for one final, overwhelming attack. But before they were ready to launch it, the *Illustrious* slipped through their fingers.

She sailed as soon as it was dark on the evening of January 23, leaving in such secrecy and haste that the repair stages were left swinging over her side. Once clear of the harbor entrance, she increased speed: ten knots, fifteen knots, twenty knots, twenty-five knots. Soon the escorting destroyers were hard put to keep up with her. She moved so fast, in fact, all that night, that she missed the cruisers sent to escort her back to Alexandria. This perhaps was just as well, since early next morning the cruisers were heavily bombed, while *Illustrious* stood undetected to the east-south east, still making twenty-five knots. She had her anxious moments. At one stage, water in the oil fuel caused her to belch volumes of jet-black smoke; at another stage she had only enough uncontaminated oil for three hours' steaming. But eventually, a little after noon on January 25, she entered Alexandria harbor. Battered. Operationally useless. But—miraculously—still afloat.

It needed eleven months' work in the dry docks of two continents before *Illustrious* was fit even for maneuvers. That wasn't surprising. The surprising thing was that she survived at all.

For no other warship of any navy ever lived through such concentrated punishment—eight direct hits (at least five of them with 1000-pounders) and seven near misses. Her ship's company, of course, were magnificent. But in any other vessel their efforts would have been unavailing. Captain Boyd realized this, and he ended his report with the words: "In conclusion I wish to pay tribute to the sound construction of the ship, which enabled her to withstand such heavy punishment."

Mr. Forbes and the shipwrights of Vickers-Armstrong could have had no finer tribute.

6

With God's help we will maintain the security of our island fortress.

—GENERAL DOBBIE

The bombs that smothered *Illustrious* were like a handful of pebbles flung into still waters; long after the splashes had died away, the waves of repercussion continued to ripple outward. For Fliegerkorps X, that fateful January afternoon, did far more than deprive Admiral Cunningham of his most valuable ship; they achieved an important strategic victory: they sealed off the Central Mediterranean to anything heavier than a cruiser. Not for another two years did an Allied battleship or aircraft carrier dare to penetrate the Sicilian Narrows, and if anyone suggested that a convoy to Malta might be escorted by capital ships right through to the island, the fate of the *Illustrious* was a counterargument that brooked no contradiction.

Thus was the pattern of future convoys irrevocably set; an escort by heavy units as far as the Narrows, and an escort by light units only for the final dash to the island.

In the five months which followed the attack on *Illustrious*, Malta received only a scattering of individual ships and one small convoy—four merchantmen westbound from Haifa; and of these, two were sunk within a few hours of their arrival in Grand Harbour. It wasn't much; but it was all that was possible. For, over the Narrows, Fliegerkorps X reigned supreme. And not only did these highly skilled Luftwaffe squadrons close the Central Mediterranean to Allied shipping; they also escorted the Afrika Korps to Libya and subjected Malta to the full horror of a long-drawn, all-out blitzkrieg.

In the case of the Afrika Korps, it was a tragedy that Malta's offensive strength had not been built up sufficiently for her forces to prevent the landing in North Africa of this formidable army with its highly mechanized equipment. As it was, Malta's submarines and night-flying Swordfish achieved no more than a very occasional success. (In March, for example, only 5 per cent of the German troops who left Sicily and only 4 per cent of their equipment failed to reach their destination.) The Afrika Korps expanded rapidly; and soon General Wavell was being bundled unceremoniously the length of Cyrenaïca.

As for the blitzkrieg on Malta, the attacks which Fliegerkorps X now unleashed on the island made the earlier raids seem, by comparison, no more than uncomfortable pinpricks. To understand why the Maltese reacted as they did to this new spate of attacks, it is necessary to look right back to the uncertain years of the mid-1930s.

The Spanish Civil War and Mussolini's rape of Abyssinia and Albania had cast dark shadows across the Mediterranean. Three times in the decade 1930–40 war had come very close to the people of Malta; but each time the crisis had receded, and the islanders had been left at peace. Then at last—on June 10, 1940—the threat which had for so long been hanging over the island materialized. Malta and Italy were at war.

The Maltese were not sure what to expect. They had been told terrible stories about the effects of bombing; they knew their own defenselessness; and—not surprisingly—they were more than a little afraid of what would happen when the wrath of the Third Roman Empire was unleashed against their small near-defenseless island. In the event, the Italian bombing turned out to be something of an anticlimax; and, incredible as it now seems, the small densely populated and virtually undefended island was able to survive an air assault directed against it by a large modern air force operating within easy range of its bases. The question one naturally asks is: How did they do it?

Many factors contributed to Malta's survival in those early days of the war. First was the epic resistance of *Faith, Hope,* and *Charity:* the three planes which took on and humbled an air force.

Second was the system of dispersal and evacuation which was put into effect the moment war was declared. It was no easy task to persuade the Maltese to dig up their roots, for they are a clannish, home-loving people, many of whom under normal conditions spend their entire lives in the dozen or so streets around their homes. Nevertheless, within twenty-four hours of Mussolini's declaration of war some 95,000 men, women, and children had been evacuated from the large towns (Valletta, Sliema, Floriana, Notabile, and Mdina Rabat) and dispersed throughout the country. One of these, a shopkeeper from the fringe of the dockyard, has given us a graphic little account of his family's upheaval. "At eight o'clock this morning," he wrote in a letter, "a car arrived to take us to a village near Rabat. We took with us sheets, blankets, and a few kitchen utensils. We tied two mattresses to the roof of the car and left without knowing the name of the people to whom we were going. We had a ticket which told us where to go, and eventually we found the house in a narrow village street. It belonged to an old man and his two daughters. One of the daughters is terrified of the air-raid signals, but the other is just like my wife and takes no notice. As for the old man, during an air-raid he laughs and goes onto the roof of his house to watch and spit at the Italian planes. They are very kind to us. But all my life I have lived in my own house. Now all of a sudden I have to impose myself on people I have never seen before. And I do not like it." Nobody, in fact, *liked* the enforced evacuation. But it saved a great many lives. And it helped the Maltese to survive, without too many casualties, the initial shock of Italian bombing.

A third reason for Malta's survival lies in the island's geology. The basic structure of Malta is tertiary limestone, a rock which is so soft internally it can be cut with a spade but which hardens, on exposure, to a marblelike consistency and toughness. All Maltese buildings, from the magnificent opera house down to the humblest croft, are built of this limestone—there is hardly a brick or a piece of woodwork on the island. And buildings of stone are not knocked down easily; nor is it easy to set them on fire. Thus, although Malta's houses suffered severely in the bombing (over ten thousand of them being destroyed in Valletta alone), they suffered less than if they had been built of timber and brick like, say, the houses of an English market town. And the limestone helped Malta in another way. It is ideal for quarrying: the perfect rock out of which to tunnel underground shelters. The Maltese Capuchin monks discovered this, and, many centuries ago, they quarried out vast underground catacombs for burial vaults; later the Knights of St. John used these vaults as store rooms, and others as their last line of defense against the invading Turks. Now, in the twentieth century, the old workings of the knights and Capuchins were opened up: new galleries were constructed; air conditioning was improvised; and within a few weeks of Italy's entering the war no fewer than fourteen miles of subterranean tunnels had been quarried out. These tunnels were anything from thirty to a hundred and thirty feet beneath the surface. They were proof against the heaviest bomb. And there was sufficient room in them for every single civilian on the island. In the days of wrath to come they saved thousands of lives. Indeed, without them, casualties might have been so heavy that Malta would have been bludgeoned into annihilation.

A fourth reason for Malta's survival was the poor quality of Italian armament. As Flight Lieutenant Burges put it: "Their guns were badly synchronized; half their bombs didn't go off, and those that did went 'pop' instead of 'bang.'" This, of course, was an exaggeration; but it did hit off an important truth. Italian bombs often broke up on impact without exploding; all those dropped in the early raids were too small to do substantial damage; and of the delayed-action bombs, over 90 per cent were unearthed and exploded harmlessly. "With better bombs and better guns," Burges said, "it might have been a different story." And that is the judgment of an expert who was on the spot.

Finally, Malta owes—or at least partly owes—its early survival to one man: Major General Sir William Shedden Dobbie, the governor of the island and commander in chief of its forces. General Dobbie, who was a shade over sixty at the outbreak of war, was a Sapper. Now, there is an old saying in the British Army that all Sappers are "mad, married, and Methodist": and it is interesting to note how General Dobbie measured up to this dictum. He was mad in the same sense that St. Paul was mad, through much learning: that is to say, he was a master in a skilled and highly technical profession. He was happily married and the father of two sons and a daughter. And his Methodism—or at least his Christianity— was of a caliber that made the army saying, in his case, particularly apt. For General Dobbie was a devout and unashamed Christian; he put his trust in God and said so; and the weapon he wielded in the exercise of his duty was the sword of the Lord and of Gideon. Such a man, in the dark days of 1940, must have seemed to the intensely religious Maltese to be a leader sent from God to inspire and sustain them in their hour of ordeal. His order of the day, for example, broadcast a few minutes after Mussolini's declaration of war, hit exactly the right note, investing the defense of the island with the sanctity of a modern crusade:

It may be [he told the Maltese] that hard times lie ahead of us, but I know that however hard they may be, our courage and determination will not fail, and that with God's help we will maintain the security of our island fortress.

I therefore call on all . . . humbly to seek God's help, and then in reliance on Him to do their duty unflinchingly.

Through proclamations such as this a bond of high purpose was forged between governor and people: a bond which, in the days to come, reached out to embrace first the pilots of *Faith*, *Hope*, and *Charity*, then the maintenance men of Hal Far and Kalafrana, and then the AA gunners and the naval personnel of the dockyard, and which finally came to include in its brotherhood all those, both service and civilian, who were working in any way, no matter how humble, in defense of the island. General Dobbie, in short, by his personal example of high, unswerving purpose lighted a torch that was not in the years to come to be extinguished by hardship, hunger, pain, or death or any other adversity; and the debt which Malta owes him is incalculable. It isn't as easy now as it was in the Middle Ages to spark off a crusade.

In the first couple of days the Italian bombing caused a certain amount of dislocation. In families which had been uprooted and dispersed to different parts of the island, the men were unwilling to go to work and leave their wives and children to face dangers all the more keenly felt because they were largely unknown. But after a while, when it was seen that the effects of the bombing were by no means catastrophic, life returned to normal. The men went back to work in the fields, coastal waters, and dockyard; and the old Maltese contempt for the Italians reasserted itself. Soon, if a bomb fell on a farmer's crop of tomatoes, he no longer took cover; he raised indignant hands to heaven and called on a variety of saints to punish the Italians' impertinence.

So month after month, through summer and into autumn, Malta carried on. At first, all civilians dutifully took cover whenever the sirens sounded; but gradually, as the epic battle of *Faith, Hope,* and *Charity* caught their imaginations, more and more people took to staying out in the open and watching the planes, high overhead, penciling history in the blue Mediterranean sky. Between June and December there were raids just about every day, sometimes only one raid, sometimes as many as eight. But damage and casualties were surprisingly light. And soon, in spite of the governor's warnings, the Maltese began to leave their country billets and drift back to their homes.

By the end of the year the streets of Valletta were as crowded as ever, and on the fringe of the dockyard families were living as close-packed as nowhere else in Europe. General Dobbie warned them of the risk they were running. But they wouldn't listen. They had developed a profound contempt for the Italians and their ineffective bombing, and they loved their homes and their old familiar surroundings. They stayed put.

Toward the end of the year rumors began to circulate that fresh waves of bombers—German bombers this time—were massing along the Sicilian shore. But by this time the Maltese considered themselves inured to the terrors of being bombed. The German planes, they reckoned, would be no worse than the Italian. There was no need for them, a second time, to uproot themselves from their homes.

They soon learned their mistake.

On the evening of January 10, H.M.S. *Illustrious,* battered to a blazing hulk but still miraculously afloat, berthed in Dockyard Creek. German reconnaissance planes spotted her at once and kept her under observation day after day. For the best part of a week there was an uneasy lull. Then, on January 16, the blitzkrieg began.

Preparations to meet the expected attacks had, of course, been made. All serviceable aircraft, including *Illustrious'* Fulmars and the two remaining Gladiators, were ready to take to the air; and a special box barrage had been positioned around the shore of Grand Harbour. But no preparations on earth could have stopped Fliegerkorps X.

The first wave of attackers consisted of twelve Ju 88s, and fifty-four Ju 87s. They came in high, in perfect formation, apparently oblivious to the island's AA. They passed directly over Valletta at midday, at a height of some 30,000 feet; then, over the center of the island, they turned, peeled off, and dived in wave after wave onto the stricken carrier. The German pilots had courage. Down the path of the pale January sun, they came streaming through the barrage, as straight as if on rails. The waters of Grand Harbour erupted into steeple-high geysers of spray, and an evil mushroom of smoke and dust rose shroudlike over the dockyard as stick after stick of bombs burst open the narrow streets and pulverized the close-packed houses to dust.

Long after Fliegerkorps X had set course for their bases in Sicily, the yellow acrid cloud hung like a pall over the dockyard, where, in the space of less than an hour, over nine hundred homes had been shattered beyond repair and over five hundred people killed or seriously injured.

That night there was a second exodus from Valletta and the Three Cities. The Maltese had learned the difference between the Luftwaffe and the Regia Aeronautica.

The savagery of the attack and the unprecedented scale of the destruction had a twofold effect on the Maltese. At first they were numbed with shock; then, when the numbness wore off, they were left with a great anger and a burning desire for revenge. Their attitude is typified by the story of the young mechanic who, on the morning after the raid, reported to Kalafrana Repair Section two hours late. His clothes were filthy, his hands were bleeding, and he was tired and distraught to the point of collapse. He explained to Flying Officer Collins that he had spent all night searching the ruins of his shattered home for his wife and child. He hadn't found them. Collins asked him, very gently, if he would like to go back. But the mechanic shook his head.

"It is useless," he said. "Besides, I work on the Gladiator. I must hit back."

That was Malta's reaction to the German blitz.

But there wasn't much chance, in those early days of 1941, of hitting back. The Maltese had simply to take it. In this they had plenty of practice; for January 16 marked the start of an air offensive of unparalleled ferocity. It fell into two clearly defined phases: first, the assault on the dockyard, then the assault on the airdromes.

In their efforts to give the *Illustrious* her *coup de grâce*, the Germans, between January 16 and 23, mounted eight large-scale raids on the area of the dockyard. They employed well over five hundred planes, of which they lost sixty-one (approximately half to the fighters and half to the AA). They hit the carrier twice; they near-missed her again and again; and they reduced the surrounding dockyard to a wasteland of rubble. It was lucky indeed that the Maltese had learned their lesson well and that after the first raid they had dispersed overnight to their inland billets. By dawn on January 17 the Three Cities were utterly deserted. Nor, after that first devastating raid, was there any more watching from the roof tops. Now, each time the sirens sounded the Maltese went underground, deep into their limestone catacombs. And so it was that, although, in the raids to come, the Three Cities (Senglea, Vittoriosa, and Cospicua) were utterly destroyed, the Maltese themselves survived. Their homes were reduced to rubble; their historic buildings were shattered beyond repair; and their churches—including the lovely Chapel of Our Lady of the Victories, built by La Valette in 1571—were razed to the ground. But their bodies, and their spirit, remained unbroken.

Many stories could be told of the courage of the Maltese during the attacks of the *Illustrious;* but one will suffice.

Joseph Gauci was employed as an Admiralty diver. Early in 1941, divers, especially skilled ones, were in short supply; and in due course Joseph was given the vitally important job of inspecting the hull of H.M.S. *Illustrious.* On January 19 he was twenty feet under water, testing the carrier's bow plates, when an attack was launched on the area of Grand Harbour. Now, the *Illustrious,* of course, was the Germans' principal objective; and bombs bursting in the water have a most unpleasant effect on anything near them—as those who have seen degutted fish thrown up in the wake of a depth charge can testify. Joseph realized his danger. Yet he refused to be hauled up. Throughout the hour and a half of the attack, with bombs bursting all around him, he carried on with his inspection. Twice he was stunned by the force of the underwater explosions. Soon he was bleeding from mouth and ears. But he finished his job. Only then did he give the signal for his colleagues to haul him to safety.

For his "courage and devotion to duty" Gauci was awarded the B.E.M. Many Maltese, during the German blitz on the dockyard, were to show equal fortitude. They followed General Dobbie's advice; they put their trust in God, kept their heads down, and carried on; and in time the *Illustrious* escaped to Alexandria, and the Germans, balked of their prey, shifted their assault to the airdromes.

They left behind them an area where literally not one single building was left standing. Within the space of a few hundred square yards over two hundred and twenty tons of bombs had been dropped in ten days, and over three thousand houses totally destroyed. Neither in Stalingrad nor in Coventry had such a weight of bombs been dropped in so concentrated an area in so short a time.

The *Illustrious* had gone; but by the end of January it was realized that the Luftwaffe had come to stay and that their attack on the carrier was only the prelude to a prolonged assault on the island. And the German intentions soon became clear: so to pulverize Malta as to render it useless as a base for either Navy or Air Force. Their first step in carrying this intention out was to obliterate the island's air defenses: to knock its handful of aircraft out of the sky.

It sounded easy. Malta had only two Gladiators and less than a dozen Hurricane Mk. Is. The Luftwaffe alone had over one hundred and eighty bombers (mostly Ju 87s and Ju 88s, but also a sprinkling of Dorniers and Heinkels) and some hundred and fifty fast modern fighters—Me 109s and 110s. And there was always, of course, the Italians. Day after day sweeps of Messerschmitts came swarming over the island, machine-gunning anything that moved, inveigling the Hurricanes into dogfights at odds of up to twenty to one; and in their wake came the dive bombers—the *Picchiatelli*—bombing airfields, hangars, and repair yards with a savage precision that put the earlier efforts of the Regia Aeronautica to shame. Yet, as soon as a Hurricane was damaged, it was invariably patched up; as soon as a landing strip was cratered, the holes were filled in. And somehow, day after day, the defending aircraft managed to struggle into the air. It was the story of *Faith*, *Hope*, and *Charity* all over again.

Ju 88

The matter-of-fact prose of the Malta War Diary paints a picture of those early days of 1941 which is vivid in its factual simplicity.

February 28th: Heavy raids on the aerodromes by three formations of at least 110 aircraft. Heaviest attack on Hal Far, with slight machine-gunning at Kalafrana. Damage at Hal Far preliminarily assessed as follows: Three Swordfish and 1 Gladiator burnt out. All other aircraft, including the last of the Hurricanes, rendered unserviceable. All barrack blocks unserviceable, two heavily damaged and one demolished. Water and power cut off. Two hangars gutted, others damaged. Airfield rendered temporarily unserviceable. Enemy losses: 4 Ju 88s, 4 Ju 87s, 3 Me 109s, 1 Me 110, 1 Do 215 confirmed; eight probables. Our losses: one Hurricane and pilot.

This was a heavy raid. Our forces were not strong enough to ward it off. If the air defence of Malta is to be continued more fighters are essential.

It seemed, that spring, as if Malta must surely succumb under the weight of such prolonged and concentrated bombing.

In the event, the island was saved by a combination of circumstances. Reinforcements of modern planes (Hurricane Mk. IIAs) were flown in in the nick of time—twelve at the end of March and a further twenty-three at the end of April.

And the German planes failed to sustain their offensive—partly because they were suffering such heavy losses, and partly because they needed the planes for their Balkan and Libyan offensives. And so, toward the end of spring, the Luftwaffe's assault began to slacken off. Just when a series of really concentrated raids might have beaten the defenders to their knees, the island was given a breathing space. And she made good use of it.

Then, early in June, the miracle happened. The Luftwaffe gave up. Fliegerkorps X was switched to the Black Sea, and the Messerschmitts and Heinkels flew east to the Pripet Marshes. For the German invasion of Russia was under way.

From June 5 to 11 there were no raids on Malta at all. Then, on June 12, the aircraft spotters along the northern cliffs sent back a report the like of which hadn't been heard for months. "Bandits, ten plus, approaching the coast. Height 20,000..." A pause. Then, incredulously, "Bandits identified as ten Savoias." The Italians were back.

The Maltese emerged from their shelters; they began once again to watch from the roof tops; in time, some of them even drifted back to ther ruined homes. Their fortitude had beaten the Luftwaffe. "A people who are bombed today," Giulio Douhet had said, "as they were bombed yesterday, and who know they will be bombed again tomorrow and can see no end to their martyrdom, are bound to call for peace in the end." The Maltese, to their undying honor, had proved him wrong.

7

*The Royal Navy offer you their congratulations on a
very fine piece of seamanship.*
                    —R.N. SIGNAL STATION, VALLETTA

The exodus of the Luftwaffe removed one of the principal
threats to another convoy; and in mid-June plans were drawn
up for Operation "Substance," the escorting to the island of
six merchantmen and a troopship. And a convoy was badly
needed. For in Malta stocks of food were running low, and as
a result of the prolonged air assault AA shells and aviation
fuel were nearly exhausted.

Since Admiral Cunningham's fleet had suffered such crippling losses during the evacuation of Crete (two battleships,
one aircraft carrier, five cruisers, and eight destroyers put out
of action within a couple of weeks), the onus of fighting
through the merchantmen now fell on Admiral Somerville
and the warships of Force H. Even without the Luftwaffe,
the forces opposing him were formidable. For it was estimated that, divided between Sicily and Sardinia, there were still
two hundred Italian bombers, strengthened by occasional
groups of German Junkers—while Axis naval forces capable of
intervention were estimated at five battleships, ten cruisers,
twenty destroyers, and some thirty to forty E-boats—craft
which had become increasingly active in the last few months.

As escort for the merchantmen, it was agreed to send one
battleship and one battle cruiser (neither, to put it politely, in
their first flush of youth), one aircraft carrier, one mine layer,
four cruisers, and seventeen destroyers: a small force in view
of the likely opposition, but all that could be spared. In
accordance with the policy of not risking capital ships in the
Narrows, it was agreed that the heavy units of the escort
should turn back at the entrance to the Skerki Channel,

leaving only three cruisers and ten destroyers to guard the convoy on its final two hundred miles.

And so, early in July, while Panzer units rolled east into the Pripet Marshes, the merchantmen chosen for Operation "Substance" started to assemble. They came together in home waters, in twos and threes, under conditions of the most stringent secrecy. Not even the masters knew where their ships were bound.

Captain Thomas Sydney Horn, master of the *Sydney Star*, was born in Alnwick, Northumberland, on June 2, 1899. At the age of fifteen he started to serve his apprenticeship on the Blue Star Line, a shipping company with a fleet of unusually fast cargo vessels. His wages were good for those days—ten shillings a month. Thomas Horn proved himself an able, conscientious apprentice. He worked hard; and eventually he achieved the ambition of every boy who starts service under the Red Duster: he became a master; master of a 12,000-ton cargo vessel, the *Sydney Star*.

Year after year Captain Horn and the *Sydney Star* followed the sun to Australia: Liverpool to Sydney with industrial machinery, Sydney to Liverpool with cotton and wool. Then came the war.

On July 12, 1941, the *Sydney Star* and the *City of Pretoria* lay side by side in the Mersey Estuary. It was raining, and a pall of haze and summer fog drifted lazily across the still water. A little before noon both ships got under way and, together with their destroyer escort, headed seaward. Soon they met up with another group of vessels: the *Port Chalmers*, the *Deucalion*, and the destroyer *Van Heemskerck*.

It was clear that a convoy was in process of forming up; but so stringent had been the security measures that nobody was at all certain who was convoy commodore. For several miles the two groups of vessels steamed parallel, peering suspiciously at each other through the haze, both waiting for orders. Then Captain Horn took the bull by the horns and ordered the others to form port column at three cables on *Sydney Star*. Rather to his surprise, they obeyed with alacrity.

A few minutes later other and heavier ships appeared to northward. They were the battleship *Nelson* and the cruisers *Arethusa*, *Manchester*, and *Edinburgh*, together with yet another group of merchantmen, which had been assembling in the Clyde. Captain Horn's spell as convoy commodore was over.

It was quite a formidable fleet which now, screened by its advance guard of destroyers, stood to the south. But still no one on board the merchantmen had the slightest idea of their destination—though, as the ships headed southward day after day, some of the more discerning masters could hazard a pretty accurate guess.

On July 20, when the ships were some hundred and fifty miles northwest of Gibraltar, a destroyer from Force H—recognizable by the lighter gray of her hull—joined the convoy. She came alongside every merchantman in turn and shot on board a sealed packet by rocket line. These packets, which the masters opened according to instructions at noon, contained a personal message from Admiral Somerville: a message which settled beyond dispute the question of the convoy's destination.

For over twelve months [the admiral wrote] Malta has resisted all attacks of the enemy. The gallantry displayed by the garrison and people of Malta has aroused admiration throughout the world. To enable their defence to be continued, it is essential that your ships, with their valuable cargoes, should arrive safely in Grand Harbour.

The Royal Navy will escort and assist you in this great mission; you on your part can assist the Royal Navy by giving strict attention to the following points:

Don't make smoke. Don't show any lights at night. Keep good station. Don't straggle. If your ship is damaged, keep her going at the best possible speed.

Provided every officer and man realizes that it is up to him to do his duty to the very best of his ability, I feel sure we shall succeed.

Remember that the watchword is THE CONVOY MUST GO THROUGH.

This message Captain Horn had typed out and displayed at key points throughout the ship.

Next night, in thick fog, the convoy passed through the Strait.

It was an anxious time. Gibraltar was known to harbor a

number of Axis spies, whose principal job was to report
Allied shipping movements. It was therefore essential for the
passage to be completed during the hours of darkness: that is,
between midnight and 4 A.M. This, in view of the fog, was
no easy task; and with visibility down to thirty yards the
troopship *Leinster* got so far out of formation that she ran
aground. The other merchantmen, however, got through
safely, in what they thought was commendably close formation. But the cruiser *Manchester,* who at dawn chivied them
yet more closely together, obviously thought otherwise.

"S stands for Straggler," her aldis flashed reproachfully at
the *Port Chalmers,* who was two cables instead of one astern
of her next-in-line. "And for Sunk!"

All that day the vessels headed east. The sea was calm; the
wind northeasterly and light; the sky cloudless. Soon after
dawn the warships from England were joined by the warships
of Force H. Admiral Somerville then divided his vessels into
two groups. He kept the lightly guarded merchantmen in the
south, close to the Moroccan shore; and took his heavy units,
including *Ark Royal,* to the north; thus interposing himself
between the convoy and the first focus of danger: the Sardinian airfields. Hour after hour, that first heat-hazed day, *Ark
Royal*'s Fulmars patrolled the cloudless sky; but of the enemy
there was never a sign. It began to look as if the convoy had
got through the Strait unobserved.

The first night east of Gibraltar—the night of July 21–22—
was uneventful.

Next morning the destroyers started to refuel, an operation
which took the better part of ten hours. During this refueling
a Cant reconnaissance plane spotted Force H in the north,
but failed to notice the convoy in the south; and the second
night east of Gibraltar passed as quietly as the first.

The following morning at eight o'clock Admiral Somerville
brought his two groups together, combining warships and
merchantmen into a single formation, and proceeded due
east at thirteen and a half knots. The merchant ships were in
two columns: *Sydney Star* being in the center of the port
column. Around the merchantmen the destroyers were spread
out in the shape of a blunt-nosed arrow; while on their port
quarter *Ark Royal* and the heavy units formed a flexible string
for free flying.

The vessels had barely taken up station when the attacks

began; and those who thought that they were in for an easy passage because the enemy was Italian rather than German were rudely disillusioned.

The first planes were reported by radar a few minutes after nine o'clock, and the attack which followed was both skillful and determined.

At nine-fifteen *Ark Royal's* Fulmars were vectored toward a group of Savoia 79s approaching the convoy from the east at 10,000 feet. These, the fighters broke up, shooting down two and forcing the rest to jettison their bombs. But while the Fulmars had been drawn away from the fleet, a second group of Savoias—seven torpedo bombers—came down in a shallow dive from out of the sun. They achieved complete surprise. Almost before a gun had been fired, torpedoes struck the cruiser *Manchester* and the destroyer *Fearless*. The *Manchester*, hit in the engine room, was forced to turn back for Gibraltar; with three of her four engines disabled, she went limping away to the west and took no further part in the convoy. The *Fearless* was not so lucky; swept by fire she capsized and sank.

Fairey Fulmar

The Italians had drawn first blood.

But for the rest of the day the convoy moved east with surprisingly little opposition. Two more attacks were made; but both were extremely halfhearted, and the Fulmars had little difficulty in breaking them up. It was clear that the dawn attack had been made by one of the crack Italian antishipping squadrons, whereas the later sorties were made by pilots half trained and less than half hearted.

At three o'clock that afternoon the convoy passed Galita Island; and a couple of hours later—if anything, slightly ahead of schedule—they approached the western end of the Skerki Channel. They were coming within range of the Sicilian airfields now, approaching fateful waters, dominated by the ghost of the *Illustrious*. At a quarter past five Admiral Somerville turned back. He took with him *Nelson, Renown, Ark Royal,* and a screen of six destroyers.

Without the great bulk of the capital ships riding beside them, the merchantmen, as they entered the channel, felt suddenly defenseless. Yet Admiral Somerville made it plain that he had not forgotten them; he left with them a reminder of his protecting strength: an air umbrella: a guard of the *Ark Royal's* Fulmars. And these Fulmars were to play a vital if unspectacular part in getting the convoy through. For a little before dark, as soon as the merchantmen and their depleted escort had passed through the channel and had emerged from its eastern end, they made an unexpected alteration of course. And it was this alteration of course—guarded and kept secret by the Fulmars—on which the whole success of Operation "Substance" depended.

For the Italians expected the convoy, on leaving the Skerki Channel, to turn southeast; to follow the usual route to Malta; hugging the African shore. And along this expected line of advance they concentrated, that night, their submarines and planes. But the convoy did not turn southeast. It turned northeast; straight for the Sicilian shore; straight, apparently, for the heart of a thickly laid mine field.

It was a carefully calculated risk which Admiral Syfret— senior officer of the reduced escort—now took. In the gathering darkness, while *Ark Royal's* Fulmars kept the sky above him free from shadowers, he led his vessels straight into the mine field. It would have been suicide if they hadn't had secret information which enabled them to follow clear water: the swept search-and-repair channel kept free of mines by the Italians themselves.

In close formation the ships moved steadily northeast. There were no alarms or excursions. No explosions. The risk paid off.

All through the early hours of the night Admiral Syfret heard the Italians searching for him. The throb of aircraft engines passed high overhead. Away to the south flares reddened the African shore. But the convoy remained undiscovered. Soon after midnight they cleared the mine field. They increased speed. They adopted a more open formation. By 2 A.M. they were less than a hundred and fifty miles from Malta.

But they were also less than a dozen miles from another island: Pantelleria. The base of the E-boats.

They approached the island from the north: from the Italians' point of view, an extremely surprising direction. They hoped to slip past in the darkest hour of the night—between 2 and 3 A.M. But it was not to be.

At six minutes to three *Cossack*'s radar picked up a group of unidentified objects, range two miles. At four minutes to three *Edinburgh*'s lookout reported the sound of engines being started, fine on the port bow. At two minutes to three pandemonium suddenly broke loose. For the convoy had run into a pack of E-boats.

Of the two, the E-boats were the more surprised. For theirs was no carefully prearranged ambush. They were simply carrying out a routine patrol, in an area believed to be far from the route of the convoy. Yet now, suddenly and unexpectedly, the convoy was bearing down on them, out of the center of their own mine field! To give the Italians their due, they rose to the occasion. There were eight E-boats, and all but one carried out a determined attack. They proved elusive targets; and their attacks were difficult to deal with, partly because they were quite un-co-ordinated and followed no set pattern; each E-boat, on the spur of the moment, acting individually, and differently.

For fifteen minutes the convoy was plunged into chaos, as fire from bofors, oerlikons, and secondary and main armament flashed from ship to ship. In the confusion several vessels, including the *Sydney Star*, were hit by the fire of those in a neighboring column: searchlights cut the sea into swaths of chalk-white light: torpedo wakes hissed through the water: vessels veered and twisted and turned. At the end of it all one E-boat was sunk by a 6-inch broadside from *Edinburgh;* one was rammed by *Cossack;* one passed at high speed between the columns of merchantmen and escaped unscathed; one was hit repeatedly by heavy fire from the *Manxman* and drifted away a blazing hulk; and the others vanished.

And when the convoy came to sort itself out, it was found that the *Sydney Star* was missing.

It was eleven days now since the *Sydney Star* had stood out of Liverpool. Not once in those eleven days had Captain Horn undressed; not once had he left the bridge. For the last sixty hours—since the convoy had entered the danger area— he had had no sleep.

Now, at 3 A.M. on the morning of July 24, he stood by the wheel, watching the streams of blood-red tracer skimming the sea, listening to the thunder of engines as the E-boats, at forty knots, tore in and out of the ships. Cordite fumes went streaming away downwind. Shells from a wildly firing merchantman scythed into the *Sydney Star*'s starboard lifeboats. Searchlights tilted, swiveled, and dipped. In the darkness torpedo wakes were almost impossible to see. But suddenly Captain Horn spotted the wake of an E-boat running parallel to the *Sydney Star*, less than fifty yards to port. He was raising the telephone tube to his mouth to order an emergency turn when the torpedo hit them.

It hit them squarely amidships, opposite No. 3 hold. For a second a pyramid of flame leaped funnel-high. Then the flame was doused: doused by the great cataract of water which came pouring in through the shattered hull. A great cavern, forty feet by twenty feet, was torn out of the ship's side. The engines stopped. The *Sydney Star* fell away. Within seconds of being hit she was down by the head and listing drunkenly to port.

Captain Horn's first thought was for the troops. For, as well as her cargo of grain, ammunition, and naval stores, the *Sydney Star* was carrying 20 officers and 464 troops (mostly of the 32nd Light A.A. Regiment). He felt the deck move heavily beneath him and wondered if the ship was about to founder. As a precaution he ordered "Abandon ship" stations.

The troops fell in beside their lifeboats. There was no panic. Everything was surprisingly orderly and quiet—even when half the men discovered that their lifeboats were useless—smashed by shellfire.

Captain Horn meanwhile had taken soundings. Nos. 1 and 2 holds appeared relatively undamaged, with only six feet of water in each. But in No. 3 hold the water level was thirty feet and rising. His ship lay stopped, listing, refusing to answer her helm, and apparently settling slowly by the head. Captain Horn did the only possible thing. He signaled the destroyer which had been screening them for help, asking her to come alongside and take off the troops.

Commander A. R. Rosenthal, R.A.N., captain of the *Nestor*, had seen the *Sydney Star* drop out of convoy. He was already on his way to investigate when Captain Horn's signal reached him. While the rest of the convoy moved slowly away to the east, the *Nestor* eased into position alongside the merchantman. In the darkness the two ships lay motionless side by side. They were only four miles from Pantelleria. And soon they heard the noise of engines: E-boat engines. The Italians were coming back to finish them off.

In the darkness it wasn't easy to disembark the troops. The swell, though slight, was sufficient to make the vessels nudge each other uneasily; and silence, with the E-boats searching for them in the darkness, was essential. But at last planks were laid from *Nestor*'s fo'c'sle to *Sydney Star*'s gunwale; Jacob's ladders were rigged aft; and at three-thirty the disembarking began. Within thirty minutes 464 troops, 20 officers, and all the nonessential members of the merchantman's crew were safely aboard the destroyer. Captain Horn was then asked if he and the rest of his crew were also coming aboard.

"No," he said. "We'll stay. We're not finished yet."

And ten minutes later the *Sydney Star*'s engines were restarted, and she got slowly under way.

This miracle was achieved by Mr. Haig (chief engineer) and Mr. Machie (chief officer), who together organized the shoring up of buckled plates, the strengthening of water tight bulkheads, and the restarting of the boilers. And while they worked, the carpenter took soundings, plumbing his way continuously from hold to hold. The figures he passed to Captain Horn were not encouraging. For the pumps weren't powerful enough to hold the influx; in No. 1 hold and No. 3 hold the water was rising; slowly but steadily.

There was nothing they could do about it. Captain Horn realized this; he realized, too, that the water would continue to flood in, whether they steamed at two knots or at twelve. His ship, by this time, had drifted to within three miles of Pantelleria. In little more than an hour it would be light. Obviously the most urgent need was to clear the Italian base by daybreak. He ordered twelve knots, praying the bulkheads would hold.

Circled by *Nestor,* the merchantman wallowed awkwardly through a sea which was mercifully calm. Her course, 116 degrees; her speed, 12 knots.

Twice the E-boats came perilously near. The noise of their engines filled the night. It seemed inevitable that they would see the merchantman and close in for the kill. But the minutes passed, the light gained slowly in intensity, and still no attack developed. (It has been suggested that the E-boats had used up all their torpedoes on the convoy and had no means of launching an attack; but if this were so they would surely have radioed Pantelleria and brought their companions out for the kill; and it seems most probable that, in spite of the approaching dawn, they simply failed to locate the merchantman.)

Sunrise found *Nestor* and *Sydney Star* alone in an empty ocean. Behind them Pantelleria had sunk beneath the horizon; ahead—a long way ahead—the rest of the convoy had entered the Malta swept channel. They still had a hundred and twenty miles to cover. And with daylight came a menace far more potent than the E-boats: the dive bombers and torpedo bombers.

At dawn *Sydney Star* had flashed the following signal to *Nestor:*

No. 1 hold up to 12 feet. No. 2 hold 7 feet. No. 3 hold 33 feet. Rest of ship dry. Have hopes I will make it.

But a couple of minutes later, out of the haze of a blood-red sunrise, came two Italian Savoias. They circled the ships warily, a fraction out of gun range.

The *Sydney Star*'s gun crews had all been transferred to *Nestor.* Her high-angle 3-inch gun, her four bofors, and her

40 mm Bofors

three machine guns lay unmanned: useless. Captain Horn called for volunteers. Out of the engine room came a black-faced collection of ragamuffins: the oilers and greasers. Most of them had never seen a bofors before; but after some hair-raising experiments, they learned quickly. And when the Savoias attacked, they were met by a fierce if unorthodox barrage. They dropped their torpedoes at long range. Both ships took violent evasive action. The torpedoes missed. Disgruntled, the Italians made for home.

But the emergency turns had strained the *Sydney Star's* bulkheads. When Captain Horn heard the next series of soundings, he felt the hairs pricking up on the nape of his neck: No. 1 hold 16 feet, No. 2 hold 7 feet, No. 3 hold 46 feet. He became suddenly aware that the ship was listing still more heavily to starboard, was settling even lower by the head, and was becoming increasingly difficult to steer.

Speed was reduced to nine knots.

But still the water gained. *Sydney Star* yawed and wallowed perversely. Already, Captain Horn estimated, she had shipped 7000 tons of water.

At seven o'clock another Savoia attacked out of the sun. Her torpedo snaked past the *Sydney Star*'s stern—so close that it exploded in her wake.

At seven-thirty two more Savoias attacked with torpedoes; but accurate fire from the *Nestor* kept them at bay.

It was now that the destroyer made a "Help" signal and received in reply two welcome pieces of news. Fighters from Malta had been sent to provide them with air cover; and the cruiser *Hermione* had been detached from the convoy to provide them with additional escort. The fighters arrived a little after eight o'clock, just as *Nestor* and *Sydney Star* altered course into the swept channel. An hour later *Hermione* came racing up from the east; and she was not a moment too soon. For now, with the *Sydney Star* quite unable to take avoiding action, a determined air attack developed.

There were five high-level bombers—probably Savoias— and three dive bombers. *Hermione* and *Nestor* put up an extremely accurate barrage, which disrupted the high-level attack; while a pair of Beaufighters from Malta attended to the dive bombers. All the bombs fell wide.

But in the *Sydney Star* the water continued to rise at the rate of fourteen inches an hour. The merchantman, by this time, had shipped a good 10,000 tons—close to her own displacement. It needed all Captain Horn's skill to keep her from yawing into the mine fields which lined the swept channel. He exchanged signals with Commander Rosenthal.

To *Nestor* from *Sydney Star:* "Pumps no longer holding No. 1. Sounding now 16 feet. Swinging badly."

To *Sydney Star* from *Nestor:* "Would a reduction in speed help?"

To *Nestor* from *Sydney Star:* "No, I don't think so at the moment."

To *Sydney Star* from *Nestor:* "I would hate to lose you now. Am considering alternative sites for beaching in case flooding progresses to a dangerous extent."

Captain Horn smiled. He, too, had thought of beaching: but only as a last resort. He passed a mass of technical information (such as his draft fore and aft and his cargo-storage arrangements) to *Nestor;* and these the destroyer relayed to Grand Harbour, making sure that tugs and a berth would be immediately available—if they made it.

And at ten o'clock that morning it began to look as if—against all the odds—they were going to reach harbor. For Malta was only twenty miles to the east.

Then came the last and most vicious assault of all.

It was as if the Italians had been watching the *Sydney Star's* progress; as if they had been hoping that she would founder without additional effort on their part, but had now suddenly realized that the prey they had been so sure of was about to slip through their fingers. Skimming low over the water came a group of Savoia torpedo planes; simultaneously another group of Savoias pattern-bombed the merchantman from 13,000 feet; while out of the sun screamed a formation of dive bombers: Ju 87s: German planes to finish what Italian E-boats had begun. It was a determined, carefully synchronized attack.

A pair of Beaufighters from Malta met the torpedo planes some ten miles from the ships. But the Beaufighter pilots were inexperienced in operating with the fleet; diverted by a feint breakaway, they pursued a couple of Savoias halfway back to Sicily, allowing the main formation to break through. Skimming the waves, weaving through the ack-ack, the Savoias swept straight at the *Sydney Star.* Captain Horn tried to swing head on; but the *Star* wallowed and ducked and yawed like a reluctant hippopotamus. Before she'd completed her turn the Savoias were on her. One was so low she passed between the masts; another had to tilt her wing tip to clear the stern. Two torpedoes flashed past the merchantman's bow; an aerial torpedo exploded with a thundering roar, showering the bridge with splinters; then the planes were past, with the oilers and greasers blazing away at them furiously even when they were nothing more than pin points on the horizon!

Before Captain Horn had time to assess the damage, *Hermione's* ack-ack opened up again. She had spotted the high-level bombers. Her first salvo burst straight in the path of the Savoias as they started their run-in. Half the formation turned away; but the other half came steadily on. There was a sudden high-pitched scream. The merchantman's crew flung themselves to the deck. And three 1000-pound bombs scythed into the sea within twenty yards of their beam. The *Sydney Star* heeled over. Waterlogged and out of control, she fell away into the churned-up troughs of the sea. The columns of water, steeple-high, collapsed over her deck, drenching the gun crews with sheets of falling spray. But they stayed at their guns; and through the spray they saw the last of their attackers—a pair of Stukas—diving out of the sun. One Stuka dived on the *Nestor;* the other, the oilers and greasers shot screaming into the sea.

Suddenly it was very quiet. The attack was over. But the *Sydney Star* now lay motionless. Her engines were stopped. She was settling slowly by the head. She was listing even more dangerously. And Captain Horn knew that it would only be a matter of hours—if not minutes—before she foundered.

The engines were restarted; and watched anxiously by *Hermione* and *Nestor,* the merchantman again got under way for Grand Harbour. Only another eighteen miles to go.

At first Captain Horn kept the engine-room telegraph at "Slow." But he quickly realized that unless he could work up more speed they would founder long before they got to the harbor entrance. Their only possible hope was to cram on all possible speed and pray the bulkheads wouldn't give way; if they did give way when the vessel was running at top speed, the odds were that she'd capsize and sink like a stone.

Captain Horn felt desperately tired. He wondered if eleven days on the bridge and seventy-two hours without sleep had impaired his judgment. He wondered if he was justified in gambling the lives of his crew against the safe arrival of his cargo.

At last he made up his mind. His hand tightened on the engine-room telegraph. He moved it steadily, in one even pull, from "slow" to "full ahead."

Two hours later they entered the searched channel at the mouth of Grand Harbour.

It was the hottest part of the day: two o'clock on a heat-hazed midsummer afternoon. The sky was cloudless: the sun a ball of gold: the sea a sheet of glass. There was hardly a breath of wind, and the storm of cheering from the breakwaters as *Sydney Star* passed in between came to them faintly, like the far-off echo of wavelets on a very distant shore.

To Captain Horn it was simply the end of another job. The entries he made in his logbook were very matter-of-fact:

2:11   Dead slow to pick up pilot off harbour entrance.
2:40   Pilot boarded off breakwater; helm and engines as requisite for approaching harbour.
2:41   Tug *Robust* fast for'ard port bow.
2:51   Tug *Ancient* fast amidships, starboard side. Tug *West Dene* assisting where necessary.
3:09   Arrived off entrance to dockyard and commenced to turn.
3:17   Vessel round and proceeding stern first to berth.
3:30   Cast off tugs.
3:34   Vessel alongside pontoon; took on board shore mooring wires.
4:00   Vessel securely moored fore and aft.

The safe arrival of the *Sydney Star* meant that all six supply ships got through to Malta. Among them they unloaded two thousand tons of frozen meat, two thousand tons of edible oil, and sufficient sugar, coffee, fats, and tea to last the island through the next three months. They also unloaded no fewer than ten thousand tons of ammunition (.303, 20-mm. cannon shell, and AA shells for bofors, oerlikon, and Lewis). They brought naval and air force spares—spare propeller screws for submarines and spare engines for the Hurricane Mk. IIs— and AA guns by the hundred. And this vast conglomeration of stores, totaling in all some 65,000 tons, was unloaded without hindrance or loss. Operation "Substance" had been an unqualified success.

Captain Horn came in for special praise. He received messages of congratulation from the senior officer of the troops embarked in *Sydney Star,* from Admiral Syfret, from Vice-Admiral Ford, and from General Dobbie. He received the O.B.E. In the House of Lords, Lord Marchwood quoted his exploits in a plea for equal awards to the men of both Royal and Merchant Navies. But the message which Captain Horn cherishes most is one sent at the request of the naval officers who served with him in Operation "Substance." It reads simply, "The Royal Navy offer you their congratulations on a very fine piece of seamanship."

8

We rigged a makeshift sail and set course for Gibraltar.
                                        —ROLAND ROUSE

The U.S.S. *West Caddoa* was old and weather-beaten; her rivets wept rust, her smokestack was as salt-caked as any dirty British coaster. For twenty-two years she had been carting pig iron and crude oil for the Western Pipe and Steel Company of San Francisco: an unusual cargo, but then the *West Caddoa* was an unusual ship, having two holds which had been specially designed for storing oil. It was this fact which led, in the summer of 1941, to her being transferred to the Merchant Navy; for, at this particular stage of the war, ships which could carry oil were, to the British, worth their weight in gold.

The *West Caddoa* was rechristened with the unlikely name of *Empire Guillemot* and sent to South Shields. Here she picked up her crew—mostly local men, though her master, Roland Rouse, came from Glasgow—and toward the end of August she sailed, with sealed top-secret orders. When Roland Rouse opened the orders he found that she was bound for Malta. He found, too, that she was routed to sail alone.

The idea of sailing single, unescorted ships violated one of the cardinal principles of naval warfare: namely, that merchantmen were safer in convoy than on their own. This principle, proved in two world wars, had, however, its exception. It was found that on the run to Malta, single individual ships fared better than those in convoy. Exact figures are hard to arrive at (for many of the individual ships sailed secretly, arrived unheralded, and departed as unobtrusively as they had come), but the following table (for ships sailing between August 1940 and August 1942) is accurate enough to prove its point:

	Set out	Sunk	Turned back	Arrived
Ships sailing to Malta in convoy	55	22	11	22
Ships sailing to Malta alone	31	9	1	21

These figures make surprising reading (in no other theater of war was it found that merchantmen were safer alone than in convoy), and they can only be ascribed to the special conditions that prevailed in the Central Mediterranean. Here, over long periods, the enemy controlled land, air, and sea. A convoy, because of its over-all physical size, was certain to be discovered as soon as it entered enemy-controlled waters; once discovered, it was certain to be attacked; and in the Narrows, mined and within easy reach of enemy air and naval bases, the odds were all in favor of the attackers. Individual ships, on the other hand, had a reasonable chance of slipping through unobserved; especially if they kept on the fringe of French territorial waters and made the passage under cover of bad weather.

The ships chosen for these individual runs were usually old, small, and slow: the sort of unobtrusive coasters which might be expected to trade along the Algerian shore. Such a ship was the *Empire Guillemot:* built in 1919, dead-weight tonnage 5641, top speed 11 knots. On September 4, under cover of darkness, she slipped quietly through the Strait of Gibraltar.

Her passage to Malta was surprisingly uneventful, possibly because the weather was dull and cloudy and the nights moonless. She reached Grand Harbour on the evening of September 19; and within forty-eight hours her cargo had been safely unloaded.

Then she waited: waited for a favorable opportunity to slip away.

But the weather now took a turn for the better, and week after week the Mediterranean skies stayed azure and perversely devoid of cloud. With visibility up to fifty miles, the *Empire Guillemot* would certainly have been spotted as she made for the African shore. Roland Rouse was a patient man and quite content to bide his time; but his crew found the delay unpleasantly irksome—for Malta had little to offer in the way of entertainment, and food was short. Early in October the skies clouded over; but now at night a hunter's moon was reaching its maturity, and E-boats and U-boats were out in force. Not until October 22 were conditions right; then, at ten o'clock in the morning, under a gray featureless sky, the *Empire Guillemot* stood quietly out of Grand Harbour.

Her crew were in good heart, reckoning their troubles were over. In fact, they were just about to begin.

The first hint that anything was wrong came a couple of days later, when a Catalina flying boat, scheduled to meet and escort the *Empire Guillemot*, failed to locate her. A Swordfish from 816 Squadron was diverted to join the Catalina, but her reconnaissance, too, was unsuccessful. Signals passed between Grand Harbour and Gibraltar, and next morning the search was intensified. But another Swordfish, another Catalina, and a Fulmar from *Ark Royal* all drew blank. The *Empire Guillemot* had disappeared. Not until October 29, a week after she had left Malta, was there a hint of what had happened. Then came an Italian radio claim: "Our torpedo aircraft operating south of Malta have sunk a large enemy

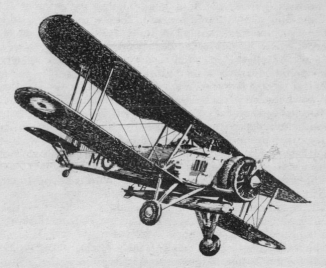

Fairey Swordfish

supply ship." And that night the following signal was sent to the Admiralty.

> S.S. *Empire Guillemot*. This ship, which sailed from Malta at 10:00/22, has not yet arrived at Gibraltar, and air reconnaissance has failed to locate her. The Italians claim to have sunk a merchant vessel west of Galita Island by torpedo on 24/10. According to the Italian radio, there were 35 survivors, of whom 2 have since died. It is presumed this vessel is the *Empire Guillemot*.

The vessel sunk was indeed the *Empire Guillemot*; but what exactly had happened to her was not known for another five years.

They reached the Tunisian shallows during the night of October 22–23. Navigation among the offshore shoals wasn't easy, and in the darkness the *Empire Guillemot* edged north at no more than quarter speed. Rouse kept her about three miles offshore, and their first night out from Malta passed uneventfully.

Dawn on October 23 found them rounding the promontory of Cape Bon. They altered course to the west-northwest and cut obliquely across the Gulf of Tunis, keeping well clear of Bizerta, where French patrol boats were known to be active. All day and all the following night they kept steadily on, through a moderate sea, beneath a slate-gray sky.

Early on October 24 they squeezed through the narrow channel between Galita Island and the shore. Galita Island was always a danger spot, and Rouse gave it as wide a berth as possible, hugging the Tunisian coast. He stood in so close, in fact, that the lookouts could see individual fronds on the palm trees lining the strand. By ten o'clock the island was hull down, and Rouse was just congratulating himself on having cleared their most dangerous hurdle when three Italian bombers came lumbering out of the cloud.

There was nothing much they could do—that was the trouble with individual sailing; if a ship was caught, she was, inevitably, in for a bad time

The Italians—slow, unwieldy Cants—circled the *Empire Guillemot* three times; then, one after the other, they came sweeping low across her deck. The thud of their machine guns echoed down from the banks of cloud. Splinters showered the merchantman's bridge; her single Lewis gun was put out of action; her rudder jammed, and in wide, erratic circles she started to drift along with the tide. Her crew took cover, waiting for the bombs. The Italians, however, were in no hurry. It was ten minutes after the machine-gunning before the first of them started her bombing run. She had a sitting target, but somehow she managed to miss, her bomb falling short. But the second Cant did better. Her bomb—a 250-pounder—landed flush amidships, on the hatch of No. 5 hold; it crashed through the hold and exploded in the engine room, killing William MacNeil, the third engineer. The *Empire Guillemot* began to settle by the stern.

Rouse ordered "Abandon ship." Two of their boats were colandered with splinters and tracer; but the other two looked seaworthy and the crew piled into them. They expected to be machine-gunned; but the Italians were merciful and left them alone as they pulled away from the sinking ship. Twenty minutes after being hit, the *Empire Guillemot* reared up her bow and disappeared. The Italians flew away. And Rouse and his crew were left alone, in open boats. It was 870 miles to Gibraltar.

In one boat were the master and nineteen officers and men; in the other were the first mate, Norman Halliday, and twenty-two officers and men. To start with, the boats kept close together, moving uneasily in the offshore swell. Even from a mile out, the men could hear the roar of breakers thundering against the Tunisian shore, and they had to shout to make themselves heard. Some of the crew wanted to make straight for land, but Rouse and Halliday persuaded them to head westward for Gibraltar. They got out their oars, rigged a makeshift sail, and set course for the Rock.

Their progress was pitiably slow. Tides and currents drifted them off course; the boats leaked; sun and a restless ground swell added to the general discomfort. In the mate's boat the men started to grumble.

All that day, October 24, they edged westward, parallel to the shore. Night brought a cooling breeze and relief from the heat of the sun. But there was no relief from the swell. The boats rolled uneasily, hour after hour, with a sickening, wayward, cork-screwing lurching. Many of the crew—some for the first time in their lives—were seasick. When, at midnight, Rouse took an astral fix, news of the boats' position was whispered uneasily from man to man. That day they had covered less than 25 miles; Gibraltar was still some 850 miles to the west.

On the second day their progress was better. They were getting the hang now of setting their makeshift sails, improving their steering, and becoming accustomed to the perpetual corkscrewing of the boats. At noon Rouse and Halliday took exact stock of their food and water, sharing equally what little they had. Water was reasonably plentiful—and there was always the chance of their being able to pull inshore at a deserted river mouth—but food was desperately short: two dozen emergency packs, a few pounds of raisins, twenty bars of chocolate, and two barrels of biscuits per boat. Master and mate took charge of their respective supplies and put the men on minimum rations: half a pint of water and a handful of biscuits and raisins per day—not the ideal diet for rowing a heavy boat through swell that rose and fell by a good twenty feet.

Nevertheless, they covered 40 miles that day, and a midnight fix placed them due north of Cape Rosa: only another 800 miles to go.

But that night the barometer started to fall.

On the third day, October 26, the sea began to rise, the boats became increasingly wayward, and a hot, blustering wind drove them away from the shore. In the mate's boat the crew became openly mutinous; they cursed Rouse and Halliday for not landing at once and pilfered one of the biscuit barrels. A little before sunset two planes, flying low over the sea, passed some way ahead of the boats. The men waved and started to flash an SOS; but in less time than it takes to describe their coming the planes had disappeared.

That day they covered a bare 20 miles; and during the night the barometer fell another four points.

October 27 dawned gray and overcast, with a hot, blustering wind slamming capriciously between south and west. It was difficult in the rising sea to keep the boats together, let alone on an accurate heading. But Roland Rouse was a determined man. He had set his course for Gibraltar, and neither wind nor wave nor the muttered complaints of his crew were going to turn him aside. The boats reeled westward into a rising gale, with the wind skimming spume off the swell crests and the noon sky as dark as an autumn twilight.

Toward sunset the storm worsened, and eventually the boats became separated. While they had been together they had felt lonely, but never utterly alone. Not as they felt now; with darkness sharpening their misery and turning their wretchedness into something very close to despair. But not until midnight—by then the wind was a full sixty knots and the waves over twenty feet high—did both Halliday and Rouse decide they would have to give up. Then, almost simultaneously, they turned their battered, near-foundering boats for the shore.

Rouse was lucky. After a couple of hours of heading south the men in his boat could hear the sound of surf pounding a distant shore. The night was dark and moonless; and whether the shore was sand or dune, rock or cliff, they were quite unable to judge. As they neared land the waves steepened; soon the sound of breakers drowned even the crescendo of the gale; and at last, dead ahead, they saw a line of spray, steeple-high, rising and falling along a half-seen curve of beach. The waves grew suddenly malicious, sweeping under the boat to a quickened tempo. They were swirled beam on. Utterly out of control, they were swept shoreward on the crest of a great wave. Spray and tumult engulfed them.

"Hang on!" Rouse shouted. And they were flung like straw out of a water runnel onto a quaking shore. Somehow all twenty of them managed to scramble out of the boat before the undertow sucked it back, beneath the oncoming wave, and it was splintered to driftwood.

Sodden, battered, hungry, and utterly exhausted, they lay on the sand, feeling the shore line tremble beneath them under the pounding of the great seas. It was an hour before they gained sufficient strength to haul themselves inland, over a low line of dunes. Here, sheltered a little from wind and rain, they tried to find shelter and start a fire; but they succeeded in neither. At dawn they were still huddled miserably together when the native coast guards found them. The few who tried to escape were quickly rounded up; and at noon they were taken to Bône and imprisoned in the barracks of the Third Algerian Tirailleurs. For them the war was over.

The mate's boat was not so fortunate.

In the storm Halliday had been swept farther west than Rouse, and when he came to head for the shore, he missed the sheltered bay of La Marsa (where the master had landed) and hit the open beach west of Cap de Fer. Here a shallow sand bar runs parallel to the beach about a half mile offshore. It is an idyllic place in calm weather, with the lagoon inside the bar as lovely as any coral-island strand; but in the early hours of October 28 the lagoon was a place of death, with the bar a frenzy of broken water and churned-up gravel. Here Halliday's boat broached to. For a moment it hung on its side, twenty feet above the bar. Then it capsized, flinging the men into the frenetic sea. Some drowned at once; others, as they struggled toward the shore. Of the twenty-three in the boat, only thirteen reached the beach; and of these, two died before dawn of exposure, shock, and cold. All were in "very bad shape" when the coast guards found them.

The area they had landed in was desolate and sparsely populated, and it was several hours before much could be done for them. But at last they were loaded into a truck and driven to a cork factory on the outskirts of Philippeville. Here they were warmed in front of an open fire and given hot tea and brandy. In the afternoon a doctor arrived, who gave them camphor injections and then took them to a small military hospital in Jemmapes. They stayed in the hospital for three days before joining the other survivors in Bône in the barracks of the Algerian Tirailleurs. Here they remained for the rest of the war: an unhappy ending to a brave venture; but an ending that had a parallel, all too often, in the fate of other merchantmen who attempted the run to Malta unescorted and alone.

Inevitably, it is the big spectacular convoys which catch the eye and hold the memory, while the passages of single ships slide unrecorded into oblivion. But when we honor the men of famous vessels like the *Illustrious*, *Breconshire*, and *Ohio*, let us remember, too, the men of the small unheard-of merchantmen who dared as much and often suffered more.

9

The sky was clear, a very bright half moon was shining on the starboard quarter, and the aircraft came in low on the port bow. It was a quite impossible night for seeing the birds, as any wildfowler will agree.

—COMMANDER GRAHAM, H.M.S. "ZULU"

The *Oribi*, a 1500-ton "O"-class destroyer, was newly commissioned. In August 1941 she returned to Scapa after her first assignment—escorting the Prime Minister across the Atlantic for his meeting with President Roosevelt. The trip had been monotonous and uneventful; and the *Oribi*'s commanding officer, Lieutenant Commander McBeath, D.S.O., hoped that their second assignment would hold more hope of action. He was not disappointed. In mid-September the *Oribi* was ordered to the Mediterranean to join a convoy assembling for the passage to Malta.

On nearing Gibraltar, the most elaborate efforts were made to conceal the arrival of the *Oribi* and other warships (which had been temporarily detached from the Home Fleet and lent to Force H). They went in to refuel individually and were passed through the Strait under cover of darkness. Next morning, September 25, they rendezvoused with the merchantmen well out of sight of land.

The convoy was a large one: nine merchant vessels, carrying among them 80,000 tons of supplies and 2600 troops; while escorting them was a formidable body of ships: three battleships, one aircraft carrier, five cruisers, and as many as eighteen destroyers—the most powerful force to attempt the passage to date. The chief object of the operation was to pass the nine merchantmen through to Malta; but it was also hoped to tempt the Italian fleet to join battle. In this hope, the unusual strength of the escort was carefully concealed, and elaborate subterfuge was indulged in to create the impression that only the customary warships of Force H (one battleship, one aircraft carrier, and a couple of cruisers) had put to sea. It was for this reason that the convoy sailed initially in two groups: Admiral Somerville and Force H keeping to the usual southern route close to the Algerian shore, where they were likely to be spotted; while Admiral Curteis and the reinforcements from home waters kept well to the north, following a little-used route close to the Balearics, where they hoped to escape detection. The two groups planned to rendezvous on the third day, before making the critical passage south of Sardinia. The *Oribi* sailed with Admiral Curteis.

The first day passed uneventfully, with both groups standing undetected to the east.

The second day brought the usual sighting, shadowing, and identifying of forces.

Soon after dawn Admiral Somerville's Force H was spotted by an Italian seaplane. Because of a radio failure, there was some delay in vectoring out the *Ark Royal*'s Fulmars; and the Italian was able to broadcast an "Enemy" report before he was chased away. This sighting of the southern group was almost inevitable and of no great consequence: but early in the afternoon there occurred something far more serious. Admiral Curteis and the northern group were sighted—most unluckily—by a Spanish civil aircraft, and their position was broadcast to the Italian fleet.

That evening Admiral Iachino sailed from Naples with a well-balanced force, including two Littorio-class battleships and four heavy cruisers. The Italian Naval High Command had guessed that a convoy was under way for Malta and had given Iachino orders to intercept.

The admiral knew that two groups of British vessels were at sea to oppose him, but since his reconnaissance reports had lacked detail, he didn't know their strength; certainly he did not, initially, suspect that the British units were more powerful than the usual and comparatively light warships of Admiral Somerville's Force H. Throughout the night the Italian battle fleet stood south by west. By dawn they were nearing Cape Carbonara, on the southeastern tip of Sardinia. Iachino hoped that Italian bombers, from Cagliari and Marsala, would soften up the convoy in the morning, and his fleet would close and liquidate it in the afternoon.

September 27 dawned fine but overcast, with patches of low thundercloud and occasional belts of haze. The wind was very light—under five knots—and shifting between south and west. This meant that the *Ark Royal's* Fulmars had difficulty in getting off the deck; it meant, too, that every time planes were flown off or landed on, the carrier had to steam into wind at top speed on an opposite course to the convoy.

As planned, the northern and southern groups rendezvoused at dawn. They had barely taken up sailing stations when the first Italian shadowers, Cants and B.R.20s, appeared on the radar screen. The Fulmars were waiting for them; but the belts of haze and the low patches of cloud gave first-class cover, and one of the Cants got away and passed back a sighting report—though this, once again, was lacking in detail. The convoy was then 120 miles southwest of Sardinia— within easy range of the airdrome at Cagliari.

All that morning the merchantmen and their escort headed east. The ships were closed up at action stations; gun crews and lookouts scanned their arcs of horizon; while eight Fulmars circled watchfully overhead. But the expected attack didn't develop; not until early afternoon. For, the evening before, Cagliari had been visited by long-range bombers from Malta; hangars, bomb dumps, and parked Savoias had been set ablaze; and it took the Italians a full morning of repair work before they could launch even a limited offensive. This was the first example of what was, perhaps, the outstanding feature of the September convoy: the excellent co-operation between Navy and Air Force.

Thus, the first attack didn't develop until close to one o'clock; then, just as the watches were changing over for lunch, a formation of twelve Cants and B.R.20s came suddenly out of the north. They came in low, less than fifty feet above the sea; but they didn't escape the Fulmars. Gunfire reverberated among the thunderheads of cumulus; planes wheeled and banked among the layers of heat haze and mist; and two of the Cants were shot flaming into the sea. Four others were forced away, without getting in an attack; and only six planes broke through to the convoy. Of these, two were shot down by the destroyer screen; the others, refusing to face the barrage, dropped their torpedoes at long range; and after fifteen hectic minutes the first assault was over.

But one of *Ark Royal's* Fulmars, while chasing stragglers, ran into a formation of six C.R.42s and was never heard of again.

At 1:15 another seven Fulmars were flown off, so that fourteen fighters were soon circling the fleet: an unusually strong umbrella. Yet it was a few minutes later that the Italians achieved their sole success of the day.

At 1:28 a second wave of attackers came in from starboard, out of the heat-hazed sun. *Oribi* sighted them first, half a dozen B.R.20s skirting a low belt of mist. At a range of two miles the destroyer opened controlled long-range fire—more as a warning than in the hope of obtaining a hit. As soon as they saw they were spotted, the B.R.20s, very skillfully handled, formed into line abreast and came on: straight for the convoy. With the range down to 6000 yards McBeath switched to barrage fire. At 3000 yards every pom-pom, oerlikon, and close-range Lewis in the starboard screen was blazing at the Italians. But they still held course. And two of them made straight for the *Oribi*. They dropped their torpedoes from under a thousand yards. One torpedo porpoised and then ran in circles; but the other was well dropped and well aimed. McBeath had barely time to swing head on before it flashed foaming past the *Oribi's* beam—so close that the lookouts could see the individual flecks of spray thrown up from its war head. As the destroyer turned, her port oerlikons were brought to bear, and tracer flashed into the Italian's tailplane. For a moment he held course; then his rudder disintegrated and, engines screaming, he plummeted into the sea.

A Fulmar accounted for one more B.R.20; but the last three broke into the convoy center. Handled with great skill and gallantry, they flung themselves, at less than mast height, at the *Nelson*. The flagship avoided two torpedoes, but the third smacked into her bow, ten feet below the water line. The great ship shuddered uneasily, and almost at once her speed started to drop.

A few seconds later the *Rodney* sighted a single aircraft coming in low and fast. She shot it down. Only as it ditched almost alongside her did she realize it was one of the *Ark Royal's* Fulmars.

Smoke and cordite fumes from the second attack were still drifting over the convoy when radar reported a third wave of aircraft coming in from the south. But this attack was never pressed home; few aircraft faced the barrage; a C.R. 42 indulging in aerobatics over the fleet (presumably in an effort to draw fire) was shot down; and nothing was achieved. By three o'clock the convoy had passed the southern tip of Sardinia. Now each revolution of their engines took them farther away from Cagliari; and soon the greatest danger—from the air—had passed.

But the danger from the sea remained: increased, indeed, with every passing minute. For at 2:30 Admiral Somerville received the following report from a Malta-based reconnaissance plane: "Two Littorio-class battleships, four cruisers, sixteen destroyers. Course 190°. Speed 20 kts." Their position was just to the north of the Skerki Bank. They were less than eighty miles from the convoy, and closing fast.

Somerville at once ordered the *Ark Royal* to fly off two shadowers and to prepare a striking force. The former left at once; but it was close to an hour before the strike was under way—since all the carrier's Swordfish had been disarmed and drained of fuel to reduce fire risk during the morning's air attacks.

By one of those unlucky coincidences, the Italian fleet made a substantial alteration of course soon after the two Swordfish had left. This alteration of course wasn't reported by the Malta-based shadower for fifteen minutes; and, because of wireless congestion, it was a further twenty-five minutes before news of it reached Admiral Somerville. An attempt was immediately made to contact the two Swordfish; but one of them had passed out of radio range, and the other, soon after receiving the admiral's signal, ran into a swarm of Italian fighters and was badly shot up. Her wing tip shredded, her fuel tank holed, and her observer wounded, she came limping back to the *Ark*. Meanwhile, in deteriorating weather, the R.A.F. shadower from Malta lost contact with the Italian fleet. Admiral Somerville was thus in the frustrating position of knowing that somewhere, within sixty or seventy miles of the convoy, Admiral Iachino was searching for him, as he was searching for Admiral Iachino. But in slowly worsening weather, the battle fleets missed each other; heat haze and the gathering thunderheads screening fleet from fleet and preventing an action which could easily have turned out to be one of the major naval engagements of the war.

It was the weather which at last caused Admiral Iachino to call off the search. By midafternoon the cloud had thickened and lowered, his promised fighter cover from Cagliari still hadn't arrived, he suspected from the volume of W.T. traffic that several British capital ships and at least one carrier were at sea, and he expected at any moment to be attacked by carrier-borne planes. At 2:45 he reversed course, increased speed to twenty-six knots, and made for home. And it was just as well for him that he did. For had he held his original course, the Swordfish would surely have found him, would, just as surely, have crippled him and slowed him down sufficiently for Admiral Somerville to come into range with his slower but more powerful units. As it was, the Swordfish searched for Iachino along his original line of advance; they searched for him until the light drained out of the sky and the petrol out of their tanks. But they didn't find him. The *Rodney*, the *Prince of Wales*, and a pair of cruisers, which had also been searching ahead of the convoy, were equally unsuccessful; and at dusk Admiral Somerville called both Swordfish and warships back to the convoy. All hope of a fleet engagement had passed.

At seven o'clock, a little before sunset, the whole force reached the mouth of the Narrows. Here was the familiar parting of the ways: the capital ships returning to Gibraltar, and the cruisers, destroyers, and merchantmen (under the command of Admiral Burrough) making the final dash alone.

Admiral Somerville judged correctly that the Italian capital ships would avoid the risk of a night action; but he thought it quite in the cards that their lighter forces would stay behind to dispute the convoy's passage east of the Narrows. He had originally ordered the convoy, on debouching from the Skerki Channel, to stand northeast, close to the Sicilian shore—the route used during Operation "Substance." But with enemy warships at sea to the north, he now had second thoughts, wondering if the southerly route, close to Tunisia, might not be safer. He signaled Admiral Burrough, asking him which route he preferred.

Burrough now made a brave decision—a decision which, in the light of events, undoubtedly saved the convoy from heavy losses. He chose the northern route, giving his reasons as follows:

(1) It seemed that the bolder course would be more likely to deceive the enemy.
(2) If the convoy moved to the southward it would be clearly silhouetted under the moon, and off the Tunisian coast could take no avoiding action.
(3) Convoy and escort in single line ahead from Cape Bon to south of Kélibia Light would extend to about seven miles, and would be very vulnerable to either aircraft or E-boat attack.
(4) On the southern route, time of arrival at Malta would be delayed.
(5) The enemy was more likely to conduct a search in the south than in the north.

Admiral Somerville concurred. At seven o'clock he turned away to the west, taking with him his three battleships, the *Ark Royal*, and a screen of nine destroyers. This left Admiral Burrough with five cruisers and nine destroyers for the final dash through the Narrows.

The ships stood quietly east, silhouetted first against the gold and crimson of a tempestuous sunset, then against the silver of a rising moon.

Italian aircraft were out in force. To start with, the *Ark Royal*'s Fulmars kept them at bay, preventing their spotting the convoy's break up and entry into the Narrows. But as it became darker, and as the merchantmen drew farther away from the carrier, so the Fulmar's effectiveness declined. By eight o'clock it was quite dark; the last of the fighters had been struck down inside the *Ark:* and Admiral Burrough was left to face the Italian bombers alone.

As the heat of the day had declined, so the thunderheads and the belts of haze had dispersed; by nightfall the sky was clear. The moon, rising on the convoy's starboard quarter, threw the advancing vessels into sharp relief; and the Italians made the most of the favorable conditions.

Their torpedo bombers came in singly, or every now and then in pairs. They came in low, fast, and up-moon: invisible throughout their attacks against the dark backdrop of sky. It was, as the captain of the *Zulu* said, a quite impossible night for them to see the "birds." But the "birds," all too obviously, could see them. Within half an hour of nightfall some dozen torpedoes had come foaming among the merchantmen. *Cossack*, *Kenya*, *Oribi*, and the *Rowallan Castle* had been near-missed; it was only a matter of time before one of the vessels was hit.

Admiral Burrough's wisdom in choosing the northerly route was now apparent. For had the vessels been silhouetted against the Tunisian shore as well as against the moon, they would have been even easier targets; and had they been strung out in single file without room to maneuver (and this would have been inevitable among the Tunisian shallows), they would have quickly lost all semblance of formation. As it was, they had difficulty enough in dodging the torpedoes and at the same time keeping station—Captain Clarke of the *Sheffield* reported several vessels "continually and grossly out of position," while at 8:30 the *City of Calcutta* and the *Rowallan Castle*, both trying to dodge the same torpedo, collided, and the latter added to the confusion by accidently loosing off her distress rockets. It was just as well that the Italian torpedo bombers, though persistent, were relatively few in number.

All this time the *Oribi* had been stationed astern of the convoy. To start with, she had a grandstand view of the assault on the merchantmen; but soon she, too, was under attack.

A few minutes after the *Rowallan Castle* had let off her rockets, an aircraft was heard approaching *Oribi* from fine on the port bow. In the darkness the plane was invisible, but the destroyer optimistically opened fire. From the bridge McBeath saw the splashes of two torpedoes, about eight hundred yards to port. He increased speed, swung stern on, and combed the torpedo tracks by asdic. As the destroyer turned, the plane, trying to follow her, ventured too far down-moon; before she realized her mistake, her silhouette was thrown into sharp relief against the horizon. Pom-pom and oerlikon hammered into her. Both her engines streamed blood-red banners of flame, and, like a great torch, she spiraled—the *Oribi*'s second victim—into the sea.

The destroyer had scarcely regained station when her asdic operator picked up a muffled underwater explosion.

"Torpedo hit on the port column," he reported to the bridge.

McBeath knew then that one of the merchantmen was in trouble. It came as no surprise when *Euryalus* signaled him: "Proceed to assistance of vessel stopped on your port bow."

The vessel hit was the *Imperial Star*, the largest and most valuable ship in the convoy. She was a 12,000-tonner: a fast, twin-screw, cargo-*cum*-passenger liner, built in 1935 by Harland and Wolff. Her cargo was a mixed one: 500 tons of refrigerated meat; 500 tons of kerosene; several hundred crates of bombs; grain; flour; .303 ammunition; and about 300 passengers. McBeath found her drifting helplessly away from the convoy, her engines stopped and her steering shattered; already, within a few minutes of being hit, she was badly down by the stern.

The *Oribi* went alongside. The *Imperial Star*'s master thought she was finished. She had, he told McBeath, been hit on the port quarter; her rudder and screws had been blown entirely away; her engine rooms had been flooded, and she was taking water. But McBeath reckoned she had one hope: one chance, albeit a slender one, of getting to Malta. Perhaps he could take her in tow.

Another destroyer, the *Heythrop*, went alongside to take off passengers; and while they were being embarked, the *Imperial Star* prepared for the tow.

Conditions aboard the merchantman were surprisingly good. Her electric supply was operating normally; all her holds (except No. 6) were dry: there was no danger of fire, and she was riding well. Only in her stern was there substantial damage. But here the damage was serious. For her electric motors had been blown two feet back from the quadrant, and normal steering was obviously out of the question. An attempt to switch over to emergency or hand steering proved abortive; for, although the rudder had been blown away, a twisted fragment of keel had jammed between the ends of the propeller shafts, and this acted as an unmovable rudder, swinging the ship continually to starboard. Nor could it be dislodged, since the propeller shafts had been buckled and refused to turn.

McBeath hoped that once the *Imperial Star* was in tow her movement through the water might dislodge the fragment of

keel. But it was not to be. At eleven o'clock the towline was
secured on both ships, and the *Oribi* set course for Malta.
But the *Imperial Star*, heavy with water and cargo, weighed
twelve times as much as *Oribi*, and it was she who did the
towing! To quote McBeath's report:

I had the *Imperial Star* in tow for two hours, occasionally
working up to eight knots. But we could only go in circles,
and nothing we could do would get the tow on a steady
course. Whenever I tried to straighten *Imperial Star* up
and head on a definite course, her way would carry her
round in a circle, and several times she dragged *Oribi*
stern first after her. Eventually at 01:20 I had to slip, as we
were again being towed stern first, and were likely to foul
the tow under the merchantman's keel.

McBeath again drew alongside. *Imperial Star* was far lower
in the water now; she was drawing thirty-eight feet and
becoming increasingly unmanageable. Also, she had drifted
to within twenty miles of the Sicilian shore and was nearing
the edge of an area known to be mined. There seemed
nothing more to be done. Reluctantly McBeath and the
master decided that at least three tugs would be needed to
tow her successfully—and there was no hope of one tug, let
alone three, venturing so far to the west. She would have to
be scuttled. It was a cruel decision to have to make—for, as
her master said, "if we'd been hit in any other place I am
convinced we could have got her in"—but undoubtedly it was
the right one. The remaining passengers and crew, 141 in all,
were transferred to the destroyer. The few flooding valves
which hadn't jammed were opened; and three depth charges
were lashed together, a little below the water line, and
ignited with a fifteen-minute time fuse. At 3:40 the *Oribi*
cast off, and eleven minutes later the depth charges exploded.

But now, perversely, the *Imperial Star* refused to sink. The
depth charges started a substantial fire; flames licked at the
hold containing the crates of bombs. But the *Star* was an
insulated refrigerator ship, and the flames wouldn't spread.
Nor did the opening of the flooding valves have any noticeable effect. At 4:20 McBeath started to shell her from a range
of 2000 yards. He shelled her for half an hour, hitting her

again and again at point-blank range with 4.7-inch salvos. But still she refused to sink.

Eventually he left her, blazing from stem to stern, listing to 20 degrees, but still miraculously afloat.

At thirty-two knots the *Oribi* cut across the Sicilian shallows following the course of the convoy. She passed within seven miles of the mainland in broad daylight, but she wasn't challenged; and at noon she caught up with the rest of the merchantmen as they were entering the swept channel.

Air reconnaissance next afternoon failed to locate the *Imperial Star.* Sometime during the early hours of the morning the stubborn ship had foundered: the only merchantman to be lost while sailing in a large scale convoy to Malta during the whole of 1941.

The rest of Admiral Burrough's force, met and escorted next morning by R.A.F. fighters from Malta, reached the island safely. The warships entered Grand Harbour first, to be greeted by a demonstration as spontaneous as it was moving. In the words of Captain Roskill:

> . . . the whole population of Malta appeared to be lined up in serried cheering masses along the shore, as the cruisers, with guards paraded and bands playing as though returning from a peacetime cruise, passed through the breakwater and up the stretch of sheltered water with which the Mediterranean Fleet had been so long and so intimately acquainted.

A few hours later the merchantmen, too, came slowly past the breakwater, and within a couple of days a further 60,000 tons of supplies had been added to Malta's already substantial stockpile.

It was reckoned that after the September convoy the island had sufficient fuel, ammunition, and food to meet her expected requirements in the next four to five months. Malta was now, in fact, a very different proposition from the near-defenseless island she had been twelve months before. Her garrison numbered close to 25,000; she had more than 330 ack-ack and light coastal-defense guns; she had 85 modern and serviceable planes; and her submarines and the warships of her famous Force K were harrying Axis shipping from the Tyrrhenian Sea to the shore of Tripolitania. Certainly few people on the island suspected, that autumn, that Malta was soon to pass through her most desperate hour and that it would be nine months before another large-scale convoy was safely unloaded at the wharves of Grand Harbour.

10

It has been decided that Malta must be obliterated.
—CIANO'S DIARIES

September 1941 provides a convenient halfway point from which to review Malta's fortunes during her first year of war.

In the summer of 1940 the Chief of Staff had stated categorically that "there is nothing practicable we can do to increase the powers of resistance of Malta"; yet within twelve months the island had been transformed from a near-defenseless encumbrance into a strongly held key point, the linchpin of our war effort in the Middle East. This transformation was brought about by three factors.

First, the strategic genius of the Prime Minister, who—almost alone—recognized the vital role Malta could be made to play and who never ceased to champion the island's cause, often in the face of very considerable opposition. It is easy now to look back and proclaim Malta's importance; easy to see how its aircraft and warships disrupted the vital Axis supply route to Libya; easy to see how it acted as the vital link between Gibraltar and Alexandria and how it contained and drained away the enemy's resources. But this importance was not so apparent at the time; and to many people—including several of the Chiefs of Staff—the island always remained an "untenable reliability." It was lucky for Malta—and for the free peoples of the world—that the Prime Minister thought otherwise.

The second factor which enabled the island to survive was that both Admiral Cunningham at Alexandria and Admiral Somerville at Gibraltar shared the Prime Minister's vision and possessed the tactical ability to put his orders into effect. Both had a host of other commitments; both suffered from a chronic shortage of warships; but their efforts to reprovision

DETAILS OF THE THREE PRINCIPAL MALTA CONVOYS WHICH SAILED DURING 1941

Date	Code name	Number of merchantmen	Number of escorting warships	Losses	Quantity of stores to reach Malta
January 1941	Excess*	3	3 battleships 2 aircraft carriers 1 battle cruiser 9 cruisers 23 destroyers 3 submarines	1 aircraft carrier badly damaged 1 cruiser sunk 1 cruiser damaged 1 destroyer damaged	Approximately 30,000 tons
July 1941	Substance	6	1 battleship 1 battle cruiser 1 aircraft carrier 4 cruisers 17 destroyers 8 submarines	1 cruiser damaged 1 destroyer sunk 1 destroyer damaged 1 merchantman damaged	Approximately 50,000 tons
September 1941	Halberd	9	3 battleships 1 aircraft carrier 5 cruisers 18 destroyers 9 submarines	1 battleship damaged 1 merchantman sunk	Approximately 60,000 tons

*The passing of a convoy to Malta was not the sole objective of Operation "Excess," and many of the warships taking part were engaged in other duties.

the island never faltered; and they took as their watchword Admiral Somerville's now classic order, "The convoy must go through."

Yet no amount of directives from above could, by themselves, have saved the island; and in the final analysis Malta's survival must be attributed to sheer guts: the guts of the Maltese in standing up to German and Italian bombing and the guts of the men of the Royal and Merchant Navies in fighting through the desperately needed supplies. The cost of running in these supplies was not light—as the accompanying table shows; but the losses that were incurred were a small price to pay for Malta's survival.

And the island did more than survive. As the months passed, her strength—albeit with painful slowness—increased until eventually her submarines and the warships of her famous Force K were harassing Axis shipping throughout the Central Mediterranean, while her aircraft were not only taking a heavy toll of Rommel's supplies but were striking at the Italian mainland as far north as Naples.

It is interesting to compare the island's resources at the outbreak of war with its resources a year later.

In the summer of 1940 Malta's garrison had consisted of less than five thousand ill-equipped troops; there were, on the island, only four obsolescent and crated planes, a mere

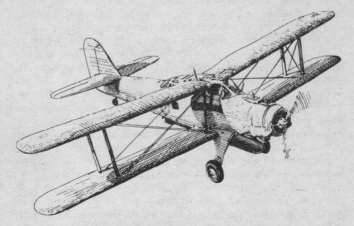

Fairey Albacore

fourteen coastal-defense guns, and sufficient food for no more than six weeks. Things were very different in the autumn of 1941. By then the garrison had risen to 30,000 men with first-class equipment; on the airfields were eighty Hurricanes and some hundred and five assorted bombers (Wellingtons, Blenheims, Marylands, Swordfish, and Albacores); the AA defenses consisted not of fourteen guns, but of close to fourteen hundred, which could, according to a Luftwaffe pilot, "put up a barrage fiercer than that over London"; while in the island's granaries and rock shelters was food for a good five months. It seemed that the corner had been turned, that the future was reasonable assured. It wasn't so. But certainly few people on the island suspected, that autumn, that Malta was about to pass through her most desperate hour.

It was Malta's growing strength that proved her undoing: that and the winter stalemate on the Eastern Front. For in November 1941 Hitler, balked of quick victory in Russia, again turned his attention to the Middle East. And it soon became clear to the German General Staff that no worthwhile scheme could be embarked on in the Mediterranean while Malta remained unconquered. For the island which only a year ago had seemed so defenseless was now proving a poisoned thorn in the Axis' side: a stumbling block to their every plan. They couldn't mount an offensive in Africa, because Malta's aircraft and ships disrupted their supply line. (In October, for example, over a quarter of Rommel's reinforcements had been sunk en route.) They couldn't prepare an offensive elsewhere, because Malta's reconnaissance planes reported every concentration of troops and shipping. And soon harbors, airfields, and railways on the Italian mainland were feeling the weight of a not inconsiderable air offensive launched from Luqa and Hal Far. There was, Hitler and Mussolini decided, only one thing to do. Malta must have her teeth drawn; she must be first battered to impotence, then captured by assault from the air. Toward the end of November, Ciano made a note of this decision in his diary. "It has been decided," he wrote, "that Malta must be obliterated."

This task of obliteration was given to Kesselring, the man who directed the Luftwaffe in the Battle of Britain. And he, as soon as he arrived in Sicily, improved on the word "obliterate." In his operational orders, promulgated early that December, he decreed that Malta was to be "Coventrated": that is, reduced to rubble by precision bombing as was the center of Coventry. He must have been confident, too, that his orders would be carried out. For forces were put at his disposal with a lavishness that turned the coming assault on the island into one of the major operations of the war.

That autumn Fliegerkorps X came back to Sicily. And they didn't come alone. Planes were also withdrawn from the airfields in front of Moscow and Stalingrad, from the reserve airdromes in France and Belgium, and from the Trondheim district of Norway. They came swarming south, squadron after squadron of battle-tested veterans, until by mid-December an air armada of unparalleled proportions was assembled on the Sicilian airfields within fifteen minutes' flying time of Malta—over 400 bombers (250 Junkers, more than 100 Savoias, and some five dozen Heinkels, Dorniers, B.R.20s, and Cants) and over 400 fighters (200 Messerschmitts, more than 125 Macchis, and an assorted bag of C.R.42s, Reggiane 2001s, and experimental Heinkel 113s). Kesselring, it seemed, was

Reggiane 2001 Falcon

taking a sledge hammer to crack a nut. With such resources he could hardly fail to give the island its *coup de grâce*.

The Germans and Italians settled to their task with studied deliberation. First, in early December, a series of reconnaissance and photographic surveys: until every detail of the island's defenses was laid bare. Then, around about Christmas, a number of probing raids on carefully selected targets. And finally, in the first days of the new year, the start of a carefully mounted offensive against dockyard, airfields, and gun emplacements. It was the beginning of a long, bitter, and desperate battle: an air assault of unparalleled duration and ferocity.

By the end of January, Malta was reeling under a continuous avalanche of bombs: raid after raid: three or four raids a day: day after day: week after week. Before long a number of shortages began to make themselves felt; a shortage of aviation fuel, of certain types of food, of belts of .303 for the Hurricanes, and, above all, of shells for the AA guns, which were now in almost constant action twenty-four hours a day. It soon became imperative to attempt to run in further supplies—although, with British naval forces weakened by the evacuation from Crete and with the Luftwaffe firmly in command of the approaches by air, the task of fighting through another convoy seemed hazardous as never before.

But by mid-March the issue was clear. Unless a convoy got through to the island soon, Malta would fall.

11

H.M.S. Breconshire: *"I have a strong tendency to
come up into wind."*
H.M. Tug Ancient: *"You're telling me!"*

The *Breconshire* and her captain were old hands in the
business of taking stores to Malta. By March 1942 they had
already completed five trips to the island, sometimes in
convoy, sometimes alone; and Captain Colin Alexander
Hutchison, R.N., and his great slab-sided vessel were well
known to the people of Grand Harbour and Marsaxlokk.

Captain Hutchison was a fine example of the old school of
seaman. A strict disciplinarian, outspoken and sometimes
intolerant, he wasn't the man to suffer fools gladly. But he
knew his job. None better.

His ship—the *Breconshire*—was officially classed as a
Commissioned Auxiliary Supply Ship. A fifteen-knot converted merchantman, she was capable of carrying 5000 tons of oil
fuel, plus roughly the same amount of general cargo. She was
rather like her captain. No airs, frills, or graces; but stouthearted,
seaworthy, and tough.

On March 18, 1942, she lay at anchor in Alexandria harbor,
at twelve hours' readiness to sail. Her destination, once
again, was Malta. She had just completed loading, and never,
thought Captain Hutchison as he checked through his inven-
tory of stores, had they taken on a more "uncomfortable"
cargo: 150 tons of .303 ammunition; 176 tons of kerosene; a
hundred crates of armor-piercing 500-pound bombs; a hundred crates of 3-inch AA ammunition; 650 tons of grain; 690
tons of coal; and several hundred boxes of depth-charge
detonators; plus, of course, their usual 5000 tons of oil fuel.
The odds were that, if hit, the *Breconshire* would explode
like a crate of fireworks.

117

In the early hours of March 20 she got underway and at dawn passed through the boom at the entrance of Alexandria harbor. With her were three other merchantmen: the *Clan Campbell*, the *Pampas*, and the *Talabot*: four ships carrying some 30,000 tons of stores: stores that were vitally needed; for no convoy had reached Malta for several months.

Captain Hutchison was convoy commodore, and he demanded a high standard of the ships which sailed with him. When the *Clan Campbell* was several minutes late in clearing the boom, he sent her a signal which fairly blistered the paint off her bridge. A few hours later he had to reprimand her again; this time for straggling. And as the day progressed it became obvious that the wretched *Clan Campbell* was going to be the convoy's lame duck—the sort of vessel that was always in trouble, always belching smoke, always steaming that vital half knot slower than the rest of the convoy. Already, after only six hours' sailing, she was lagging far behind; and eventually she was ordered to steer straight, at her maximum speed, while the other ships zigzagged on either side of her. Captain Hutchison regarded her with professional disapproval.

All that day—March 20—the merchantmen headed west, parallel to the African shore. Wind and sea were moderate; the sky overcast. Hour after hour the vessels proceeded peacefully: undisturbed.

Early next morning they were met by the main body of their escort. Four cruisers and sixteen destroyers, commanded by Rear Admiral Philip Vian, flying his flag in H.M.S. *Cleopatra*. The merchantmen felt safer now, especially since with the dawn and the warships came relays of fighter aircraft from the desert airstrips. Screened by the Navy, watched over by the R.A.F., they headed east-northeastward, butting at twelve knots into a slowly rising head sea. By noon they were into the first danger area, the narrows between Crete and Cyrenaica. But no attacks came. The ships moved on; into the Central Mediterranean; undetected; undisturbed.

But late that evening they lost their fighters; for the Hurricanes and Kittyhawks lacked the range to protect them west of Crete. And half an hour after the last of the planes had left, the convoy was spotted, purely by chance, by a group of cumbersome German troop transports flying on a routine trip between Cyrenaica and Crete. How Admiral

Vian longed for an aircraft carrier as the troop transports
skirted his convoy, observing it carefully from a little outside
gun range. Soon the Junkers' radios were working overtime;
and by sunset the convoy was no secret any more.

Germans and Italians, it seemed, were for once working in
close unison. For a little after midnight Admiral Vian received a signal from one of his submarines, P36, patrolling in
the Gulf of Taranto. "Three destroyers," the signal read, "and
hydrophone effect of heavier ships. Course 150°. Speed 23
knots." The Italian fleet was putting to sea; was heading south
to intercept the convoy.

The night of March 21–22 was uneventful; but all next
morning the convoy was shadowed and occasionally attacked
by random aircraft—mostly Savoias, dropping their torpedoes
from an excessively hopeful range. Then, a little after one-
thirty, a shadowing aircraft dropped a line of four red flares
ahead of the convoy; obviously to signal its position. Admiral
Vian knew then that the Italian fleet must be very near. But
he held course. He was determined to get the convoy through.
No matter what the cost.

The naval engagement that followed, the Battle of Sirte,
was from a tactical point of view the most brilliant naval
action of the war. For not only had Admiral Vian to engage
the vastly superior enemy fleet which had come out from
Taranto and Naples; he had also to protect a convoy. He was,
in other words, like a boxer facing a heavier opponent with
one hand tied behind his back. But he had made his plans
with painstaking care, and he had in Captain Hutchison a
convoy commodore whom he knew he could trust. So when,
at 2:10, the *Euryalus* reported "four unknowns bearing 015°,"
Admiral Vian acted at once and with splendid effrontery.
Leaving the convoy with a screen of six destroyers and a
single ack-ack cruiser, he led the rest of his ships, in divisions
in line ahead, straight at the enemy.

As the range closed, the "four unknowns" were identified.
They turned out to be a pair of destroyers and a pair of heavy
8-inch cruisers (the *Trento* and *Gorizia*); and close behind
them there soon appeared two more destroyers and the
cruiser *Giovanni della Bande Nera*. Already Admiral Vian's
force was heavily outgunned. But he continued straight for

the enemy, in five parallel columns; while behind him two ships, the *Carlisle* and *Avon Vale*, made smoke to hide the convoy.

The Italians seemed disconcerted by this bold front. At 2:36 they swung broadside on and opened fire at a range of 30,000 yards. Admiral Vian, his ships not yet within range, kept steadily on. It was more than fifteen minutes before his 6-inch cruisers were able to reply. Then, at 2:56, at a range of 22,000 yards, *Cleopatra* and *Euryalus* started to return the enemy's fire. And almost at once the Italians turned away to the northward; all except the *Trento,* who for several minutes engaged the British cruisers briskly, if not very accurately, before she, too, swung away to the north.

At 3:15 Admiral Vian turned back to rejoin the merchantmen. The first assault had been beaten off. But it had all been too easy to be true.

The convoy, meanwhile, had been subjected to a heavy and sustained bombing attack. If Admiral Vian had not left behind him an adequate ack-ack screen, the merchant ships would almost certainly have been obliterated. As it was, the concentrated barrage from the six Hunt-class destroyers and the ack-ack cruiser *Carlisle* broke up the attacking aircraft and disrupted their attacks. There were, nevertheless, several anxious moments. The bombers were German: Ju 87s and Ju 88s: and they came in in simultaneous waves, from different heights and different bearings. The *Breconshire* was straddled. The *Carlisle* was near-missed. The expenditure of ammunition was staggering (60 per cent in some of the Hunts); and conditions aboard the warships as they maneuvered at high speed soon became extremely difficult. For by now the freshening southeast wind had knocked up a heavy sea. The destroyers were washing down fore and aft; their gun crews were firing through cataracts of spray; and even the cruisers' bridges, forty feet above the sea, were being swept by sheets of driven spume. But in an hour and a half's concentrated attack not a single vessel was hit.

Admiral Vian had hardly got back to the convoy when Italian warships again appeared on the northern horizon. Only this time their silhouettes looked larger: heavier. This time, Vian realized, he had to face not only 8-inch cruisers but also a battleship—the 35,000-ton *Littorio:* a ship armed with nine 15-inch and twelve 6-inch guns: a ship whose single broadside outweighed the combined firepower of his entire fleet.

Once again he didn't hesitate. Once again, while the *Carlisle* and *Avon Vale* laid smoke to screen the convoy, he led his light cruisers and destroyers straight at their mighty adversary.

The action that followed had a classic simplicity.

The Italians were determined to get at the convoy in the remaining three hours of daylight. They had a vastly superior fleet, plus the considerable advantage of aerial spotting. Had they been given time to think, had they been allowed a breathing space in which to set in motion a plan of their own, they could hardly have failed. But this breathing space Admiral Vian denied them. His tactics were those which Kempenfelt eulogized two centuries before, at the close of the Seven Years' War; he wrote:

> [Yours] is an inferior against a superior fleet; therefore the greatest skill and address is requisite to counter the designs of the enemy; to watch and seize the most favorable opportunity for [offensive] action; to hover near the enemy; to keep him at bay; to prevent his attempting anything but at risk and hazard; to command his attention and oblige him to think of nothing but being on his guard against *your* attack.

The Battle of Sirte, in brief, was the classic proving of the adage that the best means of defense is attack.

At 4:37 Admiral Vian stood his warships straight at the Italian battle fleet, his division leaders making smoke. He was pinning his faith on one important factor. The wind: the south-south-easterly twenty-five-knot wind, in which the smoke lay perfectly, streaming diagonally in a great billowing cloud bank toward the Italian warships. This smoke served several purposes. It hid the convoy; it made it difficult for the Italian gun layers to spot their fall of shot; and, lastly and most important, it made it extremely hazardous for the Italian admiral to get at the merchantmen. For soon a gray-black billowing barrier lay between the *Littorio* and the *Breconshire*, *Clan Campbell*, *Talabot, and Pampas* (whom Captain Hutchison again led away to the southwest); and to take heavy warships through a smoke screen with enemy destroyers waiting on the far side, is, to say the least, a hazardous maneuver. It proved too hazardous, at any rate, for the Italian admiral, who soon swung away to the west and proceeded to try and get at the convoy by rounding the extremity of the smoke screen.

There followed a series of sharp encounters, in which the Italians tried to turn the westerly end of the smoke. Three times they almost rounded the barrier—on one occasion actually having a brief glimpse of the convoy—but three times Admiral Vian's destroyers closed with them, laid more smoke, and drove them back with torpedoes. At one stage it looked as though they would break through. For half an hour a slender force of four destroyers (*Havock, Lively, Hero*, and *Sikh*) had kept the Italians at bay—"a remarkable feat," to use Admiral Vian's own words. But by six o'clock the *Littorio* and the two heavy cruisers, as if suddenly realizing how slender were the forces opposing them, stood boldly toward the tattered tip of the smoke screen. At this critical moment *Penelope* and *Euryalus* came steaming back from the east, where they had been searching for the Italians to windward— in the weather gauge where the smoke was ineffective. They were only just in time. With the range down to 13,000 yards and the Italians almost clear of the smoke, they opened fire; and at the same moment *Cleopatra* swung broadside on and discharged her three starboard torpedoes. The *Littorio* was hit by a 6-inch shell, which started a fire between her after turrets; and, more important, the *Cleopatra*'s torpedoes passed dangerously close to her. Discouraged, the Italians again turned away.

Half an hour later they made another and last attempt to break through. But once again a torpedo attack, delivered through the smoke from a range of only 6000 yards, forced them back. At seven o'clock the *Littorio* swung around to the north: away from the merchantmen: back toward Taranto. The Battle of Sirte was over. Contrary to all the canons of naval warfare, a force of light cruisers and destroyers had kept at bay a force consisting of a battleship and heavy cruisers; and the convoy, for the moment, had been saved.

Captain Hutchison, meanwhile, had been having a difficult time. The Italian fleet was forcing his convoy off its prear- ranged route, was driving it southward, *away* from Malta. This was serious. For the merchantmen were scheduled to reach Grand Harbour early next morning, before it was fully light. If they were driven too far south, they would be late arriving and would have to face another morning of German air attacks. And by then, as Captain Hutchison knew, they would have lost their escort—for Admiral Vian's warships would have been forced to return to Alexandria through shortage of ammunition and fuel.

Several times Captain Hutchison altered course to the west, but each time the threat of the Italian battle fleet drove him back to the south. And at five o'clock, to add to his difficulties, the convoy was heavily bombed.

Most of the bombers were Ju 88s. They pressed home their attacks with resolution and skill; but the weather, the ack-ack barrage, and the excellent maneuvering of the convoy thwarted each assault. The weather, by this time, had become extremely unpleasant, a near gale from the southeast having whipped up a heavy sea. Soon the vessels were butting awkwardly into steep twenty-foot waves; and their gun crews were being drenched, frozen, and near blinded by sheets of driven spray. But if conditions were bad for the merchantmen, they were equally bad for the German bombers: for the succession of Junkers 88s that now came in singly, downwind, from the port bow. Smoke, low cloud, and the churned-up sea distorted their targets; while the blustering thirty-knot gale made bomb aiming a nightmare. Five bombers were shot down, one by the *Breconshire*. The rest achieved only a succession of near misses.

By seven o'clock the sun was setting, and the last of the bombers had gone.

The Italian fleet had gone too, and at the first possible opportunity Captain Hutchison hauled around to the west and stood directly for Malta.

From the bridge of the *Breconshire* he looked at the darkening sky. The bombers, he knew, wouldn't be back: not until dawn. The Italian fleet, he rightly judged, wouldn't be back either—after the mauling of the afternoon they would have no stomach for a night action in a rising storm. He knew that the important thing was to reach Grand Harbour as early as possible next morning. If they waited for Admiral Vian, they would lose time. If they stayed in convoy, the slower ships (such as the *Clan Campbell*) would hold up the faster. Their best hope, it seemed to him, was to disperse the

convoy: for each merchantman, escorted by whatever warships were available, to make her own way to Malta at her
best speed.

This, broadly speaking, had been the plan outlined in
Admiral Vian's operational orders; and now, a few minutes
after seven o'clock, Captain Hutchison anticipated the admiral's
instructions. On his own initiative he dispersed the convoy.

Bells tinkled in engine rooms. Screws increased their
tempo. Through the darkening twilight the four merchantmen
went racing west for Malta. From now on they were on their
own.

The convoy had dispersed in position 17° 10′ E, 33° 30′ N;
that is, some 240 miles southeast of Malta. They could reckon
on thirteen hours of near darkness. They had, in other words,
to average a shade over nineteen knots to reach Grand
Harbour by sunrise next morning. This speed in a rising
storm was clearly out of the question. But it did seem as if
the four vessels ought to get reasonably close to Malta by
dawn: close enough for the island's fighters to be able to
provide them with air cover for the final ten or twenty miles.

All that night *Breconshire* pounded to the west-northwest.
After a while she was joined by two destroyers: *Southwold*
and *Beaufort*, who had also been ordered right through to
Malta; and a couple of hours before midnight another warship
closed up from astern: the AA cruiser *Carlisle*. The four ships
formed into a miniature convoy. *Breconshire* in the center;
Southwold on the port bow; *Beaufort* on the starboard bow;
and *Carlisle* five cables astern. Their course, 318 degrees;
their speed, 17 knots; with *Breconshire*'s stokers fainting in
the engine room as hour after hour the great ship pounded
into the rising sea at her maximum speed.

By 6:45 next morning they were within thirty-five miles of
Malta.

By 7:45 they were within twenty miles. But already the sky
in the east was lightening.

Captain Hutchison looked anxiously at the dove gray of the
horizon. There was no sign of the hoped-for fighter escort
from Malta. He looked again at the low belts of ragged cloud.
The ceiling was down to eight hundred feet; visibility was less
than a dozen miles; he realized that the fighters would be

hard put to it to find them, even if, in the appalling weather, they could get air-borne.

He sent a signal to Grand Harbour: "All ships of convoy are approaching southwest corner of mine field south of Malta, on course 318°. Request air help." Then, restlessly, he paced the bridge. Another couple of hours, he thought, and we'll be safe. But much was to happen in those couple of hours.

At 7:50 a Cant seaplane began to shadow the *Breconshire*, its unwieldy bulk dodging in and out of the folds of cloud and early-morning mist. And it homed the bombers onto their prey. At 7:55 a single Ju 88 dived steeply out of the cloud bank; its bombs landed in *Breconshire*'s wake, less than two dozen yards astern.

The German bombers had found the convoy.

They found the ships within sight of their destination. But they also found them in a peculiarly vulnerable state: divided, lacking in air cover, and about to enter a narrow channel between mine fields and shore. And conditions that morning, for individual bombing attacks, were near ideal.

Soon from every ship in the convoy came a spate of emergency signals—"Am being bombed"—and a chain of positions between fifteen and fifty miles from Grand Harbour. It was a case of so near and yet so far.

The *Breconshire*, her ship's company closed up at action stations, kept steadily on. The two destroyers and the cruiser edged close beside her. Their ack-ack guns, too, were fully manned. And so the single Junkers which at 8:17 came sweeping out of the cloud was given short shrift; was driven off, streaming a torrent of jetblack smoke.

Soon Malta came into sight; first the premontory of Delimara Point, then the sweep of the flat northern shore. Only another dozen miles to go.

Then came the fighter-bombers. Three Me 109s, which dived suddenly out of a low belt of cloud. The *Breconshire*'s guns had barely opened up before the bombs hit her.

She was hit three times; the bombs (250-pounders) falling close to her port deck rail; one aft, one level with No. 1 hold, one close to the bridge. Captain Hutchison waited for the shattering explosion which would blow his ship into a million splinters of wood and particles of dust. But no explosion came. He realized suddenly that the holds must be flooding:

that already sufficient water must have come pouring in to damp down the ammunition and the close-packed crates of bombs. By the grace of God they hadn't blown up.

Damage reports came flooding into the bridge. Electric power, it seemed, had failed throughout the ship; the steering had jammed; and the engine room was flooding fast.

Captain Hutchison was still taking stock of the damage when, nine minutes later, another bomber came screaming out of the cloud. This time it was a Junkers 88. It was hit repeatedly by *Southwold*'s pom-poms; but it kept on; straight at the *Breconshire*. It, too, dropped three bombs; three 500-pounders, which exploded parallel to the port beam, less than a dozen yards from the bridge. The *Breconshire* heeled over. Her engines shuddered to a stop. Yawing, listing, and out of control, she fell away. In the heavy swell she began to roll uneasily.

If we're hit again, Captain Hutchison thought, even if we don't blow up, we'll founder. In a sea like this we'll break our back.

Eleven minutes later a pair of Junkers came sweeping out of the north. They came in low, almost feathering the sea, half hidden by the drifting belts of mist. One was forced away; but the other mast-high, came on, weaving through the curtain of flak. She dropped two bombs. Falling close by *Breconshire*'s starboard beam, they burst directly under the ship. The great 10,000-ton merchantman was lifted half out of the water. With a sickening crash she bit deep into the crest of a wave; then she yawed broadside on and, turning slowly in circles, started to drift toward the shore: straight for the Zonkor Beacon mine field.

In the next half hour the *Breconshire* was attacked three more times. Twice she was smothered in near misses; twice she was machine-gunned. There was no sign of the fighters from Malta.

Aboard the merchantman Captain Hutchison fought desperately to bring his ship under control. There was no hope, he knew, of getting under way; for the engine room was twelve feet deep in water. But perhaps he could steer. With much improvisation, he managed to switch over to hand steering aft; and at last he had the satisfaction of controlling his heading, if not his course. He then turned to the pumps. Since all power had failed, the mechanical pumps were useless; but hand pumps were quickly rigged, and working in shifts, the crew managed to hold their own with the onrushing water. The next priority was the No. 2 diesel-oil tank. This had been badly holed; and soon the bilges were filling with oil, which clogged the pumps. It was dangerous work to shore up and batten down the leaks; but in half an hour it was done.

And all the while Captain Hutchison made every preparation he could for the *Breconshire* to be taken in tow.

He thought at first that the *Carlisle* would try to tow them. But a little after ten o'clock another warship appeared on the scene: H.M.S. *Penelope*. The *Penelope* (having been back to Grand Harbour) had plenty of fuel and plenty of ammunition, whereas the *Carlisle* was practically out of both. The latter was therefore ordered to proceed to harbor, while *Penelope* signaled Vice-Admiral, Malta, "Intend taking *Breconshire* in tow."

But it wasn't as easy as that.

At 10:25 the *Penelope*, maneuvering skillfully in the heavy swell, passed the *Breconshire* a cable: a 6½-inch tow wire. Then Captain Hutchison's difficulties began. He had no power with which to wind in the tow; no deck space for'ard on which to flake it down; and no winch or capstan to which he could secure it. For the *Breconshire*'s deck was a bomb-scarred shambles; and even the auxiliary dynamo, which Captain Hutchison had hoped to use, had just been flooded by a near miss. Those of the crew who weren't manning guns or pumps mustered on deck and tried to haul in and secure the tow by hand. But it was too heavy. It slipped back into the sea. Eventually it parted.

Slowly the *Breconshire* drifted away, riding uneasily among the great twenty-foot waves. There seemed now to be only one chance of saving her. Tugs. But a little before eleven o'clock there came a discouraging signal from Grand Harbour: "Weather not suitable for tugs."

Watched by the four circling warships, *Breconshire* continued to drift helplessly toward the shore. She was only nine miles from the entrance to Grand Harbour; but the nine miles, it seemed, might as well have been nine hundred.

By midday she was close inshore: in thirty fathoms of water: very near the edge of the mine field. Captain Hutchison did the only possible thing. By hand he knocked out the hawser pins; and first the starboard anchor, then the port, plummeted down to the sea bed. And the anchors held. By 12:30 the ship was brought head to wind in position: 076° Zonkor Beacon 1 mile.

All that afternoon a succession of warships—the cruisers *Penelope* and *Carlisle* and the destroyers *Beaufort, Southwold, Dulveston,* and *Hurworth*—took turns at staying with the damaged merchantman to afford her ack-ack protection. And their guns saved her from further damage. For, although between midday and sunset some ten to fifteen planes made individual attacks, the *Breconshire* wasn't hit; and two Junkers and one Messerschmitt were destroyed.

Captain Hutchison used the breathing space to provide his crew with a meal—and even this, with the galley wrecked, the fires out, and the ship in darkness, was no easy task. He then set about trying to recover the tow wire, which he eventually managed to haul back on board soon after four o'clock. The rest of the evening passed uneventfully, with all hands, to quote Captain Hutchison, "employed till dark in manning the guns, clearing up the ship, and preparing towing hawsers."

A little before sunset *Penelope* made another attempt to pull the *Breconshire* away from the shore; but this, too, was unsuccessful. She did, however, manage to pass the merchantman a 500-amp. electrical lead. This, it was hoped, would enable her, when the need arose, to use her capstan to weigh anchor—though in the event it turned out that the capstan was too badly damaged and they had to cut through the anchor chain with oxyacetylene. In the gathering darkness *Penelope* drew away to seaward. "Tomorrow," she signaled, "tugs will come at 6:00. Weather permitting."

A few minutes later, just as the sun was setting, a solitary Beaufighter flew out from the island and circled the *Breconshire* twice. That was the only friendly aircraft they saw all day.

All that night the swell remained unabated: east-southeasterly and "very heavy." In the smooth, steep-sided troughs the *Breconshire* moved uneasily. She was down by the head, riding heavily, and drawing forty feet. And her pumps were barely holding their own.

Few of her crew got any sleep that night; certainly not Captain Hutchison, who hour after hour was struggling to get things ready for the next day's tow. Working in darkness, and without electric power or any type of mechanical aid, cables were shackled, collision mats were heaved into position, and the emergency dynamo was painstakingly repaired—but when, after five hours' work, it was tested, it ran for less than half a minute and then cut dead: the armature was completely burned out. And all the while the water came flooding in, finding its way through the shored-up doors and bulkheads, seeping through the holds, damaging the cargo, making the ship still heavier, still more waterlogged, still more unpredictable.

Tuesday the twenty-fourth dawned gray and overcast, with a chill wind. And the swell was as heavy as ever. In the shallow waters off Zonkor Beacon the waves seemed especially vicious, heaving *Breconshire* through a bow arc of up to thirty feet and making her roll scuppers under. And that morning, very close to the merchantman's beam, the destroyer *Southwold* spotted two dark cylindrical objects, uncovered every now and then in the troughs of the swell. Mines. So the anchors had dragged in the night. *Breconshire* had drifted even closer inshore. She lay now on the very fringe of the mine field.

At 6:30 the trawler *Beryl* fought her way out from Grand Harbour. She looked pitiably small; sometimes she disappeared completely in the troughs of the swell. Twice she tried to come alongside the *Breconshire;* but twice the waves proved too much for her.

On board the *Breconshire* conditions were by now "very trying." Apart from her crew, she had on board some sixty to seventy passengers, and it was proving impossible to provide so many men with food and water. For the gravity tanks were empty and there was no possibility of pumping water out of the main tanks; the galley and storeroom were flooded—waist-high in water; and the only means of cooking was on the blacksmith's forge. Somehow, Captain Hutchison thought, we must get the passengers off, especially the gunners and special technicians, who are urgently needed in Malta.

The *Beryl* had failed to lay herself alongside; but now the destroyer *Southwold* decided to try. She would, she signaled the *Breconshire*, approach from the quarter, shoot a line over the merchantman's stern, and transfer the passengers by breeches buoy. Extracts from the report of the *Southwold's* captain (Commander Jellicoe) describe what happened next.

10:21. While manoeuvring 1½ cables astern of the *Breconshire*, *Southwold* struck a mine, which exploded under the engine room. Both anchors were let go. The engine room at once began to flood and fill with steam. As no one [in it] could have survived, hatches were closed. ... [While waiting for] H.M. Tug *Ancient* to arrive and take *Southwold* in tow, the split in the shaft tunnel and gearing room was plugged with cotton waste and margarine.

12:58. Tow secured in *Southwold*. The cable was just tightening when the ship broke her back, the two halves being held together only by the upper deck plating.

13:30. *Southwold* again under tow.

13:30—15:54. Three attacks on *Southwold* and *Breconshire* (Ju 88s and Me 109s). One heavy bomb fell only thirty feet to port of *Southwold*. More underwater damage. Ship steadily listed to starboard. Bow rose up. Ship yawed [into trough] and began to roll over.

15:55. *Southwold* sinks.

All this Captain Hutchison watched from the bridge of the *Breconshire*.

Throughout that afternoon and evening attempts were continued to take the *Breconshire* in tow. The German air attacks continued, too. Several times the merchantman was near-missed, but no bombs actually hit her. Once again there were no fighters from Malta.

At four o'clock the *Beryl* made another effort to come alongside. This time she got near: very near. But the danger of the two vessels being flung together was too great; and eventually Captain Hutchison had no option but to order her away.

There was nothing they could do then but wait. Wait for the swell to subside. Wait until the weather was fit for the tugs from Grand Harbour to put to sea. They waited all afternoon, all evening, and well into the night. Then, at midnight, *Ancient* and *Robust*, two small 700-ton salvage tugs, fought their way out to the *Breconshire*.

Captain Hutchison, by now, had had no sleep for three days. He and his crew were wet, cold, hungry, thirsty, and close to complete physical exhaustion. But they realized that here was their last chance of saving the *Breconshire*. They set to, to try and secure the tow.

And at last they succeeded. At two o'clock they slipped both anchor cables and the two got under way.

Mr. Bromley, skipper of the *Ancient*, knew they would never get the *Breconshire* in to Grand Harbour in the prevailing east-southeasterly swell. He therefore decided to take her south to Marsaxlokk, where the harbor entrance was wider and less exposed.

Their first job was to get the merchantman well clear of the mine field. This proved unexpectedly easy, for the *Breconshire*, when heading into wind, was docile and easily led. The tugs ran at "full ahead both," one towing from either bow, and slowly but surely the great ship was drawn away from the shore at a steady knot and a half. So far, so good. After a couple of hours' towing straight out to sea the tugs started to swing her around to the south. And then their troubles began. For, heaving across wind, the merchantman took on a vicious malevolence, an almost human perversity. She started to yaw and dip and plunge, striving continually to swing her head into wind. The tugs tried to fight her, but she was too strong for them; they tried to nudge her gently, but she refused to be led. Like a wild creature caught in a trap, she flung around and about, sheering to 60 degrees on either side of her tow. At last she slammed right about: full into wind. Two of the towlines parted; and *Robust*'s engines, never too reliable, broke under the strain. Yet Mr. Bromley still hung on to her. For a long time the *Ancient* had to run at half speed, on one engine, and with her helm hard over; for a long time, too, the *Breconshire*'s progress wasn't so much a tow as a half-controlled drift. But the *Ancient* never gave up. Down in her engine room, Stoker Parsloe fed the boilers for seven hours without relief. Up on her bridge, Mr. Bromley and Captain Nicholls (of the *Penelope*) watched the tow unceasingly, hour after hour; noting every tension and drag; calculating the strength of wind and sea; checking the strain, direction, and angle of every wire. A single miscalculation, a single error of judgment, and the *Breconshire* would have broken loose. But Mr. Bromley and Captain Nicholls made no mistake; and their skill and seamanship, allied to Captain Hutchison's, kept the ships together.

Dawn found them close to Delimara Point, heading straight for the wicked hundred-yard shoal that forms the underwater tip of the island. It looked inevitable, at one stage, that the

Breconshire would run aground; but at the crucial moment the tug *Robust*, her engines repaired, came panting up from astern. She secured to *Breconshire*'s port quarter and helped to break the force of her more vicious sheers; while a few minutes later the destroyer *Eridge*, by a fine piece of seamanship, secured to her starboard bow and turned her nose those vital few degrees that took her—with less than twenty feet to spare—past the end of the shoal.

West of Delimara Point the sea was calmer, the wind less strong; and soon the *Breconshire* became easier to manage. Towed by the tugs and screened by an escort of three destroyers, she approached the entrance to Marsaxlokk at ten o'clock. By midday she was inside the small semicircular harbor and secured to No. 1 buoy. Her troubles, for the moment, seemed to be over.

Captain Hutchison knew that Marsaxlokk could afford them only a temporary refuge—for there were, in the small open harbor, no facilities for unloading. But for the moment his thoughts were only for his crew.

> By this time [he wrote] my officers and men were so tired that they could do no more. Because of flooding, mess decks were uninhabitable. There was no means of pumping. No means of cooking. No light. Very little drinking water. I landed, and proceeded to Valletta to report to Vice-Admiral, Malta. He approved my proposal to evacuate ship and give the men a rest. This was done at 15:00 hours; the ship lying comfortably to No. 1 buoy.

It was decided that evening that the *Plumleaf*, a Reserve Fleet oiler, should secure to *Breconshire* during the night and take off as much of her oil as possible; while the following night *Breconshire* would be towed around to Grand Harbour to discharge the rest of her cargo.

It was a reasonable enough plan; but it reckoned without the Luftwaffe. For during the next few days Malta was subjected to an air assault unequaled for sustained ferocity in the annals of war.

The Germans' immediate aim was to obliterate the remains of Admiral Vian's convoy. While at sea, all four merchantmen had been hit and damaged in their final dash to the island.

But only the *Clan Campbell* had been sunk. The *Pampas*, *Talabot*, and *Breconshire*, battered but still afloat, had managed to struggle into harbor.

Before they had had a chance to unload, the Luftwaffe struck.

That evening, within two hours of her securing to No. 1 buoy, the *Breconshire* was spotted at Marsaxlokk and heavily dive-bombed; while early next morning there began a series of air attacks on Grand Harbour that were to continue with unabated fury for over three weeks. The Germans' first success was to hit the *Talabot* and *Pampas*. By the evening of March 25 the *Talabot* was submerged for'ard, and her after superstructure pad been set ablaze; and the *Pampas*, repeatedly hit, had been driven aground. Of the two vessels' 15,000 tons of vitally needed supplies, it was possible to salvage only a couple of hundred tons.

The *Breconshire*, meanwhile, had survived the bombing attacks of the evening of March 25, and as soon as it was dark the *Plumleaf* soon ran into difficulties; for the merchantman proved to be so badly flooded and so extensively damaged that it was impossible to open up her tanks. A working party under Lieutenant Kennedy, the *Breconshire*'s senior engineer, came aboard at midnight; but they, too, were unsuccessful. Dawn found the *Breconshire* with her cargo still unloaded.

Soon after sunrise Captain Hutchison and the remainder of his crew, plus a special working party of fifty volunteers, returned on board and started to clean up the ship and prepare for the evening tow to Grand Harbour. There was a lot to do. The 6½ inch cable, slipped by *Ancient*, was hauled in, shackled, and flaked down, the debris on deck was cleared away with the help of oxyacetylene burners; a system of emergency lighting was rigged up; the pumps were repaired and set to work; and the guns were manned. And very necessary the guns were to prove; for soon came the bombers, wave after wave of Ju 87s and Ju 88s. Most of them peeled off over Grand Harbour; but a few came through to Marsaxlokk.

All that afternoon the *Breconshire* fought them off; and up to five o'clock they achieved nothing more than a series of near misses.

At 5:15 Captain Hutchison went ashore. He was anxious to know what damage the bombing had done in Grand Harbour.

In particular, he was anxious about the tugs due that evening to arrive for towing the *Breconshire*. He got through on the telephone to Vice-Admiral, Malta.

The news from Grand Harbour could hardly have been worse. Around the dockyard the damage had been "quite devastating." The *Plumleaf* had been driven aground; several warships had been badly damaged; and, greatest disaster of all, the tug *Ancient* had suffered two direct hits and had had to be beached. In the whole of Grand Harbour there wasn't a single serviceable, seaworthy tug. The *Breconshire*, in other words, was stranded at Marsaxlokk.

Tired and dispirited, Captain Hutchison walked back along the quay. There was, inevitably, an air raid in progress; and he could see the *Breconshire*'s guns flickering red and gold in the pale evening sunlight. Suddenly a lone Ju 88 came sweeping out of the sun haze. She was hit repeatedly; one of her engines streamed blood-red banners of flame; but somehow she kept on course; straight for the *Breconshire*. She dropped four bombs. And they were all direct hits.

The first bomb fell flush down the center of No. 4 hatch. It exploded deep in the hold, deep down in the *Breconshire*'s 690 tons of coal. It set the coal on fire. The fire spread. Soon the heart of the *Breconshire* became a red-hot inferno.

The second and third bombs fell beside the port deck rail, abreast of the bridge. For the second time, the No. 2 oil tank was badly holed. The cofferdams were opened up, and the oil fuel came flooding out; in a widening viscous pool it spread around the stricken ship.

The last bomb fell aft: again close to the port deck rail. It opened up No. 5 hold. The sea came flooding in.

Once again Captain Hutchison waited for the *Breconshire* to explode. Once again no explosion came. He got hold of an R.A.F. motor launch and rushed back to his ship. He found his crew hand-tipping buckets of water onto the blazing coal: with their pumps again out of action and their foamite long ago used up, it was all they could do. It was rather like emptying tooth mugs onto the heart of a blast furnace; but eventually two other ships—the *Robust* and *Swona*—came to the *Breconshire*'s aid. Although they knew that the merchant-man might explode at any moment, they came alongside, rigged up their fire hoses, and started to pump water into the blazing hold. Soon they were joined by another ship, the *Beryl*; and hour after hour the three vessels cascaded water into the smoldering *Breconshire*.

By sunset the fire in No. 4 hold had been brought under control, and the crew, scrambling down through the hatchway, were able to haul out the still smoldering sacks of coal. But now a new danger, less spectacular but more insidious than the fire, made itself felt. Very slowly the *Breconshire* started to settle by the stern. Soon her after-well deck was three feet under water.

In an effort to counteract this, Captain Hutchison ordered the fire hoses to play into the for'ard holds. But this he soon discontinued. For the great weight of water pumped into the ship, added to the influx through No. 5 hold, started to list her to port. She listed slowly at first, then with gathering momentum. By sunset her port deck rail was awash.

In the half light of evening Captain Hutchison went below. Down in the bowels of the ship everything was very quiet. The bulkheads were cold; but water was everywhere—knee-deep in passageways, cascading down through shattered deckheads; and the ship smelled stale and dank and lifeless. Captain Hutchison felt her moving beneath him: heavily: without resilience. He realized then that he was going to lose her: realized that soon, perhaps very soon, she was going to founder. His crew were wet, tired, and utterly exhausted. There was nothing to be gained and a lot to be lost by staying on board. At eight o'clock he gave orders to clear the ship. He was, of course, the last to leave her.

He had half expected the *Breconshire* to turn turtle during the night; but when at dawn he came down to the quay, she was still there. But the fires had restarted; great tongues of flame were again leaping out of No. 4 hold.

Captain Hutchison collected a small working party—Lieutenant Kennedy, Wireless Officer Lancaster-Smith, and some dozen ratings—and together they went out to the *Breconshire* in a borrowed launch. As they neared her Captain Hutchison could see that there wasn't a chance of saving the ship herself; the best they could hope for was to save a part of her cargo. After a good deal of difficulty they managed to clamber aboard. The *Breconshire* was listing dangerously to port. Flames were belching out of her for'ard hatchways; and ammunition was starting to explode: ammunition which had been stored next to the 500-pound bombs.

They decided their best plan was to try to get the ship to settle in such a way that at least part of her oil fuel might be recovered. This entailed flooding the boiler room beside No. 1 hold. Lieutenant Kennedy and four ratings went below to open the watertight compartments; while Captain Hutchison, the wireless officer, and the rest of the party salvaged the most valuable of the ship's stores. The *Breconshire*, by this time, was listing to over 20 degrees. The exploding ammunition had opened up her deck; and through the length of her superstructure fires were raging unchecked. Captain Hutchison ordered his crew to leave. For a few minutes longer he stayed behind, checking the flooding, gauging the way the *Breconshire* was beginning to settle. Then he, too, left his ship.

A few minutes later she heeled completely over. For a moment she lay on her beam, her funnel parallel to the water. Then, very slowly, she turned turtle.

Captain Hutchison looked at all that was left of his ship: a few feet of rusted keel, lapped by the gray uncaring waves. He wasn't a sentimental man; but he and the *Breconshire* had been through a fair amount together in the last eighteen months. He walked slowly along the quay, forcing his mind to look not behind but ahead. After a few minutes he started to work out the details of how the *Breconshire*'s oil fuel could best be salvaged.

In the fortnight after the sinking of the *Breconshire*, the Luftwaffe's air assault on Malta reached its acme of violence. In those fourteen days the island spent 168 hours under attack from the air; she endured 2159 individual raids; and in Grand Harbour 18 ships were sunk and 27 damaged. In the words of Vice-Admiral, Malta, "In spite of all that was done, nearly all the stores so successfully fought through were lost. We were just not strong enough."

But there was rather more to it than that.

The fate of the *Breconshire, Talabot,* and *Pampas* was something worse than a tragedy; it was a needless tragedy. All three vessels had survived a thousand-mile voyage—a voyage in which they had been attacked by the Italian fleet and by several hundred German and Italian bombers. They had

Spitfire

reached harbor with their cargoes practically intact. Then they had been sunk, under the very noses of the islanders who needed so desperately the supplies in their holds. Something, the powers that be decided, was wrong.

In the official inquiries that followed, two facts came to light. Malta's fighter aircraft had been proved inadequate—they hadn't control of the air even over the island itself. And the arrangements for discharging cargoes in Grand Harbour had been "inefficient"—the *Talabot* and *Pampas*, for example, had lain at anchor for the best part of twelve hours without any unloading taking place.

Two things, it was decided, were needed. A change in aircraft and a change in high places. Neither decision was easy to make, or to implement. But in the end it was decided that the Hurricanes, which had in the past performed such sterling service, should be replaced by Spitfires; and that General Dobbie, Malta's Commander in Chief, should be superseded by Viscount Gort.

No man ever did more for Malta than General Dobbie, and his departure from the island at this critical moment in its history was a personal tragedy. But such changes are sometimes inevitable.

Indeed, a thousand miles to the east, in Alexandria, another such change—though for very different reasons—was simultaneously taking place. After close to three years Admiral Cunningham was leaving the Mediterranean Fleet. He left it at a time when its fortunes were at their nadir—with 50 per cent of its warships put out of the action in the evacuation from Crete, and Malta about to enter its darkest hour. He left it with the deepest personal regret and with the affection and admiration of all who had served under him. In the months to come he was badly missed.

12

*Qalb ta' Gesu ta' Marija, itfghu il-bombi-fil-bahar
        jew fil-hamrija.*
[*Sacred heart of Jesus and of Mary, make the bombs
        go into the sea or into the soil.*]

Kesselring's orders had been to prepare Malta for capture by
airborne invasion. He made his plans carefully. His first step,
he reckoned, must be to attain complete air supremacy over
the island: to knock Malta's eighty-odd Hurricanes out of the
sky and to render her three airfields totally inoperative. His
second step would be systematically to pulverize the island's
defenses: to flatten gun emplacements and defense posts by
low-land bombing and strafing. And, his third and final step
would be to amass a fleet of gliders and paratroops on the
airstrips of Comiso and Gerbini and to escort them across to
the island. Bearing in mind that he had over eight hundred
aircraft at his disposal, he was optimistic of early success. "Six
to eight weeks," he told the German General Stag, "should
be enough."

After the reconnaissance and probing sorties of December,
Kesselring showed his hand. On January 3 the blitz on the
island began in earnest.

In the next four weeks Malta suffered as many as 107
large-scale air raids, several of them lasting well over eight
hours. These raids were carried out by a total of some 1500
bombers, which dropped, among them, over 1800 tons of
bombs. But the important point was not *how many* bombs
were dropped, but *where* they were dropped. For that
January the Luftwaffe and the Regia Aeronautica achieved
between them no fewer than 800 direct hits on Malta's three
small airdromes.. By the end of the month Takali, Hal Far,
and Luqa were as pitted with craters as the face of the moon;

over fifty British aircraft had been destroyed on the ground; and barracks, hangars, and repair yards had been reduced to so many heaps of rubble. By February 1 only twenty-eight Hurricanes out of the original eighty were left and of these half were unserviceable. It looked as if Kesselring's assault were keeping to schedule.

The attackers' methods were simple. The bombers, usually Ju 88s, came in high in waves of twenty to thirty. They had a close cover of roughly three dozen fighters, with a further three dozen as high cover stepped up in tiers in the sun. They approached their target fast, in a series of shallow dives from 20,000 to 6000 feet; the idea being to give the defending fighters as little time as possible to intercept. Having dropped their bombs, they would then turn out to sea at high speed, with their close escort forming a protective circle around them. These tactics were difficult to cope with. For the Hurricanes' top speed was not much faster than the Junkers': they couldn't interrupt them from above because of the high cover, and when they tried to intercept on the same level they had first to break through the close cover, and then, if they did get within shooting range, the pilots found that, as soon as they opened up, the recoil of their guns pushed them back out of range again. Moreover, the Junkers were heavily armored; the Hurricanes had machine guns, not cannons, and their .303 bullets skidded off the Germans' armor plating like peas off a drum. Out of the fifteen hundred planes attacking Malta in January, only twenty-three were shot down.

By the end of the month Malta was in bad shape. The heavy, bludgeoning attacks, day after day, were doing just what Kesselring had hoped: they were grinding the island's air defenses to pulp. Then came a heaven-sent respite. From February 1 to February 14 Malta enjoyed a fortnight of low cloud and near-continuous rain. The bad weather didn't, of course, stop the air offensive; but it did cause the attacks to slacken off. And in the comparative lull the garrison worked desperately to patch up their defenses.

The chief problem was the airfields. They were vulnerable targets: hangars, barracks, planes, and petrol bowsers being crammed tightly together in the only available patch of level ground. In the crowded parking areas, aircraft, throughout the whole of January, had been destroyed on the ground at an

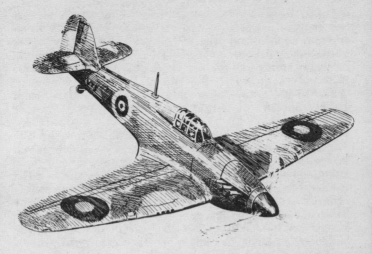

Hurricane

average rate of two a day. If this went on, Malta, it was clear, would soon be defenseless.

The answer, as everyone realized, lay in bombproof dispersal pens built outside the airdromes' perimeter. But to build such pens was easier said than done. There were two difficulties: space and labor. And neither was easy to surmount. For the airdromes were hemmed in either by solid rock—to cut through which would have been a veritable labor of Hercules; or else by arable small holdings—to appropriate which would have reduced Malta's already too small quota of home-grown food. And even if space had been available, few airmen could have been spared for work on the pens. For servicing the planes and repairing the landing strips were jobs which were now keeping Malta's four thousand airmen working day and night, in shifts of fourteen to sixteen hours. Yet something had to be done. And at the end of January the Air Officer Commanding did the only possible thing; he appealed to the Army for help.

There were, on February 1, less than three dozen dispersal pens in Malta; and there were four haphazard things, built out of sandbags in odd corners of the airfields. But in the next two months an amazing transformation took place. For soon everyone on the island—Army, Navy, Air Force, and civilians— were working flat out on the vital job of constructing properly dispersed bombproof shelters for Malta's remaining aircraft. It was work on which the fate of the island depended. Without pens, the aircraft would be destroyed on the ground; without aircraft, the island would be laid wide open to air-borne invasion.

Now, building a dispersal pen sounds easy. But it wasn't. The first difficulty was to find a site. This was eventually solved by creating a special dispersal area: a strip of ground three miles long and three quarters of a mile wide connecting Hal Far and Luqa. This area, known as the Safi Strip, consisted of ravines, nullahs, rocky plateaus, and a patchwork of tiny fields surrounded by high stone walls. The whole had to be leveled; and leveled by manual labor—for there wasn't a single bulldozer or pneumatic drill on the island. Once the site had been cleared, work could begin on the pens. The earlier pens had been built of sandbags; but these had not proved sufficiently blastproof; and by experiment it was found that the strongest pens were those built of used five-gallon petrol tins filled with sand and earth and lashed one to another by wire. Just think what building such a shelter involved. The pen for a Wellington, to give a concrete example, comprised three walls, each ninety feet long, fourteen feet high, and consisting of twelve tins at the base and tapering to two at the top. Such walls involved the use of 60,000 petrol tins, filled with 3500 tons of earth and stone and linked together by 2½ miles of wire. And every stage of construction—filling the tins, heaving them into position, wiring them together—had to be done by hand. The construction of each pen required 39,600 man-hours (200 men working 18 hours a day for 11 days). One would have thought that half a dozen such pens a week would have been good going. But, in fact, throughout February and March, they were constructed at an average rate of over 40 a week; until, by early April, Malta could boast some 350 large, strongly built, linked, dispersed, and camouflaged pens—one for every aircraft, petrol bowser, control van, and steam roller on the island.

It was a herculean labor, of which the Air Officer Commanding (Air Marshal Sir Hugh Lloyd) has painted a vivid picture.

The soldiers [he wrote] built most of the pens. . . . There were always 1500 of them working on the aerodromes and sometimes as many as 3000. Civilians helped, too. In fact, everyone helped: and every contribution—even for an hour a day—was very welcome. Officers, clerks, photographers, storemen, wireless operators, aircrew, in fact, anyone with a few hours to spare would arrive with their sandwiches and work for an hour or so, regardless of the weather or the enemy. It was a magnificent effort.

And it saved Malta. In January over fifty aircraft had been destroyed on the ground. But in February losses dropped to eleven; and in March—although the raids that month were heavier than ever—to nine. For on the ground the planes were safe now from everything except a direct hit. They could be serviced, repaired, and refueled in comparative safety. And they were ready, day after day, to join battle with Kesselring's raiders.

Kesselring, of course, soon spotted the new dispersal area and bombed it heavily. But the pens were well scattered and extremely durable. They made unpromising targets. And so, early in March, the Luftwaffe switched their attention to the landing strips. If they couldn't destroy the aircraft on the ground, they would do the next-best thing: make it impossible for them to take to the air.

Day and night, week after week, the bombs rained down on Luqa, Takali, and Hal Far. Five-hundred-pound bombs, thousand-pound bombs, incendiary bombs, delayed-action bombs, and bombs linked together by heavy chains so that as they fell they tumbled over each other like kittens at play. Each day craters, hummocks of flung-up earth, and shattered debris pockmarked the landing strips. But no matter how great the devastation, somehow, after every raid, the damage was made good. For once again the Army came to the rescue. To each airfield a pair of regiments was allocated (West Kents and the Royal Artillery to Luqa, Inniskillings and Manchesters to Takali, and Dorsets and Buffs to Hal Far), and for these regiments the defense and repair of the airstrip became a full-time job. As soon as each raid was over, some five hundred to a thousand men would come swarming onto the airdromes armed with buckets and spades and pounders and rollers. The debris would be carted away, the craters filled in, the rocks pounded to dust, and the landing strips again rolled level and firm.

Sir Hugh Lloyd gives a vivid account of the sort of thing that went on, day after day.

> Seventy-five to eighty Junkers over this evening [he writes]. A big attack on Takali, and soon I could see immense clouds of dust and smoke rising over the aerodrome. . . . I went out with Satchell and Woodhall to review the damage. . . . Walking over the aerodrome in the dark was an eerie experience. Everywhere there were huge mounds of earth with great holes in the middle of them, and big blocks of rock. Other parties were also out, looking for wounded and assessing the damage; and, in avoiding the mounds, we became mixed up and lost. We shouted; they shouted back; and each thought the other needed help. It was as if we had been stranded on the moon, separated one from another by deep craters and crumbling ridges. Even the most optimistic person would have reckoned the aerodrome must have been unserviceable for at least a week; but as a result of an all-night onslaught by the Inniskillings and Manchesters, it was in use the following afternoon. It was a near miracle; and when the German photographic planes came over next day I'm sure they couldn't believe their eyes. For from the air Takali looked just like the cratered battleground of the Somme.

For a fortnight Kesselring pounded the airdromes, losing in the process thirty planes destroyed and a further thirty damaged. He came perilously close to success. Fuel, water, and power were cut off; literally every building on or around the airfields was destroyed or damaged; while the unremitting bombing, day and night, week after week, made maintenance work a nightmare. Then, once again at the crucial moment, Kesselring changed his tactics. Unable to destroy the defending Hurricanes on the ground, unable to prevent their taking off, he now embarked on a scheme of destroying them in the air—not by the usual tricks of inveigling them into impossible dogfights or sending over decoy bombers with a posse of shadowing fighters up in the sun, but by an elaborate, exactly timed assault on the fighters as they landed back on the airstrips.

What happened was this. Early in March, Kesselring began to send over some two or three dozen Messerschmitts and Macchis about half an hour before the main raid was due to start. These would get the Hurricanes into the air and attempt to make them use up ammunition and fuel. Then came the . main raid, resulting in confused air fighting for anything up to an hour, at the end of which time the bombers would be departing for Sicily and the Hurricanes, short of petrol and ammunition, would be waiting to land. But just as the fighters were about to return to Luqa, Hal Far, or Takali, Kesselring would send over a fresh influx of Messerschmitts and Macchis, which would circle the airfields ready to pick off the Hurricanes the moment they went into the landing circuit. It was a horrifying sight to see a Hurricane, approaching the landing strip with its flaps and undercarriage down, being machine-gunned by a pack of Messerschmitts. Time and again the pilots would pull up their wheels at the last moment and turn away. But there was a limit to that. Their fuel wouldn't last forever. And eventually they'd be forced to run the gantlet: to make the slow, straight landing run which kept them—for sixty to ninety seconds—at the mercy of the German fighters. In a week eight Hurricanes were destroyed in the act of touching down, three were damaged, and three more ran out of fuel and crash-landed in clouds of dust on the airfields with the Messerschmitts' cannon shell rocking their already splintered fuselage.

By March 23 only eleven Hurricanes were left.

The answer to all this, of course, ought to have been staggered take-off and special airdrome patrols to protect the returning fighters. But there weren't enough Hurricanes for that. Outnumbered by anything up to twenty to one, the few British fighters that were left had to concentrate on the most vital of their jobs: intercepting the bombers. Everything else —including airfield defense—had to go by the board. It was small wonder that losses were heavy. But at least Kesselring wasn't having things all his own way; he was falling behind schedule; and the end of the month saw Malta's air defenses battered thin and stretched to breaking point but still holding out.

How long they would have held out if Kesselring had continued his assault on the airdromes is problematical. Maybe a week; maybe a fortnight; not, almost certainly, more. But the assault on the airdromes didn't continue. At the critical moment Kesselring made the mistake which cost him the Battle of Malta. On March 23 he switched his attacks to the dockyard.

It was the same mistake that the Germans had made in the Battle of Britain. At the end of September 1940 another fortnight of pounding the Kent and Sussex airdromes and the Luftwaffe would have won control of the skies over southern England; but at the critical moment they shifted their attacks to the London docks—a couple of weeks too soon. Now in Malta, at the end of March 1942, the Luftwaffe had the island's air defenses reeling: a few more hammer blows would have seen them completely knocked out. But the hammer blows were never given. At the critical moment the Luftwaffe shifted their attacks to the dockyard—once again a couple of weeks too soon.

There was, on the face of it, a very good reason for Kesselring's change of plan. For on March 23 the merchantmen of Admiral Vian's convoy were approaching the entrance to Grand Harbour. Kesselring knew how urgently Malta needed the 50,000 tons of supplies in their holds. He reckoned it more important to sink the merchantmen than give the airdromes their *coup de grâce*. He transferred his attack to Grand Harbour.

In the week March 23–29 over 2000 Axis planes rained death on the area of the dockyard. It was the heaviest piece of sustained bombing in the history of war: 2600 tons dropped into a couple of square miles; 2600 tons of bombs which pulverized ships, wharves, docks, warehouses, and harbor installations into a holocaust of laminated scrap. And as, under this vicious assault, the dockyard suffered, so the surrounding Three Cities suffered with it. It was like the attacks on the *Illustrious* all over again, only magnified ten times.

Now, Malta is very small; its area is less than that of Greater London; and only one place in the world—Macao—is more densely populated. Inevitably the bombs that didn't hit military targets hit civilian ones; and soon in the area surrounding the dockyard not a single building remained standing.

Everything—churches, hospitals, schools, public buildings, shops, and homes—was razed to the ground.

The rock shelters were crowded that March as never before. With the raids on the dockyard lasting twenty hours out of twenty-four, the Maltese buried themselves in their catacombs, emerging only in the brief intervals between raids to bring down fresh supplies of water and food. Each of their shelters, no matter how small, had its own shrine, with candles burning day and night. And beside these the Maltese women murmured their prayers, hour after hour, while above them their homes were pulverized to rubble. *"Qalb ta' Gesu ta' Marija, itfghu il-bombi-fil-bahar jew fil-hamrija* [Sacred heart of Jesus and of Mary, make the bombs go into the sea or into the soil]," they prayed. Or, more prosaically, "Oh Lord, send over the Italians."

In March over nine thousand Maltese homes were destroyed. And by the end of the month only five serviceable Hurricanes were left. Out of the eighty-one planes which had lain at Luqa, Hal Far, and Takali at the start of the year, seventy-six had been destroyed.

But German and Italian losses were even heavier, and in the assault on the dockyard they rose to a level that not even Kesselring could afford. The official figures speak for themselves.

German and Italian aircraft:

shot down over Malta in January	23
damaged " " " "	21
shot down over Malta in February	22
damaged " " " "	37
shot down over Malta in March	87
damaged " " " "	109

At the very end of the month Kesselring's attacks eased off: just for a couple of days: and in those couple of days a small reinforcement of twelve Hurricanes got through to the hard-pressed defenders. It wasn't the sort of relieving force that could save Malta; but it was enough to keep the struggle alive.

Glad as the islanders were to see the reinforcements, it was clear that small driblets of Hurricanes were an alleviation, not a cure. Only one thing could put an effective stop to Kesselring's assault. Spitfires. Fast, maneuverable planes, possessing a far greater range and firepower than the semiobsolete Hurricanes. "Malta's need," wrote the Air Officer Commanding, "is for Spitfires, Spitfires, and still more Spitfires. And they must come in bulk, and not in dribs and drabs." This need was generally recognized; but the difficulties in getting Spitfires to the island were apparently insuperable. For Spitfires needed a much longer takeoff run than Hurricanes: there was no possibility of their getting off the deck of a small carrier like the *Argus;* and of the larger carriers which might have been available, the *Eagle* was laid up for repairs and the *Victorious* had such small lifts that she couldn't get a Spitfire into her hangar. Sir Hugh Lloyd, however, was a determined man. He knew that Spitfires alone could save Malta, and he was determined to have them. At the end of March he sent an unofficial "ambassador" to London: Squadron Leader Gracie. Gracie's orders were to bring back Spitfires—"and plenty of them." No matter how many difficulties were put in his way, no matter how many official toes he had to tread on, he had somehow to get the planes.

Gracie left for London on March 31, and next day the assault on Malta was renewed.

The island had suffered heavy enough punishment before. But now, with its defenses crumbling under a pounding which had already lasted three months, the devastation increased to the point where it seemed more than flesh and blood could stand. For all through the first three weeks of April the Luftwaffe pounded the near-defenseless island more or less at will. In those few weeks 5715 bombers dropped 6750 tons of bombs—the equivalent of the blitz on Coventry repeated every eighteen hours for thirty days. Another 10,000 homes were razed to the ground; AA and defense posts were flattened; the airdomes became more and more pock-marked and cratered; all the island's reservoirs but one were destroyed; water couldn't be pumped out of the wells because there was no oil for the pumps; stores were set on fire and food became desperately short; by the middle of the month everyone on the island was suffering from chronic strain and lack of sleep. It was Malta's darkest hour. It seemed impossible for the island to survive.

Then, in mid-April, two things happened which marked the turning of the tide.

For months the attention of the free world had been pinned on Malta. There was something about the island's heroic stand that caught at the imagination: the tiny pin point of rock bludgeoned to bloodiness by the air forces of two great empires, but still unbowed. "Malta, the Unconquered Isle" was a typical press heading; and the island's praises were sung in towns as far apart as Helsinki and Chungking, Kiev and Kansas City, Capetown and Santiago. Now, quite suddenly, the admiration and sympathy of the free world found expression in one inspired gesture.

On April 15, His Majesty King George VI made the following announcement: "To honor her brave people I award the George Cross* to the island fortress of Malta, to bear witness to a heroism and devotion that will long be famous in history."

Never before had such an award, for collective heroism, been made. There was a very good reason for this. Never before had it been so deserved.

The cross itself was handed to the islanders by their new governor, Viscount Gort. At a great public ceremony in the bomb-blasted Palace Square he told them: "How you have stood up to the most concentrated bombing in the history of the world is the admiration of all civilized people. The Axis powers have tried again and again to break your spirit, but your confidence in the final triumph of the United Nations remains undiminished. Battle-scarred George Cross Malta stands firm, undaunted, and undismayed, waiting for the day when she can call: 'Pass, friend; all is well in the Island Fortress!'"

Such a day, in April 1942, must have seemed very far away: a paradise too remote to have much substance. But at heart it was a vision: something to hang on and hope for.

So the Maltese hung on and hoped.

And exactly a week after the ceremony in the Palace Square, they were given a sign: an omen that the long night of devastation—though by no means over—had passed its darkest hour.

Early on the morning of April 22 the air was filled with a

---

*The civilian equivalent of the Victoria Cross.

great roaring. Yet the sirens were silent. Uncertainly, the Maltese looked up. They saw that overhead the sky was filled with unfamiliar planes; planes with strange elliptical wings. The Spitfires had come at last.

13

Who said a wasp couldn't sting twice?
                                    —SIR WINSTON CHURCHILL

When Squadron Leader Gracie arrived in London he found that the urgency of Malta's needs was by no means fully appreciated by people outside the island. It is true that those in authority in Whitehall knew that Malta wanted Spitfires; but it was generally hoped that somehow the island would be able to muddle through without them, and the official attitude was summed up by the Wing Commander who said apologetically to Gracie, "In any case, old chap, there just isn't a way of flying the Spitfires in. So I'm afraid that's that." The Air Ministry was quick to point out, too, that simply to get the planes to Malta would not be enough; ground crew and spare parts would be needed as well, but since no convoy was being planned for several months there didn't seem any possible way of getting them through.

A lesser man would have given up. But Gracie had been told to get Spitfires, and Spitfires he intended to get. After a series of rebuffs and frustrations he took his plea for reinforcements to the very highest authority; and it was largely because of his persistence that early in April a personal telegram was sent across the Atlantic.

Former Naval Person to *President Roosevelt*.
     Air attack on Malta is very heavy. There are now in Sicily about 400 German and 200 Italian fighters and bombers. It seems likely from [these] extraordinary enemy concentrations that they hope to exterminate our air defences. . . . Would you be willing to allow your carrier *Wasp* to do one of these [air ferry] trips, provided details are satisfactorily agreed between the Naval Staffs? With her broad lifts,

U.S.S. Wasp

capacity, and length we estimate that *Wasp* could take fifty or more Spitfires.... Thus a powerful force could be flown into Malta at a stroke, giving us a chance to inflict a very severe and possibly decisive check on the enemy.

The response was immediate and generous.

President to *Prime Minister.*
   Admiral King will advise Admiral Pound that *Wasp* is at your disposal as you request.

The Admiralty wasted no time, and next day the following signal reached the C. in C., Home Fleet.

   It is of utmost importance to reinforce Malta with as many Spitfires as possible in the immediate future. No British aircraft carrier capable of operating Spitfires is available.

It is therefore requested you will arrange for U.S.S.
Wasp to embark as many Spitfires as possible. It will
probably be considered necessary for *Wasp* to carry a
certain number of fighters for her own protection, and this
must be accepted in spite of the loss in carrying capacity for
Spitfires. Request early report as to the number of Spitfires
Wasp will be able to transport.

The wheels had been set in motion. So much, Gracie
thought, for the planes. Now for the ground crew and spares.
He took his problem to the Admiralty, where he found My
Lords Commissioners none too sanguine about being able to
meet his requirements. For warships were desperately short,
and with the Luftwaffe in firm control of the Central Mediterranean a convoy was considered impractical. However, after a
deal of discussion it was agreed that plans should be drawn
up for shipping men and stores to the island by submarine. It
was realized that this would prove a slow and arduous job,

and that it would have the disadvantage of reinforcing Malta in dribs and drabs; but it seemed all that was possible under the circumstances. The Admiralty did promise to keep an eye open for alternative methods of transport; but Gracie—as it turned out, wrongly—thought this promise was no more than routine politeness. In the second week in April, having done all he could to insure that the necessary ground crew and spares would be forthcoming, he flew north to help embark the Spitfires on U.S.S. *Wasp*.

The operation which followed was a remarkable piece of Anglo-American co-operation. In the latter stages of the war it was quite customary for British and American task forces to operate together; but not even in those days (when the machinery of liaison had been much tested and greatly improved) did the planes of one navy ever operate from the carrier of another. It is therefore greatly to the credit of all concerned that Operation "Calendar"—the flying off of British Spitfires from the U.S. aircraft carrier *Wasp*—should have proceeded with such smooth efficiency.

Early in April the *Wasp* and her destroyer escort put in to the Clyde: the first American warship to enter the European theater of war. Off the Tail o' the Bank the destroyers refueled, while the great carrier proceeded upriver to King George V Dock to embark Spitfires and pilots.

Elaborate security measures had been adopted to prevent the *Wasp*'s destination becoming known, rumors having been carefully spread that she was transporting planes to Russia. This subterfuge, however, rather lost its value when the Spitfires arrived on the quay; for they had obviously been tropicalized! Throughout April 12 and 13 the loading of the planes proceeded smoothly; early on the fourteenth the pilots came aboard, and soon after sunrise the *Wasp* and her destroyers stood south out of the mouth of the Clyde.

Operation "Calendar" was under way.

On board the carrier, as at eighteen knots she stood steadily to the south, were fifty-two Mk. 5B Spitfires; each plane tropicalized, fitted with V.H.F. and jettisonable long-range tanks, and armed with four cannon and four machine guns. Also on board were fifty-two pilots of 601 and 603 Squadrons.

To start with, everything was strange to the pilots; for few had been on board a carrier before, let alone an American one. One of them, Flight Lieutenant Barnham, has left us a vivid account of his first impressions of the *Wasp*.

It was with a mounting sense of adventure [he writes] that I followed two of my American hosts through a labyrinth of corridors. Twisting and turning, we passed through the openings of watertight doors and ascended clanging ladders. We were in artificial light all the time: predominantly orange, but sometimes blue. These lights played over the uniforms of the two American officers, changing the immaculate Naval Air Arm green into unusual hues. . . . [They took me first to] the wardroom, where I learnt that ships of the American Navy are "dry" ships, serving soft drinks, mostly Coca-Cola, and where we each had an excellent cup of coffee served by a negro barman. Here, too, I first heard the characteristic Tannoy message, "The smoking lamp is out throughout the ship, gasoline system in operation." After coffee the Americans led me down more corridors, past the hum of dynamos, through the hangar deck filled with aircraft and smelling of dope, and into other creaking passages where cigar smoke lingered outside half-opened doors.

"Well [they said], here's your cabin; your kit's been put in. We've got a library, and, if you like music, we've got lots of records—Bach, Mozart, Beethoven, Schubert. Just make yourself at home. Here, have a cigar!"

And to each of the British pilots, as they arrived on board, the same friendly welcome was invariably extended. Which helps to explain, perhaps, why Operation "Calendar" was such an outstanding success. Not only were the Americans out to prove their operational efficiency; they were also out to prove themselves the perfect hosts. In each case they achieved 100 per cent success.

For four days the great carrier stood southward, screened by the *Renown* and her destroyers; until on the afternoon of April 18 the Rock of Gibraltar was sighted dead ahead.

Operation "Calendar" had, up to now, been a rest cure for the pilots; but with *Wasp* standing well into the Mediterranean their testing time was approaching: the time when the planes would be wheeled out of the hangar and up onto the flight deck, ready for take-off. On April 19 both squadrons were carefully briefed, their drill for ranging and take-off was rehearsed and perfected, and they were given information cards for their 550-mile flight. These information cards had been compiled with a care and accuracy very different from the almost casual orders which had been characteristic of Operation "White." Among other things, the tracks to be flown had been worked out only at the last minute, after the *Wasp* had received an up-to-date weather report from the Malta Channel. Other points, too, such as height, airspeed, and procedure if lost, had been carefully calculated: a glance at Flight Lieutenant Barnham's card will show in what detail.

INFORMATION CARD

PILOT'S NAME: F/LT BARNHAM.
AIRCRAFT NUMBER AND LETTER: 969/R.
ORDER OF TAKE OFF.   SECOND SQUADRON.

TAKE OFF
As normal except:—
(a) Throttle *fully* open
(b) Tail trim in central position.

AIRBORNE
Wireless—Switch on to receive on Button B.
Undercarriage—Retract as soon as possible.
Climb—Straight ahead up to 400 feet. Then reduce revs to 2400 at +2 lbs. boost at 170 m.p.h.
Trim—Close hood, trim for hands and feet off, then climb to rendezvous height.
Petrol—At 2000 feet *switch on* overload tanks and then *switch off* main tanks.

FORMATION
Join up as soon as possible in predetermined positions. *Wide formation*.

CRUISING
Revs and petrol—Once in formation reduce to 2050 revs. Adjust throttle to get 160 m.p.h. at 10,000 feet. Fly on overload tank until it runs dry. Then *switch on* main

tanks and *switch off* overload tanks. Note: jettison overload tank if necessary when empty—gives 50 miles extra endurance.

Compass—Check on deviation card. Swung very recently. Also on coast line.

Wireless:

V.H.F.—Maintain *strict* R/T silence after leaving carrier. Only transmit in emergency.

I.F.F.—On at E.T.A. minus 30 minutes (approximately 90 miles from Destination).

Tracks:	Leg	Track	(Mag)	Distance		Time
	1st	096°		305		1.54
	2nd		096°		52	19½
	3rd	109°		77		29
Last	4th		169°		73	27½
leg	5th	105°		160		60

If separated or lost—On last leg head *North*.

Turn *East* on reaching land (Sicily) and follow coast to easternmost point, then set compass to 222° (M) for destination. Don't flap or worry.

E.T.A.—Zero + 4 hours 10 mts.

Throughout the night of April 19 *Wasp* stood steadily to the east. There was no enemy activity by either air or sea; both asdic and radar screens remained encouragingly blank; the weather was good; and a little before sunrise on Monday, April 20, the carrier and her escort were coming up to the position for flying off: 37° 30′ N, 03° 20′ E. In the pale half light of dawn the *Wasp's* Martlet fighters roared off her flight deck—their task to cover the carrier while she launched her Spitfires—and at 5:18 A.M. the first of the Malta-bound fighters climbed into the lightening sky. The pilot, fittingly enough, was Squadron Leader Gracie.

Few of the pilots had ever taken off from a carrier before; few had any experience of long-distance sea flying. The strangeness and tension of both the launching and the flight itself are apparent from Flight Lieutenant Barnham's account.

Grumman Martlet

I'm strapped into my Spitfire [he writes] and I can feel the heaving and shuddering of the ship's engines racing more vigorously than they have ever raced before...strapped tight I can't look round; but glancing into the mirror above my windscreen I observe that the Spitfire behind me, with the C.O. inside, is being wheeled backwards towards a great lift—a pause—then, with the propeller turning in a transparent arc, the perspective of his plane changes as it disappears bodily, the floor with it, up into the blackness of the girders. Then the lift comes down again...this time for me. Mechanics grab my wings. A last glimpse of the hangar, as the floor heaves beneath me. Then I'm on the deck in white daylight. Clouds: sea: flight deck in front: the superstructure halfway down, right. A white-sweatered American mechanic, much closer, wearing goggles—a red skullcap on his head. With his legs wide apart, he's bending forward like a Rugger player, clenching his hands high in the air: I put on the brakes. His hands begin to rotate rapidly: I open the throttle. The engine is roaring; a checkered flag falls: release brakes, throttle wide open, gathering speed, tail up, looking over the nose: deck's very short. Going faster. The overhanging bridge on the super-structure sweeps towards me: pink faces, pink blobs with no features on them: a quick goodbye wave to the Americans. Grab the stick again: end of the deck. Grey waves. Keep her straight—stick back. Out over the sea. Waves nearer. Stick further back—at last she begins to fly. Gaining more speed. I now start climbing. I don't suppose any enemy pilot could see the battleship, just below on my right, as close as this and survive. Changing on to long-range tanks, I'm circling away to the left, climbing steadily—the engine does not falter—this is fine! With the ships looking like toys, I take position well to the left of the C.O., while the other three Spitfires which I have to lead clamber into formation behind me.

As we set course towards the east the sun rises out of the sea, filling the whole of space with light. . . .

We have been flying through turquoise and silver space for four hours, with the long Mediterranean unwinding below us. For a time, after climbing to 10,000 feet, the russet-coloured mountains of Algiers accompanied us, but finally they retreated into the haze. The sun, mounting higher, has been a blinding light in our eyes. I watch its reflection glistening in the ruffled surface of the sea. With nothing else to look at, I watch the strange patterns blown on the seascape by the wind, but then, about an hour ago, a sheet of white cloud extending below us obliterated the ocean. Because this cloud hid some rocks that should have been our first navigational check, we didn't know we were off course. The wind must have blown us nearly 100 miles from our estimated position, for, as the clouds started to break up, the C.O. discovered that he was about to steer us along the north coast of Sicily! . . . Glancing south, in which direction we have now been ordered to fly, I see the clouds draw back like a curtain to reveal an island, a brown conical hill, floating innocently on the blue water: Pantelleria, an enemy fighter base. That was several minutes ago. Since then we have been flying onwards in a southeasterly direction, with our fuel levels sinking lower and lower, and with a thousand miles of sea between us and Egypt; and I can well believe the stories that pilots, flying this route by night, have been lured by false vector calls on to enemy aerodromes and their machines and crew captured. . . . The clouds have disappeared now. Empty sea stretches in all directions; but soon a disturbance of colour on the horizon grows steadily nearer. From navigational logic it's just where I expected it to be. We change formation as two islands, like autumn leaves floating on the water, grow larger and larger. The steep cliffs of the smaller and nearer, which must be Gozo with Malta lying beyond it, rush towards us. White walls crinkle a hilltop. The small fields are yellow. Blue water in front of my propeller and, as we cross the channel between the two islands, I can see waves breaking on the sunlit rocks ahead. Then we are leaping inland over the island of Malta.

Operation "Calendar" had been successfully carried out. The Spitfires had arrived, Malta, it was thought, had been saved.

But it was not so.

It is true that out of the forty-eight planes which had left the *Wasp*, forty-six had managed to reach the island. But the great things that had been hoped of them never came to pass. For, incredible as it sounds, within seventy-two hours of their arrival, every single one of the Spitfires had been either destroyed or rendered unserviceable; and Malta, once again, was left bereft of aircraft, as defenseless as before.

This was both a tragedy and a disaster. It was a tragedy that the fruits of so much careful planning should never have been gathered in; it was a disaster that Malta should have been left, at this crucial moment, wide open, once again, to the threat of air-borne invasion.

How and why did it happen?

It happened, firstly, because the Spitfires arrived too late. For months General Dobbie and Sir Hugh Lloyd had been crying out for planes; but nobody had taken them seriously. With typical optimism (born of mental laziness) it had been hoped by those at home that Malta, somehow, would muddle through. By the time the seriousness of the island's position had been realized. Malta's air defenses had been worn too thin to protect the relieving planes as they came in to land. The Germans got to know the Spitfires were coming. They lay in wait for them. A few minutes after touchdown wave after wave of Junkers came screaming down on the airfields. Six hundred tons of bombs were unloaded within a quarter of an hour, and on the very morning of their arrival over half the desperately needed planes were destroyed on the ground, bombed to obliteration before they had time to refuel and take to the air.

A second cause of the disaster was the inadequate measures taken to greet the arriving planes. It is easy here for those who were not on the spot to be overcritical: easy to point out that the pens chosen to harbor the Spitfires were too far from the landing strips and were inadequately stocked, manned, and signposted; easy to criticize the delay in servicing and fueling the planes, the delay in briefing the newly arrived pilots, and the muddle as to which squadrons should fly which planes. And there is indeed no doubt—in view of what was accomplished later—that the arrangements for greeting the first batch of Spitfires could have been greatly improved. On the other hand, it is only fair to remember that conditions on the Malta airdromes were such that simply to keep them operational was a full-time and creditable achievement. Three months' continuous and devastating bombing had shattered dispersal pens, obliterated ack-ack defenses and petrol bowsers, and necessitated the continual rebuilding of the cratered runways after every raid. Little time and few men could be spared for laying on a large-scale receiving service.

The final reason for the failure of the "Calendar" Spitfires was the difficulty experienced in keeping the few aircraft which were not bombed serviceable. The trouble here sprang from two sources: (1) the poor condition of the Spitfires when they arrived and (2) Malta's chronic shortage of spare parts and skilled ground crew.

The first defect was inexcusable. After the planes had been loaded onto the *Wasp* it was found that 90 per cent of their long-range tanks were defective (and caused serious flooding in the carrier's hangar); 95 per cent of their guns were dirty and unsynchronized; 70 per cent of their radios were inoperative; and that there was, in brief, "a very great deal wrong with them"; a state of affairs which reflects little credit on the R.A.F. Embarkation authorities.

The second defect was neither so simple nor so easy to

remedy. Malta had been operating Hurricanes for years; her ground crew had become familiar with them and had evolved a system for improvising spares (which were always in short supply). When Spitfires replaced Hurricanes this system ran up against inevitable snags, for the planes' component parts were radically different. Sir Hugh Lloyd puts the position very clearly and simply.

Our main difficulty [he writes] was spares, which were always being used at a far quicker rate than they were being delivered. At the risk of being facetious, may I point out that an aeroplane is a most complicated piece of machinery. Men would rob parts from every unserviceable Spitfire to make others serviceable; but there was a limit to that, particularly with engines. We needed new radio equipment too, and tyres, inner tubes, hydraulic oil, and all the complicated parts and nuts and screws and bolts which are necessary to keep an aeroplane flying. . . . I also wanted at least 200 spare engines. But we couldn't run to an aircraft factory for help, and the few Hurricane spares we had were useless; it was a hopeless situation. . . .

So it was that the handful of Spitfires which managed that first day to survive both bombing and air fighting became grounded through lack of spares and lack of ground crew experienced in servicing them—for the reinforcements promised by the Admiralty had got only as far as Gibraltar.

Operation "Calendar," in fact, which had met with such apparent success, proved in the end to be a mockery; and the last few days of April saw Malta once again defenseless, with German bombers ranging at will over the length and breadth of the island.

The end of April saw, too, another sinister development. Photographic reconnaissance revealed that in the vale of Catania a chain of satellite landing strips were being built beside the fields at Gerbini, Catania, and Comiso: take-off strips for gliders. The air-borne invasion of Malta was clearly imminent; and the need to reinforce the island with a further batch of Spitfires now took on an added urgency. Hence the decision to make another air-ferry trip: "the wasp's second sting."

Only this time the detailed and meticulous planning which had previously insured the successful launching of the planes was applied also to their landing. This time the Spitfires didn't simply arrive; they arrived in good condition; they were greeted by a superbly efficient system of reception which enabled each plane to be air-borne and fully operational within ten minutes of its touching down. And—what was more—it was arranged that skilled ground crew and spares (including the vitally needed engines) would reach the island within a few hours of the planes. For the Admiralty had discarded by this time their original scheme of reinforcing the island by submarine. They had hit on a better idea. And early in May one hundred and five Spitfire ground-crew members and close to one hundred Spitfire engines were embarked in a specially camouflaged blockade runner: the mine layer H.M.S. *Welshman*, which had been disguised as a Vichy-French *Léopard*-class destroyer, with the idea of running her to Malta along the fringe of French territorial waters.

On the night of May 7 both the *Wasp* and the *Welshman* were aswing at their anchors within a few hundred yards of the Rock. By dawn both vessels had sailed, independently, for Malta.

This second air-ferry operation was known under the code name of "Bowary." It was planned that *Wasp* should follow the same procedure as for "Calendar," embarking Spitfires and pilots in the Clyde, sailing with her escort to a position south of Sardinia, and flying the planes off at dawn on Saturday, May 9.

The operation, however, got off to a bad start. In fact, it nearly didn't start at all, the culprit once again being the R.A.F. Embarkation authorities, who for the second time running supplied planes with defective fuel tanks. This was a far more serious matter than appears at first sight. It was serious from the point of view of the Spitfires, which relied on their extra tanks to reach Malta. It was equally serious from the point of view of the *Wasp*. For in an aircraft carrier the most elaborate precautions have to be taken to insure that petrol is kept permanently sealed in airtight tanks—the danger of fire is too great to risk leaving it exposed. Once already the defective tanks of the "Calendar" Spitfires had spewed

H.M.S. Welshman

petrol all over the *Wasp*'s hangar. Now it happened again. Of the first half dozen planes to be hoisted aboard, four had faulty tanks. The commanding officer of the *Wasp*, with every justification, refused to continue loading.

The whole unhappy incident, and its inevitable repercussions, are clearly set out in a letter which Flag Officer in Charge, Glasgow, wrote to the Admiralty.

On Thursday, April 30th [he writes] U.S.N. aircraft carrier *Wasp* proceeded upriver to K.G. V Dock to embark Spitfires. Previous to arrival of vessel, the R.A.F.

Embarkation had been informed of the importance of having machines ready, so that the least possible time need to be spent upriver. . . . The ship secured at 1400 and the first plane was ready for hoisting at 1402. . . . After some twelve machines had been taken on board, the U.S. officers raised the question as to whether the tanks had been tested and rendered serviceable. On receiving a negative reply, Captain Reeves, Commanding Officer of U.S.S. *Wasp*, ordered all embarkation to cease, and re- fused to take any more machines on board, until they had been tested and serviced. The reason for this order was that on the previous trip, it was found that, on filling the jettisonable tanks, ninety per cent of them leaked and flooded the hangar.

By working all night a number of tanks were tested and rendered serviceable, and Captain Reeves finally agreed to sail for the Tail o' the Bank and to carry out such further repairs as were necessary with his own labour.

I am informed that if the operation is repeated a U.S. Air Officer will be sent in advance to Renfrew [where planes and tanks are prepared for embarkation].

The fact that the planes were provided on both occasions with tanks which had not been tested and had not been rendered serviceable is unsatisfactory, and has unfortunately created a very bad impression. . . .

Thanks to the hangar personnel of the *Wasp*, every tank had been repaired by the time the carrier reached Gibraltar. But a legacy remained. A half-formed doubt in the minds of the U.S. Navy as to British standards of operational efficiency: a doubt which was only removed, years later, by the feats of British task forces in the Pacific.

Like "Calendar," "Bowary" was favored by good weather and little opposition; and soon after sunrise on Saturday, May 9, sixty-three Spitfires were flown safely off. Sixty-one of them arrived in Malta; and that weekend they gave the German bombers such a mauling that, in the words of Malta's War Diary, "from that moment massed daylight raiding was brought to an abrupt end."

For this time the Spitfires didn't just arrive. They were met, directed to their pens, refueled, and serviced with such clockwork precision that many of them were back in the air within four minutes of their touching down. The German bombers which followed them in found their "victims" not, as they had hoped, on the ground, but in the air. They got more than they had bargained for; and they suffered losses from which they never recovered. It was an amazing transformation from the chaos which had followed Operation "Calendar": an apparent miracle: a miracle brought about by a group of officers working with Squadron Leader Gracie, whom the A.O.C. had put in charge of the organization for receiving the planes.

Gracie's problem was how to turn the Spitfires around with the least possible dealy. In his own words:

> . . . we went to our pilots, ground crew, and administrative staff and told them we were going to give them an organization which would enable us to win the Battle of Malta, which at that time we were in grave danger of losing. We told them that it would mean the hardest possible work under very difficult conditions; that we were going to enlist the aid of the Army, both in men and materials; and that the battle would be lost unless they all pulled their weight one hundred per cent. The response was tremendous. Every man felt himself an important item in the battle, and not merely an insignificant unit. . . .

The first step to be arranged was how to meet and direct the planes immediately after their touchdown. This was solved by the airdrome control officer at each of the three airdromes having beside him a representative for each dispersal pen; as soon as a plane touched down, the control officer would call out the number of a pen, and the representative in question would run to meet the plane at the end of the runway and would jump onto its wing root and direct the pilot to his pen.

These pens had been specially built around the airdrome perimeters and on the Safi Strip; each was a self-contained, self-supporting unit, equipped with petrol tins for refueling, glycol coolant for the engines, ammunition for the guns, and three specialist ground crew, who, the moment a plane was taxied into their pen, set to work to make it one hundred per cent combat-worthy. They stripped off the long-range belly tanks, refueled the main tanks by hand from five-gallon petrol tins, tuned up the radio, and checked the synchronization of the guns. It was hoped that no more than a quarter of an hour would be needed to get each Spitfire serviced and back into the air.

In the event, this estimate proved to be overconservative. For on May 8 some planes were back in the air within four and a half minutes of touching down; and the average turnaround was seven minutes. It was, that day, not the pilots who saved Malta, it was the ground crew.

For the turnaround was so quick that the Junkers and

Savoias, following the Spitfires in as they had done after "Calendar," were met head on over the airfields. Thirty-seven were destroyed for the loss of three Spitfires.

One of the pilots, recently flown in from the *Wasp*, describes this first day on the island as follows:

Took off again at 1100 hrs. Climbed to 4000 feet, and saw the terrific barrage put up by the harbour defences. As the first wave of 87s dived into the barrage the C.O. followed them down, and I stayed close beside him. We flew to and fro in the barrage, trusting to luck to avoid the flak. Then I spotted a Ju 87 climbing out of the fringe of the barrage; I turned and chased him. I gave him a one-second burst of cannon, and he broke away sharply to the left. At that moment another Ju 87 came up in front of my nose, and I turned into him and let him have it. His engine started to pour out black smoke, and he began to weave. I kept the tit pushed hard, and after a further two-to-three second burst with one cannon (the other having jammed) he keeled over at 1500 feet and went straight into the sea.

I then spotted an Me 109 firing at me from behind, so I pulled the Spit round to port and after one and a half turns got on his tail. Before I could fire, another 109 cut across my bows from the port side, and I turned straight onto his tail and fired till my cannon ran out of ammunition. He was hit and his engine poured black smoke; but I couldn't see what happened to him, as I was now defenceless and two more Me 109s were on my tail. I spiralled straight down to the sea at full throttle, and then weaved violently towards land with the 109s still firing at me. I went under the fringe of the smoke screen to try and throw them off, but when I came out the other side I found them both sitting on top waiting for me. So I kept right down at zero feet, and steep-turned towards them, noticing the smoke from their gun ports as I did so. After about five minutes of this I managed to shake them off.

I landed back at Takali and made out my report, claiming one Ju 87 destroyed and one Me 109 damaged.

Scrambled again after lunch, and again after tea, but no luck. . . .

The tempo of life here is just indescribable. The morale

of all is magnificent—pilots, ground crew, Army, civilians, the lot—but life is certainly tough. The bombing is pretty well continuous all day. One lives only to destroy the Hun and hold him at bay; everything else—living conditions, sleep, food, and all the ordinary standards of life—have gone by the board. It all makes the Battle of Britain and fighter sweeps over France seem like child's play in comparison, but it is certainly history in the making; and nowhere is there aerial warfare to compare with this.

And next day the fighters met with even greater success. For the Germans, from sunrise to sunset, attempted to mount an attack on Grand Harbour, where the *Welshman* had just arrived with her vital cargo of spares. But once again they met the Spitfires head on, and in a day of bitter and continuous air fighting, sixty were destroyed.

This was air fighting that couldn't, at such a tempo, last for long; one side was bound to crack. Up to May 9 it had seemed inevitable that it would be Malta which cracked: that the island's few remaining fighters would, in the end, be whittled away. But the air fighting of May 8 and 9 brought about a remarkable change. In those two days the Luftwaffe lost ninety-seven planes to the Royal Air Force's eight. Quite suddenly it was Kesselring who was reeling. And dawn on May 10 found the Luftwaffe, for the first time, seriously short of aircraft; while in Malta a force of new and formidable fighters—the dreaded Spitfires—were established in strength.

From that moment Kesselring's attacks began to ease off. They didn't, of course, stop completely: but the continuous massed raids of March and April were never repeated. And at the end of the month the gliders started to disappear from the airstrips of Comiso and Gerbini. The Spitfires had done the trick. Invasion had been averted. Malta had weathered the storm.

And at this juncture it is worth bearing in mind the debt that the island owes to President Roosevelt. For in the final analysis Malta's survival was due to his generosity. If Roosevelt hadn't allowed the *Wasp* to enter the Mediterranean, Malta would almost certainly have fallen. For no other carrier could have ferried Spitfires to the island in April or May, and without Spitfires Malta would have been bombed to annihilation.

It was recognized at the time that the island was indebted to the President, and that summer the following signal was sent from the Admiralty:

> To Task Force 39.
>
> Please pass the following message to the Commanding Officer, U.S.S. *Wasp*.
>
> The British Chiefs of Staff send their heartiest congratulations to yourself and all ranks and ratings of U.S.S. *Wasp* on completion of Operations "Calendar" and "Bowary". . . . These operations were one hundred per cent successful, and their success augurs well for future combined operations undertaken by the American and British Services.

But only in retrospect does the magnitude of the debt become apparent; only in retrospect can it be seen how the President's decision marked the turning of the tide.

Yet the planes by themselves would not have been enough. Ground crew and spares were needed as well. And the blockade runs of the *Welshman* must be regarded as an essential complement to the air-ferry runs of the *Wasp*.

The *Welshman*-class mine layers were hybrid in appearance, being too large for destroyers and too small for cruisers. They were fast modern ships, heavily armed, and with plenty of internal storage space, which was usually, of course, taken up with mines; they had three funnels and a heavy box-type bridge. The French *Léopard*-class destroyers were equally hybrid. Being substantially over 2000 tons, they, too, looked rather like light cruisers, a resemblance which was heightened by their three funnels and heavy box-type bridge.

At the end of April a member of Admiral Somerville's staff came forward with a happy suggestion. Why not disguise one of the mine layers as a *Léopard* destroyer and try to run her to Malta along the North African coast on the fringe of French territorial waters? The idea was put to the Admiralty. It was just the alternative to running in ground crew and spares by submarine that they had been trying to find.

Early in May the *Welshman* put in to Gibraltar. Her commanding officer, Captain W.H.D. Friedberger, was given secret instructions; and a few days later a mysterious assortment of flags, pennants, and false partitions started to arrive aboard the mine layer. In the early hours of Thursday, May 7, she embarked her passengers and cargo: 540 tons of stores, of which the most important were six dozen crates of smoke-making compound and eight dozen Spitfire engines; also 120 passengers, of whom over a hundred were R.A.F technicians: the ground crew for Malta's Spitfires.

That evening, as soon as it was dark, the *Welshman* drew a little away from the quay, and her ship's company started to manhandle the false partitions into place, enlarging the *Welshman*'s bridge, building up her superstructure aft. By midnight the metamorphosis was complete, and the disguised mine layer was standing out to sea. At 3 A.M. she passed Europa Point, less than an hour after U.S. *Wasp*—bound eastward on her second ferry of Spitfires.

Friday, May 8, dawned fine, with a light southwesterly breeze, a calm sea, and good visibility. All day the *Welshman*, disguised as the *Léopard* and flying French colors, stood quietly east, zigzagging at her most economical cruising speed—a shade under twenty knots. At noon she sighted a solitary merchantman, hull down on the northern horizon, and gave her a wide berth; and at three o'clock a civil aircraft passed high overhead but made no attempt to close and identify her. Apart from these two, sea and sky remained empty hour after hour. And soon the first night had come and had passed as uneventfully as the day.

Saturday, May 9, found the *Welshman* some thirty miles off the African shore, heading as if toward Algiers. From her masthead and sternpost fluttered the Tricolor and Ensign of France. At seven o'clock speed was increased to twenty-five knots, and the miles began to slide effortlessly by. The port watch was just settling down to breakfast when out of the west came a low-pitched hum, a hum that deepened quickly into great pulsating roar. Aircraft: wave after wave of them: the *Wasp*'s Malta-bound Spitfires. They passed directly over the *Welshman*, making for their Galita Island landfall. For several minutes the air trembled; then the aircraft were gone; and the mine layer was alone once more; alone in a great emptiness of sunlit sea and azure sky.

Then, at a few minutes to ten o'clock, came their first test. Out of the north came a single and highly suspicious Ju 88.

She circled the *Welshman* once at a radius of four miles. Captain Friedberger could sense the pilot's reaction—"Looks

like a French destroyer. But we'd better make sure." The
Junkers closed in. She circled them twice this time, at a
radius of fifteen hundred yards. Once again Captain Friedberger
could guess what the pilot was thinking—"Looks like a *Léopard*
destroyer. But there's something funny about her. Something
not quite right. And what's she doing heading east, and
outside territorial waters?" The Junkers' circles grew tighter:
closer. Soon she was so near that they could read her identifi-
cation letters. Suddenly she broke off circling. In a shallow
dive she came straight toward them. Threateningly. As if on a
bombing run. Captain Friedberger kept his turrets trained
fore and aft. His pom-poms were not even manned. A couple
of his crew waved cheerfully at the German pilot. From their
masthead the French Ensign streamed away downwind.

The bluff was one the German pilot didn't dare to call.
After a second dummy attack, at mast height, he broke away.
He waggled his wings, and, apparently satisfied, made off to
the east. The *Welshman* steamed steadily on.

Half an hour later another aircraft came into sight. This
time a Catalina, an antisubmarine flying boat of Coastal
Command. She circled the *Welshman* several times, obviously well aware of who she was. Captain Friedberger signaled
her by aldis to keep her distance; for, much as he valued her
antisubmarine protection, it would obviously be out of keeping for a British aircraft to be screening a Vichy-French
destroyer. And it was well that he did. For, a few minutes
after the Catalina had disappeared, another Ju 88 came in
sight. Again the *Welshman*'s disguise served her well, and
this second Junkers, after a cursory inspection, also went on
her way.

That afternoon the mine layer edged close inshore, skirting
the fringe of territorial waters, heading as if for a Tunisian
port. Soon she was passing between Galita Island and the
northwestern tip of Tunis. There followed two anxious moments.
Off Bizerta a Vichy float plane circled her twice; and a little
later a shore station, high up in the cliffs, ordered her to show
her signal letters. Captain Friedberger disregarded both; he
didn't deign to answer; he kept on course; and he got away
with it.

At last light the *Welshman* cut southeastward into French
waters. She increased speed. Her navigating officer took

last-minute fixes on the fading shore. The crucial stage of the voyage was about to begin.

There followed as nice a piece of dead-reckoning navigation as anyone could wish for. At close to thirty knots the *Welshman's* navigating officer, Lieutenant Commander Gellatly, took the mine layer through the complicated skein of shoals that fringe the Tunisian shore; and at the end of eight hours' blind, full-speed steaming he made an exact landfall at Malta next morning, within two minutes of sunrise. And all this was on a dark, near-moonless night, the date having been especially picked to afford maximum darkness as a cloak against E-boats. Their only excitement came with the dawn, when, as they were rounding the breakwater at the entrance to Grand Harbour, their starboard paravanes cut two mines, which narrowly missed their stern as they swung into harbor. By six o'clock they were secured to the wall of No. 5 dock.

There was about Grand Harbour an air of desolation and disrepair; the hulks of half-sunk ships littered the basin; bomb rubble lay strewn to the water's edge; everything was very quiet.

It was certain that German reconnaissance planes would soon spot the *Welshman*, and that once they spotted her they would make every effort to obliterate both ship and cargo. Speed in unloading was therefore essential; and Captain Friedberger aimed to discharge his passengers and cargo, refuel, and load up for the return journey all in a single day. He was therefore much relieved to find that gangplanks were quickly provided, and his passengers were disembarked at once. By six-thirty the last of the vital R.A.F. ground crew was ashore, and the unloading of the cargo was under way. Soon *Welshman* was surrounded by lighters; working parties were busily manhandling out the stores—assisted by Malta's last remaining crane; and columns of motor transport were conveying the vital crates from dock to supply dump. The men worked quickly: efficiently. And it was just as well they did. For at eight o'clock that morning came the German reconnaissance planes. They spotted—and evidently identified—the *Welshman;* for a couple of hours later some eighty planes made her the centerpiece of a vicious and sustained attack. The mine layer's disguise was useless now. She had to fight for her life.

One of the things the *Welshman* had brought to Malta was smoke-making compound: six dozen crates of it. And it was this compound which now came to her aid. For soon, over Grand Harbour and French Creek, there floated a white miasma: a canopy of artificial smoke. In the light northeasterly wind it lay well, confusing the bombers, hiding their target. But inevitably there were gaps. And through these came the Junkers. They were met by the newly arrived Spitfires, and by the heaviest gun barrage Malta had ever concentrated over one particular spot. Over French Creek alone eighteen were shot down; twenty-three were damaged; and the *Welshman* wasn't hit.

But it was a near thing. Time and again the mine layer was deluged with water, splintered with near misses, and showered with debris—four tons of steel girders, for example, ex H.M.S. *Fermog*, were blasted off the quay and flung on top of her for'ard oerlikons. While the center of No. 5 dock, which half an hour before had been piled high with naval stores, was reduced to a vast smoldering crater, seventy feet wide and twenty feet deep.

But by then the last of the stores had gone.

At eleven-fifteen, a few minutes after the raid was over, Lord Gort arrived on board the *Welshman*. He found her listing to starboard, covered with debris, and badly holed above the water line. But she was, Captain Friedberger insisted, still seaworthy; and soon after midday she was able to limp across to the Canteen Wharf to oil.

There were at that moment less than two thousand tons of diesel oil in the whole of the island. Captain Friedberger was loath to deplete the stock by taking more than a bare minimum; but Vice-Admiral, Malta, insisted that he take "at least three hundred tons," so that the *Welshman* could make good speed for the first and most dangerous part of her journey home.

Having oiled, the mine layer was resting quietly in the open water of French Creek when another raid developed. This time the smoke was thin, but her guns operated effectively. One aircraft was shot down; and once again the ship escaped damage. After this, the embarking of passengers for the return to Gibraltar was completed in peace; and soon it was dusk.

At a little after eight o'clock the ship cast off and proceeded out of harbor. Everything was very quiet. The water was as still as glass; and the half light softened the ravages of two years of near-continuous bombardment. Captain Friedberger had been to Malta before the war: before the dockyard had been reduced to a broker's yard of scrap; before Valletta and Senglea had been smashed to unstable heaps of rubble and Grand Harbour had become littered with the half-sunk hulks of merchantmen and men-of-war.

> Our departure [he wrote] was most affecting. The quiet of a shattered dockyard frontage . . . a circle of five burnt-out or sunken merchant vessels . . . then a ring of cheers which seemed to come from the bastions of Valletta and Senglea, and the singing of "Roll Out the Barrel," a tune which is *vieux jeu*, but nevertheless expresses the spirit of Malta.

Welshman was swept out through the breakwaters by Malta's last remaining mine sweeper. Almost at once she increased speed to thirty-four knots, and soon the island disappeared in the quiet evening haze. Two days later she was back at Gibraltar.

The *Welshman*'s first trip had been an unqualified success, and the ground crew she took to Malta were soon playing a major role in the island's defense.

Coming at a time when a convoy had been impractical, the mine layer's passage had bridged a dangerous gap, had spanned a critical period when the island's link with the outside world had been almost completely severed. What had been done once could be done again, and it was inevitable that Lord Gort and Vice-Admiral, Malta, should press for further storing trips. The Admiralty agreed, and the mine layer made two more trips to Malta; one in June with glycol coolant, 20-mm. cannon shell, and another batch of Spitfire engines; and one in July with flour, edible oil, and paravanes. On each occasion she ran the blockade successfully—though by no means uneventfully. Then, in August, the need for further storing runs came to an end.

For that month an all-out effort was made to meet the island's needs by fighting through one of the largest convoys of the war: fourteen merchantmen escorted by sixty-five warships. Compared with this vast armada, now preparing to sail, *Welshman*'s storing runs might be thought to be mere fleabites, the cargoes she carried to be an insignificant trickle. But this was not so. For her three trips got through vital supplies at a time when no other vessel could have managed to fight her way through—for the *Welshman* alone possessed the essential speed, carrying capacity, and fighting ability. The debt Malta owes her is incalculable; and if ever a list were compiled of the half dozen vessels that did most to save the island, then the *Welshman*, together with the *Breconshire*, *Wasp*, and *Ohio*, would certainly be included.

Vice-Admiral, Malta, fully recognized this.

> I wish to bring specially to your notice [he wrote to the Admiralty] the debt which Malta owes H.M.S. *Welshman*, for the three voyages she has made for the purpose of bringing vital supplies to the island. . . . I have the highest opinion of the manner in which the ship was handled by her Commanding Officer (Captain W.H.D. Friedberger, R.N.), and of the conduct of her officers and Ship's Company throughout these arduous and hazardous operations.

It is pleasant to record that the *Welshman*'s services did not pass unrecognized. After the third voyage her crew were given no fewer than twenty-one awards, including the D.S.O. for Captain Friedberger and the D.S.C. for Lieutenant Commander Gellatly. The awards were richly deserved. For it was largely because of the *Welshman*'s three storing runs that Malta's Spitfires were able to operate throughout the summer with such effective efficiency.

14

It is impossible for us to carry on without further supplies of food and ammunition.

—C. in C., MALTA

The *Wasp* and the *Welshman* had between them averted the danger of Malta's being bombed to obliteration; but the question of how to provide the island with food, ammunition, and fuel still remained. For out of the March convoy less than one twentieth of the much needed supplies had been saved, and by early April the governor was sending urgent signals to the War Office, stressing the island's desperate need.

From C. in C., MALTA.
To WAR OFFICE.
4/1/42
Our supply position has been reassessed and may be summarized as follows:

(a) Wheat and Flour. No material cuts seem possible, as these are staple foods. Present stocks will, with care, last until early June.

(b) Fodder. Issues already inadequate were recently cut; stocks will now last until end of June.

(c) Minor foodstuffs. Meat stocks are entirely exhausted. Most other stocks will last until June.

(d) White oils. Aviation fuel till mid-August; benzine till mid-June; kerosene till early July.

(e) Black oils. We have only 920 tons of diesel oil (5 weeks' supply) and 2000 tons of furnace fuel, all of which will be needed for fuelling H.M. Ships now in dock. The black oil position is thus becoming precarious, and very urgent action appears necessary to restore it.

(f) Coal. Welsh coal will last only until end of May...
    other grades until mid-June.
(g) Ammunition. Consumption of ack-ack ammunition
    has greatly increased in the recent heavy raids...and
    we have only 1½ months' stocks left. . . .

The governor ended his report by pointing out that, unless
supplies were brought in soon, the island would be too weak
to provide adequate cover for their unloading. He pressed for
the sending of at least five ships, with late May as the
deadline for their arrival.

But to those in London, the dangers and difficulties of
another convoy in the immediate future appeared insuperable:
air cover over the island was not yet sufficiently assured, and
the warships were simply not available. The governor therefore received, on April 18, a brief note from the Secretary of
State for Colonies stating that "a convoy in May will not, repeat not, be possible."

This provoked another despairing appeal.

FROM C. in C., MALTA.
    The decision not to run a convoy for the present is based
on general considerations which are outside my sphere. I
can only speak for Malta itself, and our situation here is so
grave that it is my duty to restate it in the clearest possible
terms. This decision [not to run a convoy in May] material-
ly reduces our chance of survival, not because of any
failure of morale, but simply because it is quite impossible
for us to carry on without further supplies of food and
ammunition. It is obvious that the very worst must happen
if we cannot replenish our vital needs, especially flour,
kerosene, and ammunition. . . .

But even this *crie de coeur* failed to produce a convoy.
Malta was told she had to wait; her rations were reduced to
starvation level, her ack-ack guns were limited to fifteen
rounds a day, and before long the Maltese were suffering all
the privations and heartaches of a full-scale siege.

The shortages were cumulative. As soon as stocks of one
commodity were seen to be low and steps were taken to
restrict its use, this, in turn, invariably led to other shortages.
Take coal and coke, for example. When stocks were seen to

be shrinking, the power station had their rations cut, and throughout the island household electricity was turned off; this led to more kerosene being used for both lighting and heating, and soon there was a shortage of kerosene; for a time this was alleviated by the use of candles and wood fires, but after a few weeks supplies of candles and wood were completely exhausted. And so the shortages built up: in commodity after commodity, week after week, month after month, until there came a time when no amount of ingenuity and no amount of improvisation could obscure the unpalatable truth: the island was being strangled to death.

The process of strangulation was, of course, a gradual one. It constituted a danger that was less spectacular than the bombing and less immediately apparent. But the danger was very real; it was all the greater for being veiled, all the greater, too, because there was nothing the Maltese themselves could do to avert it. They could alleviate its effects (by stricter rationing and greater ingenuity in stretching their resources to the uttermost), but the ultimate solution lay beyond their power to control. Only by running in another large-scale convoy could the problem be met. And another convoy, the governor had been told, was out of the question for several months.

So the people of Malta tightened their belts and set to make their meager resources hold out to the last possible moment.

The most acute shortage was of cooking fuel. Throughout the island gas and electricity had been turned off, and the ration of kerosene was sufficient to cook only two hot meals a week—quite inadequate for a people being bombed day after day anything up to eighteen hours out of twenty-four. To start with, the problem was met by each household having its own individual "fire drum," a Heath Robinson apparatus consisting of a five gallon petrol tin with the lid knocked off, and a supply of cotton waste. The technique of using a "fire drum" was simple. You filled the bottom with cotton waste, onto which you dripped kerosene and water—two drops of water to one of kerosene. You then set fire to the waste; the parts impregnated with kerosene burned fiercely, turning the water to superheated steam, over which food could be cooked on an iron plate. Soon the streets were filled with "fire drums" (they were far too dangerous to light indoors; roaring away like a series of miniature blast furnaces. But eventually the supply of cotton waste began to dry up; and it was then that Lord Gort instigated the "Victory Kitchens": a series of self-contained mobile canteens which were equipped with utensils made out of dockyard scrap and staffed by volunteers from the Army. By the end of May communal cooking was firmly established throughout the island, and over 200,000 people were daily bringing their food to the "Victory Kitchens" —where, of course, it could be cooked in bulk: a process which effected a great saving in kerosene.

The next most serious shortage was that of bread. Now, bread is a Maltese's staple diet. He eats little fish and practically no meat, but in peacetime he eats anything up to fifty ounces of bread a day. This bread comes to him in large circular loaves; he scoops out the center and stuffs the cavity with a mixture of garlic and tomato soaked in edible oil; and three such loaves a day are standard diet. But now, in the spring of 1942, the bread ration was down to ten ounces (half a loaf) a day and there seemed no doubt it would have to be reduced still further. Ten ounces of bread a day may sound more than adequate, being nearly double the standard wartime ration in England and Italy; but in England bread is a subsidiary food to meat, in Italy it is subsidiary to spaghetti, whereas in Malta it is the basic diet. To have cut the ration still further would have led to widespread despondency and a consequent drop in morale. Lord Gort realized this. The food experts who had been specially flown in from England assured him that alternative diets would provide the Maltese with an equal number of calories and vitamins and that the ration could safely be reduced. But the governor knew better. And by enforcing a stringent campaign against waste at the mills, by scraping every available source of supply, and by supplementing the flour with a mixture of strange ingredients (of which potato peel was one of the more mentionable), he managed to keep the ration at ten ounces. It was a near thing. On more than one occasion there was only sufficient flour on the island for ten days' bread. But always, as each crisis came to a head, a relieving shot in the arm enabled the bread to be made: a few hundred tons of flour unloaded from the Welshman, an early harvesting of the island's crop of barley, a new method of swelling and processing the dust from the mills. Somehow, by luck or hard work or ingenuity, the supplies of bread kept coming through.

And as it was with bread, so it was with other supplies. By mid-May there wasn't a cow or a tin of milk on the island. But there were several thousand goats; and the milk from these was pasteurized (to prevent undulant fever), bottled, and distributed under government supervision. By mid-June, Malta couldn't raise a tablet of soap or a pat of butter; but by the end of the month substitutes had somehow been improvised. And so the battle of supplies went on; with the Maltese—to quote an eyewitness account—"embarking on a period of enforced frugality the like of which had not been endured by any British community within living memory."

It is worth remembering, too, that, although by this time the air raids had slackened off, they were still, by normal standards, heavy. It isn't easy to be brave on an empty stomach.

Improvisation is all very well, but it can't last forever. The barrel is not so bottomless that it can go on being scraped ad infinitum; and so, inevitably, there came a time when Lord Gort had to admit that Malta was very close to being starved into surrender. He did the only possible thing then. He fixed a "target date": a date beyond which no amount of abstemiousness and no amount of ingenuity could make his supplies hold out. And he put the position, quite plainly, to London. Unless a convoy got through to the island before the target date, Malta would have to surrender.

The powers that be in London were beginning to realize by this time the strategic importance of Malta. They were anxious to relieve her. But they had always stipulated that before another convoy tried to force its way through, two conditions must be met: air supremacy over the island had to be assured, and sufficient warships had to be available.

By the end of May the first stipulation could be met; the *Wasp*'s second consignment of Spitfires had driven the Luftwaffe out of the Maltese sky. But the problem of ships remained. It was a problem to which there just wasn't an answer. For Britain's sea power, in the spring of 1942, was stretched to the breaking point and her warships were scattered throughout the seven seas, from North Cape to Tierra del Fuego and from Singapore to Buenos Aires. Ships for a convoy to Malta simply weren't available; especially the capital ships and modern aircraft carriers, whose presence was almost a requisite of success. There were, however, a number of light warships which could be spared in midsummer from both home waters and the Indian Ocean; the former could be in Gibraltar by the end of May, the latter could get to Alexandria early in June. It was therefore decided to run two lightly escorted convoys simultaneously in the second week of June, one leaving from Gibraltar and one from Alexandria. It was hoped that this arrangement would force the enemy to divide his forces and would enable one of the convoys to slip through relatively unopposed.

It was a reasonable scheme; but events were to prove that two nibbles at a problem are less effective than one good bite.

The convoys were scheduled to sail early in June; and as soon as Lord Gort heard the merchantmen were assembling (six in Gibraltar and eleven in Alexandria) he set to work on plans to receive them. He was determined that the mistakes of March should not be repeated; that every vessel which managed to fight its way through should be unloaded swiftly and efficiently and its cargo dispersed to underground supply dumps with the minimum delay. Preparations were made to meet every foreseeable eventuality—the ships arriving all together or singly or damaged; attacks on them by bombers, dive bombers, fighter-bombers, E-boats, or paratroops. A protective smoke screen was laid on to cover the whole of Grand Harbour. Relays of stevedores were detailed off to manhandle the stores from ship to quay and then from quay to the waiting columns of lorries and trucks. Specially picked drivers were chosen to lead the transport columns to the various dispersal points. An elaborate scheme of colored arrows and lamps marked the different routes; while at key points policemen were standing by to insure a smooth flow of traffic.

On the airdromes, too, special arrangements were laid on. A number of aircraft were carefully tuned up and put into reserve; tactics were discussed, rehearsed, and perfected; and AA defenses were redistributed and strengthened around the harbor. At the end of all these preparations Lord Gort felt confident he could protect the merchantmen once they got through.

But would they get through?

That was a question the Maltese couldn't answer. On their beleaguered island they had done everything humanly possible to insure the convoys' success. Now they could only wait and watch and pray. And they prayed hard. For they knew that if none of the merchantmen which were assembling in Gibraltar and Alexandria were able to fight their way through to them, Malta would have to surrender.

15

Events proved with painful clarity that our air striking force had nothing like the necessary weight to stop the Italian fleet.

—ADMIRAL HARWOOD

For the convoys in June seventeen merchantmen and seventy-six warships assembled at either end of the Mediterranean: six merchantmen and twenty-nine warships at Gibraltar and eleven merchantmen and forty-six warships at Alexandria: two great armadas, dedicated to the task of fighting through the desperately needed supplies. The convoy from Alexandria was commanded by Admiral Vian, that from Gibraltar by Admiral Curteis. It was planned that both should leave harbor on the same day—June 11—so as to force the Axis to divide the weight of their attacks; but once at sea, they were to proceed independently.

The chief effort was to be made in the east, where great things were expected of Vian's convoy from Alexandria. For only three months earlier a convoy from this port had been fought through after one of the most brilliant naval actions of the war (the Battle of Sirte); and the vessels now assembling were led, at least nominally, by the same man, Rear Admiral Vian, and were faced by apparently similar problems. Yet the similarity between the two convoys was more apparent than real; and the convoy in June started off under several serious disadvantages.

It started, in the first place, without Admiral Cunningham, who a couple of months earlier had left the Mediterranean to take up the important post of head of the Admiralty delegation in Washington. Admiral Cunningham's great experience and his happy flair for formulating simple and concise operational orders were sadly missed. His successor, Admiral

Harwood, had a brilliant war record; but he lacked his predecessor's experience in planning large-scale operations.

In the second place, the June convoy had to contend with far less favorable weather conditions. In March the vessels had enjoyed a certain amount of protection from cloud cover, from poor visibility, and, above all, from a nightly cloak of at least ten hours' darkness. But in June the weather was fine, with bright sun, little cloud, unlimited visibility, and less than six hours' darkness. The chances of secrecy, evasion, and delaying tactics were therefore very much reduced.

A third weakness of the June convoy was the composition of its escort. This may have looked, on paper, stronger in June than it had been in March (the early convoy was protected by only five cruisers and seventeen destroyers, while the later one had eight cruisers and twenty-six destroyers); yet the second assembly of warships suffered from one great weakness: they were a hybrid force, many vessels being on temporary loan from the Far Eastern Fleet; they had enjoyed no opportunity of working up together, and therefore they lacked something in cohesion and *esprit de corps*.

But the most vital difference between the two convoys was in their machinery of command. In March the man in charge of operations, Rear Admiral Vian, had been actually on the spot, sailing with the convoy. But in June the operations were directed by remote control: by Admiral Harwood and Air Marshall Tedder, working together from a combined operations room back in Alexandria. This, in the event, led to a rare muddle. It led also to an inflexibility of command which cramped the style of everybody, from the senior officer of the escort down to the commanding officer of the humblest corvette. For gone now was the freedom of individual action which had been allocated, with such excellent results, to flotilla leaders during the Battle of Sirte. The whole force, including the unfortunate Rear Admiral Vian, had in June to dance to a tune piped from Alexandria. No amount of careful and ingenious planning could outweigh the cumbersome impracticability of such a scheme.

It is interesting to see how the basic plan of the operation came to be adopted.

After the March convoy Admiral Harwood had expressed the opinion that "before another convoy is run, air superiority over the island (of Malta) must be assured." By June this air superiority had been achieved, and Harwood could now reckon that if he got his merchantmen to within a hundred miles of their destination they would be virtually safe. Thus, the final dash to the island, during which so many ships had previously been lost, now caused little anxiety. But the early stages of the convoy route, on the other hand, promised to be unusually hazardous. For in North Africa the Allied position had greatly deteriorated. Here, General Auchinleck had been repeatedly urged by the Prime Minister to launch an all-out attack. But he had delayed, and the delay had proved fatal—for Rommel's reinforcements had built up more quickly than Auchinleck's; it was the German general who struck first; the British were rolled back to the Egyptian border; the desert airstrips were lost; and the Royal Air Force became far too occupied with problems of its own to be able to devote their attention to affording convoy protection. Admiral Harwood, in other words, had to face the unwelcome fact that his vessels would have little if any air cover. For no carrier was available and the R.A.F. had lost its airdromes. From the moment the ships left Alexandria the Germans would be able to shadow and bomb them at will.

And there was another danger, even more potent than the Luftwaffe: the Italian fleet.

Here was the real crux of the problem: what could Admiral Harwood do if the Italian fleet put to sea to intercept the convoy? In March, weather conditions and darkness had helped Vian and his destroyers to ward the Italians off. But—rightly or wrongly—it was not considered possible for a similar success to be achieved in midsummer. The answer *ought* to have been simple. A single armor-decked carrier, with an effective striking force of modern planes, would have solved every difficulty. But no such carrier was available. It is a sad reflection on those responsible for prewar naval planning that Admiral Harwood was now obliged to turn to another service for help; was forced to go cap in hand to Air Marshal Sir Arthur Tedder and ask if the Royal Air Force—notwithstanding its other commitments—could protect the convoy from the Italian fleet.

Tedder was not the man to refuse a colleague help—no matter at how inopportune a moment, from his own point of view, the request came. And thus the basic plan for Operation "Vigorous" was born: the plan whereby the convoy

would defend itself against air attack, but would rely on the
R.A.F. to ward off the Italian fleet. And from this arrangement sprang the twin evils of inflexibility and remote control.
For it was obviously essential for a single brain to co-ordinate
the movements of the convoy and the sorties of the R.A.F.
bombers; and such a brain, it was decided, could best operate
from R.A.F. headquarters in Cairo.

Once the basic plan of co-operation between the two
services had been agreed upon, Harwood and Tedder got
down to details. They soon ran into difficulties; for the R.A.F.
had a host of other obligations to fulfill, and few of the
available bomber crews had been trained for antishipping
work. It was found in the end that rather fewer than forty
planes could be spared to take part in the operation, some
fifteen to eighteen from Malta and some twenty-one from
Egypt: a pitiable slender force with which to try and halt a
modern battle fleet. However, the Egyptian force included
nine Liberator bombers, equipped with the latest top-secret
bomb-aiming apparatus, and the experts were confident that
these planes—together with the few available Wellingtons
and Beauforts—would be enough to cripple the Italians and
prevent their closing with the convoy.

The main outline of "Vigorous" having been agreed upon,
Harwood and Tedder proceeded to indulge in a wealth of
ingenious subterfuge. The old target ship *Centurion,* for
example, was hauled out of her retirement, coaxed from
Bombay to Suez, and positioned in the convoy center to
masquerade as a capital ship and draw the enemy's fire. All
the merchantmen were loaded with great secrecy and at
small isolated ports. A feint convoy was scheduled to sail
thirty-six hours early in an attempt to draw the Italians
prematurely to sea. A number of Commando raids were
planned on Luftwaffe airdromes; and all available submarines
were ordered to form a surfaced screen between the convoy
and the expected line of advance of the Italian fleet.

Having made these arrangements, Harwood and Tedder
retired to their special room in the headquarters of the Naval
Co-operation Group, Royal Air Force, Alexandria. Here they
settled down to wait. They had made their plans and there
was nothing more they could do.

The feint convoy sailed from Alexandria on the evening of
June 11. It consisted of four merchantmen, escorted by the

cruiser *Coventry* and eight destroyers; and for the first night its passage was uneventful. Next morning the ships were about to reverse course to join the main convoy when the Junkers found them. There were fifteen Junkers. They near-missed a destroyer and the largest of the merchantmen, the *City of Calcutta*, so shaking the latter's engines that she had to drop out of convoy and proceed independently to Tobruk. The loss of a merchantman before the convoy proper had even sailed was serious; but far more serious was the fact that information as to what was happening only filtered back to headquarters in a slow and unreliable trickle. Thus, from the moment "Vigorous" got under way Harwood and Tedder found themselves bedeviled by lack of news, and it soon became impossible for them to obtain an accurate up-to-date picture of what was happening. But by the time it was realized that communications were proving inadequate, the main convoy had sailed. And it was too late to call it back.

The main convoy, consisting of seven merchantmen, seven cruisers, and eighteen destroyers (plus the various corvettes, rescue ships, mine sweepers, and torpedo boats), sailed at noon on June 12. Their start was not auspicious. For within a couple of hours of sailing one of the merchantmen, the *Elizabeth Bakke*, began to drop astern. She turned out to be too foul to maintain the convoy speed of thirteen knots and was therefore detached and escorted back to Alexandria.

A few hours later the convoy was further depleted. Two corvettes, the *Erica* and *Primula*, developed engine trouble and were sent limping back; while the merchantman *Aagterkirk* suffered the fate of the *Elizabeth Bakke;* proving too slow, she was ordered to return to port. But by this time the Germans had got to know that a convoy was at sea; their bombers found the *Aagterkirk* some dozen miles from Tobruk. Forty Stukas came screaming out of the sun and the *Aagterkirk* vanished in a smother and flurry of bombs.

Nor was this an end to the convoy's troubles. For on the second day out the sea started to rise, whipped up by a hot blustering wind. In the heavy swell the motor launches suffered extensive damage—one was so badly battered that she subsequently foundered—and they, too, had to be or-dered back to Alexandria.

Thus, by the end of the second day the convoy had already lost three merchantmen and six warships. And the Narrows—

Curtiss Kittyhawk

and the full weight of the Luftwaffe's bombing—were still to come.

During the night of June 13–14 enemy aircraft, shadowing the convoy, were continually overhead. Throughout the six hours of darkness flares fell in a near-continuous stream, throwing the silhouettes of the warships and merchantmen into garish relief. The flares did no harm, but, as Admiral Vian remarked, "they gave one a very naked feeling." The weather that night remained fine but overcast, with an intermittent gale and a heavy southerly swell.

Dawn found the convoy standing into the Narrows.

Throughout June 14 German and Italian aircraft circled the advancing ships. In the morning their attacks were not heavy, largely because two squadrons of Hurricanes and Kittyhawks had been switched at a moment's notice from the Western Desert to the Narrows; and seldom were planes more welcome, for they broke up any number of threatening attacks and shot down or damaged over a dozen bombers. But in the afternoon, as the convoy moved steadily westward, the fighters were forced to operate increasingly close to the limit of their endurance. Soon—because of the loss of the advanced desert airstrips—they were able to spend only a few minutes over the convoy center, and by evening the ships had progressed so far to the west that the fighters were no longer able to help them. And as soon as the Hurricanes and Kittyhawks had disappeared, the German attacks increased in tempo.

Between six o'clock and nine o'clock as many as seven separate waves of bombers came sweeping down on the convoy. Most of the planes were Junkers. They attacked in groups of ten or twelve, approaching the convoy from astern at about 10,000 feet and diving to 3000 feet to release their bombs. Several ships were damaged by near misses; but only one was sunk—the *Bhutan*, a 6000-ton merchantman, bringing up the rear of the port column. She was hit by at least three bombs and sank in twenty minutes. Most of her crew were picked up by the rescue ships *Antwerp* and *Malines*.

Even more serious than the loss of yet another merchantman was the warships' vast (and unprecedented) expenditure of ammunition. For more than twelve hours now the gun crews of the destroyers had been continually in action; they had become dazed and exhausted in the sweltering heat, deafened by the crescendo of noise, jarred by the blast and recoil of pom-poms and oerlikons; in several warships it was found, by that evening, that over 50 per cent of the ammunition had been expended in the single day. And even after sunset the gun crews had little rest; for, as day gave way to night, so the Junkers and Savoias gave way to the equally dangerous E-boats.

The E-boats closed in as soon as it was dark. But Admiral Vian was ready for them, assuming a prearranged night disposition which, as he remarked, "proved a very unattractive proposition." This disposition consisted of a tight-packed core of merchantmen; an advanced anti-U-boat screen ahead and on either bow; a special night screen of two cruisers and four destroyers on either quarter; and a solitary destroyer five miles out on either quarter and bow. And throughout the first part of the night this formation kept the E-boats at bay. Shadowing aircraft droned high overhead, continually illuminating the merchantmen with flares; and the sound of the E-boats' engines as they circled the convoy throbbed throughout the night. But always they were driven back; not once did they penetrate sufficiently close to launch an effective attack. Not until the early hours of June 15 did they have even a taste of success. Then, suddenly and unexpectedly, the convoy played right into their hands.

For at a few minutes to 2 A.M. Admiral Vian's night disposition was thrown into chaos. An emergency signal was received from Admiral Harwood that the Italian fleet was at sea: was racing to intercept the convoy. "Turn back," the admiral ordered, "along the same track."

It was the start of a series of marches and countermarches which sealed the fate of Operation "Vigorous."

The immediate effect was bad enough. In the inevitable confusion of turning some forty ships on their axis in the darkest hour of the night and in the middle of a pack of E-boats, two vessels were lost: the cruiser *Newcastle* was torpedoed in the bow and obliged to reduce speed, and the destroyer *Hasty* was torpedoed amidships and became a total loss. But the long-term effect was even more disastrous. For the reversal of course entailed the burning of yet more oil fuel and the expenditure of yet more ammunition. And by dawn on June 15 both fuel and ammunition were running dangerously short.

That morning, in gradually paling light, the convoy retraced its steps, back into the Narrows between Cyrenaica and Crete, back into "Bomb Alley." And the ships' companies waited anxiously for the signal to say that the R.A.F. had halted the Italian fleet, and that they could, once again, set course for Malta.

The Italian fleet had been sighted at seven o'clock on the evening of June 14. It had been sighted by a reconnaissance plane from Malta, and the pilot's "enemy report" was concise and accurate: "Two battleships, four cruisers, eight destroyers leaving Gulf of Taranto. Course 160°. Speed 20 knots." This report was confirmed an hour later by another Malta aircraft, which photographed the naval base at Taranto and discovered that two *Littorio*-class battleships, four cruisers, and some ten destroyers had put to sea. But—and this brings us to the chief reason for the failure of Operation "Vigorous"—it was five hours before Admiral Harwood received the first sighting report and seven hours before he received the second confirmatory report. Nor, in the case of Operation "Vigorous," was this delay the exception; it was the rule. And throughout the early hours of June 15 Harwood and Tedder were fatally hamstrung by their lack of up-to-the-moment information.

However, as soon as they realized the Italian fleet was at sea they ordered the various R.A.F. striking forces into the air.

First away were the Wellingtons from Malta. And this earliest sortie was a pointer to how little the Air Force appreciated the magnitude of the task they had taken on. For the sortie consisted of four obsolescent Wellingtons, armed with a couple of torpedoes apiece: a pathetically unrealistic force to throw against a modern fleet.

The courage and skill of the Wellington crews were beyond question; but the result of their attack was a foregone conclusion, and the story of it is soon told.

They sighted the Italians at 3:40. The warships turned stern on to the aircrafts' flares and made smoke. The Wellingtons became so confused that only one out of the four even dropped its torpedoes, and they ran wide by a couple of hundred yards. By four o'clock the Wellingtons were heading disconsolately back for Malta; and the Italian fleet, undamaged, was standing steadily on.

Next to attack were the Beauforts. They left Malta at 4 A.M. and for the first part of their flight enjoyed the cover of darkness. They sighted the Italian fleet at dawn and attacked at once in the pale deceptive light. Three aircraft concentrated on a pair of heavy cruisers stationed on the bow of the main formation, and one of these—the *Trento*—was hit and driven out of line. The other nine aircraft concentrated on the battleships. Their attacks were pressed home with great courage, several aircraft flying flush over the warships' decks after dropping their torpedoes from as close as two hundred yards. They claimed two hits on each of the *Littorios*. But, in fact, they hit neither. By 5:30 the Beauforts were heading back for Malta. Their crews were jubilant. But, in fact, their only achievement was to slow down the *Trento*. The rest of the Italian fleet continued south, cutting across the path of the convoy.

Next to arrive on the scene were the Liberators. By an extremely skillful piece of navigation they reached the Italian fleet exactly on E.T.A. after a flight of five and a half hours and were able to synchronize their attacks with those of the Libyan Beauforts. There were eight Liberators, and they approached the fleet from the bow, coming in at 14,000 feet out of a rising sun. They concentrated their attack on the two battleships and the undamaged eight-inch cruiser. Their bombing was accurate, and the three warships at which they aimed disappeared in a flurry of bursting bombs. The Liberator crews—unbelievable as it sounds—claimed to have made twenty-three hits. In fact, they made one: a single bomb, which burst on the *Littorio's* "A" turret, killed one man and did no damage whatsoever except for shaking the *Littorio's* seaplane off its launching platform. The rest of the "hits" were near misses, which merely deluged the battleships in harmless columns of spray. The Italian fleet held course.

Last to attack was a squadron of Beauforts from an airstrip close to the Libyan border. Twelve planes took off a little after sunrise; but only five reached the Italian fleet, for the squadron was intercepted en route by a group of Messerschmitts. The surviving Beauforts, however, attacked most gallantly, head on. Two were heavily damaged, but all managed to drop their torpedoes from close range. None hit: though the Liberator crews, watching from high above, optimistically reported damage to a cruiser and a heavy destroyer.

So ended the last of the air attacks. The R.A.F. had done its best; but its best was nothing like good enough; for the sum total of all their efforts had been to disable one cruiser. In the words of the official Naval Battle Summary, "All the gallantry of these airmen, all the skilful leading that enabled the little striking forces to find their targets, had not availed; the Italian fleet stood on."

The failure of the R.A.F. attacks, however, was not known at the time to Harwood and Tedder; and at dawn, feeling that the perils of a return to Bomb Alley were more to be feared than the perils of encountering the remnants of the Italian fleet (which they felt sure would be at least substantially damaged), they decided to reverse the course of the convoy and again head it for Malta.

Thus, at seven o'clock Vian was ordered to turn once more to the west-northwest. And so he reversed course and stood, in blissful ignorance, straight for the still-advancing Italian fleet.

Harwood and Tedder then waited, impatiently but optimistically, for news of the R.A.F. attacks. But the hours passed and no news came.

Then, at 8:30 A.M., a most unwelcome signal was picked up at R.A.F. headquarters: a signal from a reconnaissance seaplane which reported that two Italian battleships, three cruisers, and nine destroyers were still heading straight for the convoy, were within 150 miles of the merchantmen. Believing the R.A.F. attacks to have failed entirely, Harwood ordered Vian to retire at full speed to the east; and once again the unfortunate convoy reversed its course.

A couple of hours later, however, Harwood and Tedder received the reports from the Malta Beauforts. These reports, which claimed two hits on each battleship, were untimed; but, not unnaturally, Harwood presumed them to be subsequent to the seaplane's reconnaissance report which he had received at 8:30. He therefore ordered the convoy back to the west-northwest.

This order, Vian received at 1:45 P.M. It was the fourth signal ordering him to reverse course that he had received within twelve hours; and it reached him at a bad moment, in the middle of a heavy air attack in which one of his key ships—the *Birmingham*—had just been disabled. Like Nelson, he turned a blind eye to his C. in C's. signal and continued to withdraw to the east.

Naval officers are not encouraged to disobey orders, especially orders to close with the enemy; and Vian's decision to hold his course was one of considerable moral courage as well as one of correct judgment. For had he again headed for Malta he would have run straight into the Italian fleet, and his whole force would certainly have been annihilated.

Harwood and Tedder, meanwhile, were receiving a spate of contradictory (and often untimed) signals: signals from the Liberators claiming twenty-three hits, and signals from reconnaissance planes reporting that the Italians were undamaged and were sweeping down on the convoy. They were in the impossible position of having to direct an operation in which they no longer knew what was happening. At noon Admiral Harwood did the only possible thing: he sent Vian a discretionary signal—"I must leave it to you whether to comply with my earlier signal, or whether to again retire. . . ."

For Harwood and Tedder, this signal was an admission of

defeat, an admission that they were no longer in command of the situation. For Vian, it was the final confirmation of what he had long suspected: that the whole basis of the operation, the co-operation between the R.A.F. sorties and the convoy's movements, had broken down; from now on, he realized, he was on his own.

There was only one thing he could do. Retire. And quickly, before the Italian fleet overhauled his convoy.

So all that afternoon the vessels stood to the east under a clear sky: a sky which was never empty of enemy bombers. For now, once again, they were in Bomb Alley, in the dangerous waters between Cyrenaica and Crete; and the German bombers were out in force.

They attacked in groups of between twenty and thirty, splitting up on the fringe of the convoy and diving in threes onto individual ships. They co-ordinated their attacks with a skill and precision which the R.A.F. had never managed to achieve; and in spite of heavy and concentrated ack-ack several planes broke through the barrage. The *Birmingham* had two of her turrets knocked out of action. The *Airedale* was smothered in hits and near misses and had to be sunk. The *Centurion* was hit repeatedly. The *Arethusa* was damaged, and the *Nestor* was so badly holed that she had to be scuttled.

At 6:42 P.M., at the height of these attacks, Vian received yet another signal from his C. in C. The Italian fleet, it seemed, had at last given up the chase, had hauled around to the northwest, and was heading back for Taranto. "Now," Admiral Harwood signaled optimistically, "is the golden opportunity to get convoy to Malta. Have Hunts, *Coventry*, mine sweepers, and corvettes enough fuel and ammunition for one-way trip? If so, I would like to turn convoy now...."

To Admiral Vian, harassed and battered by constant assault from the air, the prospect was anything but golden, the demand for yet another reversal of course anything but opportune. He checked his reserves of ammunition and found that the majority of his destroyers had little more than 20 per cent left. He therefore told the C. in C. that he considered his ammunition "insufficient for the passage to Malta"; and at sunset that evening Harwood gave the sad but inevitable order: "Return to Alexandria with your whole force."

Operation "Vigorous" had reached its inglorious end. Of the fifty-seven ships which had set out, with such high hopes, for Malta, not one had reached its destination.

Post-mortems are not often profitable; but in the case of Operation "Vigorous" several useful lessons can be learned from an analysis of the causes of failure.

The first lesson is that effective liaison between two services cannot be achieved without the most detailed and meticulous preoperational planning—planning on a far more intensive scale than was attempted for Operation "Vigorous." The second lesson is that the man in charge of an operation ought to be actually on the spot and not directing affairs from a distance of several hundred miles. The history of war is littered with disasters which can be attributed to the evils of the system of remote control—to give an example adjacent to "Vigorous" in both time and place, General Auchinleck's debacle in the Libyan Desert.

It is interesting to note that the vast interservice projects later set in motion in the Mediterranean were planned with meticulous attention to detail; while the system of remote control was never used again in a convoy to Malta. So although Operation "Vigorous" was a failure—and a failure which came near to losing us Malta—at least its lessons were well learned and its mistakes were never repeated.

Meanwhile, the Gibraltar convoy, given the name Operation "Harpoon," had left the Clyde on the night of June 5 and entered the Mediterranean a week later. It consisted of six merchantmen; one ancient battleship (H.M.S. *Malaya*); two obsolescent carriers (H.M.S. *Argus* and *Eagle*); four cruisers; seventeen destroyers; and four mine sweepers—the latter being specially provided to sweep ahead of the convoy as it entered the approaches to Grand Harbour. The unenviable task of fighting through with this patchwork and pitiably weak armada was given to Vice-Admiral Curteis. His problems were not made easier by the fact that very little air help could be expected from Malta, for the island's major effort was to be directed at helping the convoy from the east.

As usual, the ships passed through the Strait in darkness, and their first day in the Mediterranean, June 12, passed uneventfully.

Next morning the destroyers were due to start refueling from the *Brown Ranger*; but the oiler had hove to several miles short of her rendezvous, and fueling didn't commence until late in the afternoon. And while the destroyers were spaced out, searching for the oiler, they were spotted by Italian shadowers, who, in the evening, followed them back to the convoy. All that night the shadowing Cants circled Admiral Curteis' ships. There was nothing he could do to shake them off; and tomorrow, he knew, they would home the bombers onto them.

August 14 dawned bright and clear: no clouds and very little wind. And what wind there was came from astern, making it difficult for the carriers to operate their planes—especially the ancient *Argus*, who, having hauled around into wind for flying off, had barely sufficient speed to rejoin the convoy!

By nine o'clock the shadowers had been driven off; but the bombers would soon be coming. Admiral Curteis ordered the convoy into the open and somewhat novel cruising disposition. The carriers, each with its attendant escort, he ordered out to the port wing to form a flexible string for free flying. The two columns of merchantmen, each led by a cruiser, he positioned in the convoy center. The destroyers, he arranged in a circle around the merchantmen at a distance of three and a half miles. The *Malaya* and the four mine sweepers, he put in the rear, to afford a good volume of fire for rescue operations, should they be needed. "This disposition," Admiral Curteis later wrote, "proved very satisfactory, as all ships fired both outwards and inwards with a freedom which would have been impossible in a closer (more orthodox) screen."

Certainly for the whole of June 14 the convoy stood up to the bombing remarkably well. In the first attack, which started at ten-thirty, no damage was suffered, and two C.R.42s were shot down. In the second and heaviest attack, a little before midday, a cruiser and a merchantman were disabled; but thirteen bombers were shot down, six by fighters and seven by ack-ack. While in the evening attack, from Sicilian bases, no damage was sustained and a further three torpedo bombers were destroyed. Admiral Curteis had reason to be more than satisfied with the day's events. His novel cruising disposition and his small but highly skilled force of fighters had taken heavy toll of the enemy and had kept them effectively at bay.

At nine o'clock that evening they came to the Skerki Channel. Here, according to plan, Admiral Curteis with his heavy units hauled around to the westward, leaving only the light units under Captain Hardy to cover the final two hundred and fifty miles.

And never before had such a slender force attempted to penetrate the Narrows. For Captain Hardy, as he stood that evening into the Skerki Channel had, to guard his merchantmen, only a single AA cruiser and nine not very modern destroyers. Given good fortune, they might, it seemed to Captain Hardy, beat off U-boats and planes; but if the Italian fleet put to sea their fate would almost certainly be sealed.

The five merchantmen formed into line ahead and, screened by the warships, stood boldly into the Narrows.

As they passed along the Tunisian shore they were silhouetted sharply in the glare of the setting sun; and a few minutes later, in the brief Mediterranean twilight, the half-expected attack began to develop. There were nine bombers: Junkers 88s: and, their engines cut, they came drifting out of the evening haze. They met with a warm reception. Two were shot down; all their bombs fell wide; and soon it was quite dark. Undisturbed, the ships moved quietly on through the Narrows.

But a little before midnight disturbing reports began to filter through to Captain Hardy: reports that the Italian battle fleet was putting to sea.

For the last forty-eight hours reconnaissance aircraft from Malta had been keeping a close watch on the Italian naval bases of Naples, Taranto, and Cagliari. On the evening of June 13 large concentrations of warships had been spotted in the Gulf of Taranto, and it was known that from here a powerful battle fleet was putting to sea to intercept the convoy from Alexandria. At first it seemed that no warships were assembling to oppose the Gibraltar convoy. But then, on the night of June 14, a report reached Captain Hardy of two Italian cruisers and five destroyers standing out of Palermo. Unfortunately their course and speed on leaving harbor was not reported, so he had no means of judging whether they were a lone force intending to intercept his convoy or reinforcements intending to join the Italian battle fleet in the east. He could only hold course and hope for the best.

The same dilemma was perplexing Admiral Curteis, who was now withdrawing toward Sardinia. He also had received the report from Palermo. He wondered whether he ought to send reinforcements to Captain Hardy, who, he knew, had too slender an escort to cope with an attack by enemy cruisers. In the end he decided not to. One of his key ships, the *Liverpool,* had already been damaged, and he was anxious to keep the rest of his force to screen the highly vulnerable *Argus* and *Eagle.* This decision—whether or not to send reinforcements—was, as the admiral himself admitted, "a gamble either way." It so happened that the gamble didn't pay off; that Admiral Curteis' force remained unmolested, while the Italian cruisers, all that night, headed straight for Captain Hardy.

By dawn they were less than twenty-five miles from the convoy.

A few minutes after six o'clock on the morning of June 15 a solitary Beaufighter, on its way from Malta to provide the convoy with air cover, spotted the Italian fleet in the pale half light of dawn: two six-inch cruisers and five destroyers, heading south-southeast at top speed. They were then less than twenty miles from the convoy and were closing fast; and they were, by extremely skillful navigation, interposing themselves exactly between the merchantmen and their goal.

Captain Hardy had only just received the Beaufighter's warning signal when the Italians came in sight: seven warships, hull down, outlined against the brightening sky to the east. Hardy recognized the enemy as cruisers and knew that he was heavily outgunned. There was, it seemed to him, only one chance of saving the convoy. He ordered his five "fleet" destroyers to close with the enemy, and at the same time he turned the merchantmen back to the southwest under cover of smoke; his immediate intention being, as he put it, "to gain time by fighting a delaying action, in the hope that an air striking force from Malta might be sent to our aid."

At 6:40 the Italians opened fire at a range of 20,000 yards—far outside the range of Hardy's destroyers. Their shooting was unpleasantly accurate, their second salvo straddling the *Cairo* and their third and fourth falling among the merchantmen. Then the smoke screen started to take effect, the destroyer attack forced the Italians to shift their fire, and

Bristol Beaufighter

the merchantmen—for the moment, made good their escape, scurrying behind the rolling banks of smoke toward the Tunisian shore.

But in saving the merchantmen the destroyers suffered heavily.

There were five destroyers in the attacking force—*Bedouin, Partridge, Ithuriel, Marne,* and *Matchless*—and they headed straight for the Italians. Their attack, however, was delivered with more *élan* than discretion; for, instead of closing with the enemy cruisers in line abreast (thus presenting a number of targets calling for simultaneous engagement), they became strung out over a distance of nearly a mile in loose line astern (thus presenting a series of targets which could be engaged one by one). The leading ships, *Bedouin* and *Partridge*, soon came under heavy and very accurate fire; before they could bring their guns to bear, both were hit, the *Bedouin* amidships, the *Partridge* flush on her stern. Both lost way, and the fight passed them by. The three remaining destroyers—*Ithuriel,*

Matchless, and *Marne*—met with better fortune. The *Ithuriel*, holding her fire with admirable restraint, was at last able to engage one of the cruisers, the *Raimondo Montecuccoli*, with good effect; at a range of 8000 yards she hit her twice, forcing her to turn away. The *Marne* and *Matchless* meanwhile turned their attention to the enemy destroyers; they hit one and drove the others off.

In spite of the crippling of *Bedouin* and *Partridge*, the opening phase of the action had been not unsuccessful. But there now came two most unwelcome developments. First, a sudden shift in the wind exposed the *Cairo* behind her smoke screen, and the Italian cruisers were quick to spot her. They divided their fire, using two turrets apiece on the destroyers, and two on the *Cairo*. At 7:10 they hit her amidships. At the same time the five merchantmen, deprived of the bulk of their escort, were heavily attacked by a squadron of German dive bombers. One, the *Chant*, was sunk; and another, the *Kentucky*, was disabled.

Faced with a combined assault by air and sea, Captain Hardy did the only possible thing. He concentrated his forces. The *Ithuriel*, *Marne*, and *Matchless* were recalled; and soon the entire force was retreating northeast, followed at a respectful distance by the Italian cruisers. As soon as his ships were together, Captain Hardy made several minor alterations of course; then for the second time he made smoke, and once again the dark billowing clouds went swirling across the convoy's wake. This seemed to disconcert the Italians, who obviously feared a torpedo attack if they approached the smoke too closely. At first they swung away to the southwest, trying to work their way to windward; then, a little after eight-thirty, they hauled right around to the northeast and stood away from the convoy. For a while Captain Hardy kept them in sight, shadowing them with the *Cairo* and his remaining "fleet" destroyers; then, when it was clear that they had for the time being given up, he returned to the merchantmen.

By ten o'clock the convoy was again in formation and heading for Malta. They had to leave behind them the disabled *Bedouin* and *Partridge*. They had lost one merchantman—the *Chant;* and another—the *Kentucky*—was damaged and in tow. But they had driven the Italians away; Malta was only 150 miles to the west; and it must have seemed to

Captain Hardy as if the worst was over, especially as Malta's long-range Spitfires were now providing sporadic but very welcome air cover.

The Spitfires, however, were operating at extreme range. They couldn't stay over the convoy for long; and often there was a few minutes' gap between the departure of one formation and the arrival of the next. In one such gap the Junkers struck.

There were ten aircraft. In the few minutes that the convoy lay unprotected, they delivered a carefully co-ordinated attack; and yet another merchantman, the 6000-ton *Burdwan*, was disabled.

Captain Hardy now made a brave decision. Two of his merchantmen had been sunk and two disabled; two of his largest destroyers had been crippled; his flagship had been hit three times; and several other vessels had suffered minor damage; to enable the casualties to keep station, the whole convoy had had to reduce speed to five and a half knots. Captain Hardy decided to cut his losses, to sacrifice the disabled vessels, and to concentrate all his efforts on saving the two undamaged merchantmen. It was a cruel decision to have to make. The idea of leaving behind the helpless destroyers was especially invidious; but without doubt it was a decision that was entirely justified; a decision which, as it turned out, was to save Malta.

At noon the crippled *Burdwan* and *Kentucky* were torpedoed (their crews being taken off by the *Badsworth* and *Hebe*); the *Bedouin* and *Partridge* were left to their own devices; and the rest of the convoy, at top speed, started its final dash for the island. Soon they came within radius of the short-range Spitfires; and a final dive-bombing attack, which developed at one-fifteen, met with a warm reception, three Junkers being destroyed without damage to the convoy. By two o'clock the vessels were within ninety miles of Malta, being watched over by relays of patrolling fighters, and the danger from the air had passed.

The danger from the sea, however, still remained; and early in the afternoon the enemy cruisers put in another appearance. They had learned from the Junkers that several of the convoy were disabled and straggling; that easy pickings were theirs for the taking. They came closing in for the kill.

Their first victims were the derelict merchantmen. Then they turned their attention to the *Bedouin* and *Partridge*.

The two destroyers had been struggling for hours to effect repairs and get under way. Eventually the *Partridge* was able to get up steam and move slowly off; but the *Bedouin* lay helpless, completely disabled. At ten o'clock the *Partridge* prepared to take her in tow, and by noon the two vessels were under way, limping slowly east in the wake of the convoy. But the Junkers spotted them, they called up the Italian fleet, and soon the two six-inch cruisers again came in sight. There followed a battle as brave as it was one-sided.

As soon as she saw the cruisers, *Partridge* slipped her tow, laid smoke around the *Bedouin*, and stood toward the enemy, attempting to draw their fire. She succeeded all too well. For nearly an hour she lay under heavy and accurate bombardment from the Italians' six-inch salvos; she was also attacked from the air, and eventually two near misses jammed her rudder hard to port. Soon she could move only very slowly in tight erratic circles. From where she lay disabled she could see the Italians finishing off the *Bedouin*. A series of torpedo bombers dived on the crippled ship; for a while her gunfire kept them at bay; but at last she was hit. She sank in eight minutes, her last gesture of defiance being to shoot down her assailant. *Partridge* watched the Italians picking up her crew. It seemed inevitable that it would be their turn next. But suddenly, to their amazement, the cruisers hauled around and started to retire at high speed.

It was a striking force of Malta's Albacores which had, at the last minute, reprieved the *Partridge*. As the Italians, attacked by the torpedo planes, withdrew to the north, so the damaged destroyer again got under way. Unmolested, she limped south, making for the Tunisian shallows. That night, under shelter of land, she made good her various defects, and early next morning set course for Gibraltar. Two days later she arrived at the Rock: battered but—miraculously—still afloat.

The convoy meanwhile had been making good progress; all that afternoon they headed steadily east. Dive bombers and torpedo bombers were still about; but the patrolling Spitfires kept them at bay and blunted the edge of every attempted attack. Not until the evening, when the convoy was within sight of land, did the bombers succeed in breaking through. Then, at seven o'clock, a last desperate assault by twelve Stukas resulted in several near misses but no serious damage. As soon as this attack had been beaten off, the convoy prepared to enter the swept channel.

Only one danger now remained: mines. For the last two months the Germans had been industriously mining the approaches to Grand Harbour; all the island's mine sweepers had been put out of commission in the heavy raids of April and May, and the sea lanes approaching Grand Harbour were now thickly sewn. This state of affairs had been anticipated; and it was hoped that the mine sweepers which had sailed with the convoy would sweep ahead of the merchantmen as they entered harbor, while the rest of the warships returned to Gibraltar. This plan, however, had to be modified; for the *Cairo* and the destroyers, in two days' heavy fighting, had exhausted both ammunition and fuel, so that they, too, needed to enter harbor. There followed one of those tragedies which are so liable to occur when an operational plan has to be changed on the spur of the moment. For, owing to a misunderstood signal, the destroyers stood into the channel ahead of the mine sweepers. Within sight of Grand Harbour, two of them, the *Kujawiak* and the *Badsworth*, were mined. In the confusion that followed, with the vessels trying to regain their proper order, a merchantman and a sweeper strayed into a mine field; and soon four ships were lying disabled within sight of Grand Harbour. Luckily three of them managed to struggle into the dockyard, but the Polish destroyer *Kujawiak* was lost. It was an unhappy end to an otherwise successful operation.

For, although two merchantmen out of six may not appear, at first sight, a very favorable proportion to have been fought through, the difficulties that the convoy had to face were such that for any vessels at all to have reached Grand Harbour was a major achievement. And, as good fortune would have it, the two merchantmen that survived—the *Troilus* and *Orari*—were unusually large and heavily loaded. Within a few hours of berthing they had discharged 20,000 tons of vitally needed supplies, including the flour and ack-ack ammunition on which the fate of the island depended. In view of the complete failure of the convoy from Alexandria, the arrival of these two merchantmen assumed a massive significance. For it was their cargo which tipped the scales that hung so precariously between survival and defeat; with the help of what they had brought, Malta was able to tighten her belt and survive until another and larger convoy could be fought through; but if the *Troilus* and *Orari* had been sunk, Malta would almost certainly have fallen. That is the measure of the achievement of the men who sailed under Admiral Curteis and Captain Hardy.

16

Rorqual to Alexandria for special duty.
> —ADMIRALTY SIGNAL

Operations "Harpoon" and "Vigorous" cost the Royal and Merchant Navies eleven ships sunk and eleven damaged; they cost the Royal Air Force upward of forty planes; and they achieved only partial success. Malta was still desperately short of food, ammunition, and all types of fuel.

The food situation was the worst. Rations, already down to starvation level, suffered a further cut in early July; and how close the island was to starvation can be seen from the following table.

Weekly rations for July 1942
per person per week

BREAD	73½ ozs.	EDIBLE OIL	Nil
SUGAR	Nil	TOMATOES	3 lbs.
RICE	Nil	POTATOES	1½ lbs.
FLOUR	Nil	LAUNDRY SOAP	¼ lb.
FATS	3½ ozs.	TOILET SOAP	Nil
CHEESE	1¾ ozs.	MATCHES	1 box
TEA	Nil	JAM	Nil
COFFEE	1¾ ozs.	MEAT	Nil
MILK	Nil	KEROSENE	⅜ gal.
GOAT'S MILK	3 pints		

No people could exist for long on such a diet as this. And as soon as the results of the June operations were known, plans were immediately drawn up for another and larger convoy, to sail this time from Gibraltar. It would, however, inevitably be well over a month before the ships could even assemble; and in the meanwhile Malta had—somehow—to be kept going. The *Welshman* made an emergency run to the island with a cargo of general stores; a number of small blockade runners sailed independently from Gibraltar and Alexandria; and the submarine *Clyde* ran no fewer than six storing trips.

The idea of using submarines as store carriers was not new. The French Navy indeed had designed the gargantuan *Surcouf* expressly for such a purpose; and as early as 1941 a number of British submarines had been used to carry provisions to Malta.

These early trips, with their experiments, improvising, and teething troubles, were in a way more interesting than the later runs, when things went smoothly almost as a matter of course. And certainly the *Clyde* could never, during the summer of 1942, have carried so much, so safely, so many times, if it hadn't been for the early experimental runs made by submarines like the *Rorqual* and *Cachalot*.

Rorqual and *Cachalot* were originally built for mine laying. They were big for submarines: over 1500 tons and over 270 feet in length. Their normal complement was fifty-five; they carried a single four-inch gun and six torpedo tubes; their top speed was fifteen knots, and they had, of course, when empty of mines, a wealth of storage space in their long external mine casings. They needed, in fact, only a small amount of conversion to become store carriers capable of carrying up to 200 tons of supplies. The Admiralty was quick to see their possibilities.

Early in May 1941 *Rorqual* was taken off her petrol run "for special duty." Her commanding officer, Lieutenant Napier, brought her to Alexandria; and for three weeks she lay in the sun-drenched harbor while dockyard workmen swarmed through her labyrinthine passageways, stripping her bare of batteries, torpedo tubes, and every item of nonessential equipment. Then, on June 3, she started to load.

Her cargo reflected Malta's most pressing needs. Apart from two officers and twenty-one other ranks, she carried:

2	coils of wire
2	tons of medical stores
147	bags of mail
45	tons of kerosene

    15   tons of 100-octane spirit (in bulk)
  1478   cases of 100-octane spirit.

It took Lieutenant Napier the better part of forty-eight hours to load these stores, the limiting factor invariably being space rather than weight. The 100-octane spirit proved especially difficult. It arrived at the ship in lightweight 4½-gallon tins, hermetically sealed. These tins were fitted, two at a time, into small wooden crates; the crates, which had been specially designed to run exactly over the mine rails, were then lashed externally to the submarine's casings. It was hard, laborious work, calling for much time, patience, strength, and rope; and it was only finished a couple of hours before the ship was due to sail.

She left Alexandria on June 5, a little after sunrise; and for the whole of her passage to Malta the weather was mercifully fine. This was lucky. For even with a sea as calm as the proverbial millpond, her cargo shifted uneasily; and whenever she dived the stench of petrol vapor all but suffocated her crew. She therefore made practically the whole voyage at periscope depth.

For the first few days her progress was uneventful. Then, early on June 9, her lookout spotted a Ju 52 and a single Messerschmitt 109 heading south for Cyrenaica. *Rorqual* dived. Lieutenant Napier took her down to seventy feet. For an hour he waited anxiously, while in the overcrowded quarters his passengers and crew became hotter, shorter of air, and increasingly sickened by the nauseating reek of 100-octane fuel. Then he surfaced. Cautiously. And he found that the planes had gone.

Two days later *Rorqual* nosed into Grand Harbour.

Her cargo was difficult to unload, for seven of the crates had shifted, and water absorption had caused the wood to swell. Nevertheless, she managed to achieve a quick turnover, discharging and reloading within forty-eight hours. She left Malta early on June 15, and five days later was back in Alexandria.

Almost at once she started to load again. Only this time, acting on Lieutenant Napier's recommendation, the 100-octane spirit was stowed somewhat differently. In place of the small wooden crates, holding only a couple of tins apiece, the dockyard carpenters were told to provide large wooden "tanks"—3 feet 6 inches wide, 14 feet 9 inches long, and high enough to fit exactly into the mine casings. Only four of these could be built in the few days before *Rorqual* was due to sail; but four was enough to test the effectiveness of Lieutenant Napier's idea.

Loading commenced on June 22; and this time the *Rorqual* carried twenty-one passengers, and

90	bags of mail
2	tons of foamite refills
11	fire hoses
2	"U"-class submarine propellers
2	tons of Army clothing
11,700	gallons of kerosene
14	tons of 100-octane spirit (in tins)
50	tons of 100-octane spirit (in bulk).

She left Alexandria on June 25 and once again enjoyed good weather and a moderately uneventful passage. Indeed, this time what little incident there was arose from mechanical defects rather than the nature of her cargo. For the new method of storing petrol proved an unqualified success. *Rorqual* was able to dive to ninety-five feet, and Lieutenant Napier found he could proceed underwater for several hours at a stretch without undue discomfort from petrol vapor.

On *Rorqual*'s return to Alexandria, toward the end of July, it was agreed that in the future every submarine making the run to Malta should be equipped with tanks for carrying petrol in bulk. This insured quicker loading and unloading, safer transit, and less discomfort for the crew. And it was largely thanks to the pioneer work of the *Rorqual* that a year later the submarine *Clyde* was able to carry some 1200 tons of vitally needed kerosene to Malta within the space of a couple of months.

Another of the pioneering submarines was the *Rorqual*'s sister ship the *Cachalot*. In midsummer she made a difficult and most frustrating voyage to Malta, a voyage which demonstrated not only the complex problems of store carrying but also how little those problems were understood by those who received the stores at Malta.

Cachalot carried a difficult cargo: 10 tons of medical stores,

30 tons of armor-piercing shells, 42 tons of kerosene, and 1380 tins of petrol (stored in the old-fashioned crates). She sailed at noon on June 6, and almost at once her commanding officer, Lieutenant Newton, ran into difficulties. Soon after leaving harbor he went into a shallow dive to test the storing arrangements. He found the submarine difficult to control; she porpoised alarmingly and refused to keep at a steady depth. On surfacing, he found they were leaving a "very considerable" track of oil, a track which would be all too clearly visible from the air. All that afternoon and evening hoses sprayed the *Cachalot*'s keel, and later, working by moonlight, fourteen seamen scrubbed away, hour after hour, at the oil-coated deck plates. By dawn the telltale streak had been considerably reduced. But soon came another difficulty; for, as the wooden storage crates absorbed water, the *Cachalot* became increasingly intractable. Soon Lieutenant Newton was finding it impossible to keep her submerged for more than a few minutes at a time. He tried pumping out, to compensate for the absorption of water; but the *Cachalot* still porpoised dangerously. There was only one thing to do: stay on the surface.

So began the long crawl to Malta at periscope depth, with the *Cachalot* trailing her oil streak, the midsummer sun blazing out of a heat-glazed sky, and a short sea knocking up ugly little cross waves. It was a nightmare voyage, made under conditions of extreme physical discomfort, and discovery and consequent obliteration an ever present threat.

But at last, after seven days, the *Cachalot* limped into Grand Harbour.

When she unloaded, it was found that, of her 1380 tins of petrol, 3 had shifted and become buckled and 10 had leaked and become contaminated with sea water. Nevertheless, to deliver safely 1367 tins out of 1380 must have seemed to Lieutenant Newton a satisfactory enough performance. But certain members of the R.A.F. apparently thought otherwise. An irate wing commander came storming aboard the submarine an hour after she had unloaded. It was not very encouraging for the *Cachalot*'s crew, after their difficult and dangerous voyage, to hear him dismiss their contribution as "a miserable fleabite . . . enough for a bare three days' flying . . . and hardly worth the bringing." The wing commander's parting shot was that, having seen the "filthy" condition of the *Cachalot*, he was having a tin of the petrol flown back to Alexandria for testing—"as it was probably contaminated and no use at all!"

Fortunately the wing commander's views were not shared by many of his service colleagues, or by the people of Malta; and submarines continued to play an important role in reprovisioning the island right up to the autumn of 1942.

During the latter half of 1941, for example, sixteen storing trips were successfully run: three from the United Kingdom, two from Gibraltar, and eleven from Alexandria. The cargoes were usually aviation fuel, with a leavening of mail and medical stores; the average weight per cargo being roughly 160 tons. During the spring of 1942—when Malta's needs were at their most acute—the tempo of these storing trips was stepped up, and by the end of July another twenty runs had been successfully carried out. Once again the usual starting point was Alexandria, and the usual cargo, aviation fuel; but now, thanks to the idea of storing the fuel in bulk, more could be carried, and the average weight for each cargo soon rose to close to 200 tons.

Thus, all in all, British submarines carried to Malta some 65,000 tons of stores. The amount itself was not great; but the supplies in each case could be hand-picked to satisfy the island's most urgent need of the moment. And they always got through. In supplying the island not a single submarine was lost.

Nevertheless, the storing trips were not popular with submariners, to whom each run to Malta meant three weeks of uncomfortable overcrowding; three weeks, too, without hope of making a sinking—for, with the torpedo bays full of medical stores and bags of mail, offensive action was obviously out of the question. The storing trips, in short, were arduous and inglorious, and the men who made them were usually accorded neither laurels nor thanks. Nevertheless, they played a not unimportant part in keeping the island supplied, and the men of *Rorqual*, *Cachalot* and *Porpoise*, *Urge*, *Osiris*, and *Clyde* must all be numbered among those who contributed to Malta's survival.

17

*Many of these fine men and their ships were lost.
But the memory of their conduct will remain an
inspiration to all who were privileged to sail with
them.*

— VICE-ADMIRAL SYFRET

PART I

For the convoys of June 1942 a vast concourse of shipping had
assembled at either end of the Mediterranean; but of the
great armadas—in all, some hundred vessels—which had set
out for Malta with such high hopes, only two merchantmen
had managed to struggle through to Grand Harbour. The
effort had been great and costly; but success had not been
achieved.

Over half the warships taking part in these convoys had
been borrowed, specially for the occasion, from the Home
and Far Eastern Fleets. These warships could not stay in the
Mediterranean. They were too badly needed in their own
commands: the Home Fleet for an important convoy to
Russia, the Far Eastern Fleet to establish their new base at
Kilindini. Thus another attempt to reprovision Malta was, for
the time being, out of the question; the warships simply were
not available.

Yet never before had the island's need been so desperate.
Food was now pitiably scarce—at the end of June the already
meager rations had suffered a further cut; aviation fuel was an
ever present anxiety, while supplies of diesel oil had sunk to
their nadir—in the whole of the island there were, that July,
less than 4000 tons of oil fuel (enough for a single battleship

212

to make the two-way passage to Alexandria). It was calculated
that, unless a substantial convoy could reach Malta by mid-
August, the island would be starved into surrender.

The moment the Home Fleet had fulfilled its obligations in
the Arctic, its warships were therefore again rushed south to
the Mediterranean. And this time they came in force. This
time there were no half measures. A grand-scale operation
was carefully planned: a convoy so vast that, it was hoped, it
would solve, once and for all, the question of the island's
survival.

There followed an epic encounter.

For the August convoy was planned and prepared for on so
vast a scale that secrecy was out of the question; and the
Germans were able to watch the build-up of Allied forces and
make their counterplans accordingly. Thus, while the warships and merchantmen were still assembling, German bomber
squadrons in Sardinia and Sicily were heavily reinforced;
E-boat flotillas were brought to full strength; and U-boats
were given top-secret patrol areas. Germans and Italians, in
short, were as determined to destroy the convoy as the
British were to fight it through. For both knew that on the
outcome of the impending battle hung nothing less than the
fate of Malta: the island which had for so long been a thorn in
the side of the Axis and which Allied strategists had at last
come to recognize as the key to the Middle East.

Allied forces, at this vital moment in the history of British
sea power, were commanded by Vice-Admiral Syfret: an
officer of great resolution and imperturbability who had
considerable firsthand experience of the dangers and difficulties of the passage to Malta. Syfret had at his disposal such an
armada as had not been seen in the Mediterranean since the
days of Lepanto: fourteen merchantmen (big, fast ships,
carrying among them over 120,000 tons of supplies); two
battleships; seven cruisers; twenty-four destroyers; two fleet
oilers; one tug; four mine sweepers; seven motor launches;
and eight submarines. And—most important of all—three
"fleet" aircraft carriers, which carried among them exactly a
hundred planes.

Opposing him was a powerful, well-balanced fleet (which
the Italians failed to use); some four hundred and twenty
bombers, torpedo bombers, and long-range fighters; some

eighty E-boats; and about two dozen submarines—half of them operating in the Western Basin and half in the Narrows.

The combatants were evenly matched.

On August 2, some 3000 sea miles from Malta, Admiral Syfret, on board his flagship *Nelson*, hoisted the signal which set in motion Operation "Pedestal"—the last and greatest of the epic convoys to Malta.

That night the fourteen merchantmen and their powerful escort began to assemble off the Scottish coast. Of the ten-thousand-odd men who sailed that night under Admiral Syfret, not more than a couple of dozen were supposed to know their destination.

Largest of Admiral Syfret's merchantmen was the S.S. *Ohio*.

She was an American-built tanker of 14,150 tons, owned by the Texas Oil Company and now on loan to the Ministry of War Transport, who had placed her under the management of the Eagle Oil and Shipping Company. Tankers, in general, are sturdily built and often have a beauty of line that is lacking in more prosaic cargo vessels. The *Ohio* was no exception. She was a very modern vessel, having been built in 1940; and her design embodied both strength and grace in generous proportions. Her all-British crew of fifty-three had been hand-picked; so had her master, Captain D.W. Mason, a quiet, soft-spoken man of thirty-nine. They had been hand-picked because the *Ohio* was the most vital and vulnerable ship in a peculiarly vital and vulnerable convoy. She was vital because in her holds was the oil fuel on which, above all else, the fate of Malta depended. She was vulnerable because a single hit could turn her, all too easily, in a matter of seconds, into a blazing funeral pyre.

By dawn on August 3 the merchantmen had taken up their sailing stations, in three parallel columns. Soon, screened by heavy units of the Home Fleet, they stood to the south, skirting the Irish coast.

At 8:45 A.M. Captain Mason mustered his crew in the petty officers' mess. He told them exactly where they were going and exactly what was expected of them. He read letters from the owners and from the First Lord of the Admiralty, and by taking the men into his confidence, at once established a happy atmosphere.

This atmosphere embraced not only the *Ohio*'s regular crew but also the twenty-four R.N. and Maritime Regiment gunners who manned the tanker's ack-ack. This ack-ack was unusually formidable—one five-inch, one high-angle three-inch, one bofors, six oerlikons, two Brownings, and four P.C.A. Rockets and Kites—and all on board the *Ohio* knew that very soon they would be needing every gun and all the skill of their gunners.

For seven days the convoy headed south. Their passage to Gibraltar was unopposed but far from uneventful. For hour after hour Admiral Syfret exercised the merchantmen in making emergency turns and in altering speed and formation, until, in his own words, "they attained an efficiency in maneuvering comparable to that of a fleet unit." In between times, planes from the *Argus* carried out dummy attacks, giving the gun crews practice in aircraft recognition and in lining up on target. The days passed quickly, the nights uneventfully; and on the morning of August 9 the convoy approached Gibraltar.

It was foggy: a mixed blessing, since poor visibility lessened the chances of their being spotted, but at the same time increased the danger of collision. Admiral Syfret's maneuvering practice now bore fruit; the vessels bunched together, and keeping close and accurate station, passed through the Strait without mishap. They were, however, spotted by a couple of fishing boats, trawling in the swept channel without lights. It seemed highly probably that the "fishermen" were Axis spies; but this was something of which they couldn't be certain. They could only give them as wide a berth as possible, and hope for the best.

Next morning, well out of sight of land, the convoy took up its normal cruising disposition. The fourteen merchantmen were in the center, in four parallel columns; close around them were the heavy units (cruisers, carriers, and battleships), fanned out ahead was the advance screen of destroyers, while away on the port quarter the two fleet oilers, *Brown Ranger* and *Dingledale*, began the long business of refueling.

And almost at once came evidence that the convoy was in for a rough passage. For at noon a Spanish civil airliner, obviously spotting for the Italians, flew high over the fleet; and an hour later a submarine—U73—surfaced fine on the convoy's starboard quarter and torpedoed the aircraft carrier *Eagle*.

The U-boat had taken her opportunity with great skill and daring. She had dived under the screen at a moment when refueling and the flying off of planes from the *Furious* had disrupted the destroyer guard. Now four torpedoes smacked into the carrier. Instantly the great ship heeled over; the planes on her flight deck slithered into the sea; smoke poured darkly out of her air vents; and, vibrating heavily, she rolled onto her side. Within eight minutes she had capsized and sunk. Of her ships' company, over nine hundred were picked up, but of her planes, only four—on patrol at the time of torpedoing—were saved. Within a few hours of entering the Mediterranean the convoy had lost one of its most vital ships. And its exact position had been given away.

U73 had found the convoy neither by chance nor by herself. She was one of a pack: a pack whose patrol line stretched from Algiers to the Balearics and who for twenty-four hours had been lying in wait along the convoy's expected line of advance. Now that they had scented their quarry, now that they had drawn first blood, the whole pack—some dozen strong—came swarming in for the kill. All that afternoon and evening they probed and worried at the fringe of the convoy. But they couldn't get through to the merchantmen. For Admiral Syfret extended his destroyers to form an all-around protective screen; and time and again his warships gave warning of U-boat contacts, and the merchantmen, in perfect formation, swung aside. They made in all, between 2 P.M. and 8 P.M., seventeen emergency turns; and thanks to the destroyers' vigilance and the merchantmen's proficiency and maneuvering, every attack was thwarted, and though several torpedo tracks were seen, not a single vessel was hit. By evening the U-boats had dropped astern; and the convoy—except for the loss of the *Eagle*—had survived its initial test.

It had been a hot airless day. Sunset brought relief from the glare, the heat, and the U-boats; but it also brought the planes; first the shadowers, then, in the gray uncertain twilight, the bombers.

There were thirty-six bombers, Junkers 88s and Heinkel 111s. The Junkers came in high, spiraling in from 8000 feet out of the darkening sky. The Heinkels came in low, their wing tips almost feathering the sea. Their attacks were syn-

Heinkel He 111

chronized to a split second and timed exactly to coincide with the striking down of the last of the fighters into the aircraft-carrier hangars. Ack-ack patterned the sky—the *Ohio*'s gunners had a chance to prove their mettle now. Three Junkers and a Heinkel were shot flaming into the sea. Several vessels disappeared in a flurry of steeple-high bomb splashes; several torpedoes exploded in the froth of churned-up wakes. Then, quite suddenly, it was dark and the planes were gone.

They claimed to have hit a cruiser, an aircraft carrier, and a merchantman. But, in fact, not a ship was touched, though several had near-miraculous escapes. The convoy had survived its second moment of crisis.

All that night the fourteen merchantmen, undamaged, headed east. But Syfret knew that other—and heavier—attacks were still to come. For they were now being shadowed. Hour after hour three long-range Cants from Cagliari could be heard circling high overhead, their radios reporting the convoy's every move. The vessels altered course and speed; their ack-ack cracked open the sky; but there was no throwing the aircraft off. At midnight the monotonous throb of their engines filled the night; at dawn the sky still vibrated to their mocking syncopated beat.

But the *Indomitable* flew off her Martlets early; before dawn; before the Cants expected them. In the white deceptive half light of an hour before sunrise two of the shadowers were shot blazing into the sea. But the third escaped; from the shelter of a bank of cloud she continued to observe the convoy. An hour later new shadowers came creeping onto the radar screens; and an hour after that, the bombers.

Wednesday, August 12, had dawned eventfully. It continued eventfully, at a mounting tempo, right up to midnight.

For the convoy had now passed Longitude 5° E and was nearing the Sardinian Narrows. Admiral Syfret knew that sometime during the next few hours the first wave of attacks, from the airfields around Cagliari, would mount to their climax. And soon after these attacks had ended, a second wave would come flooding in, this time from the Sicilian airstrips. Wednesday, August 12, it was generally agreed, would prove the convoy's most vital day and would provide the merchantmen with their most crucial test.

There were, in fact, two attacks from Sardinia that morning; and though both of these, especially the second, was heavy, neither was pressed home with quite the expected severity. For during the night of August 11–12 bombers from Malta had visited the Italian airstrips; once again planes were destroyed on the ground, hangars set ablaze, and supply and fuel dumps gutted; while (according to official Italian reports) the wakeful night—"*notte di veglia*"—handicapped the air crew in their sorties against the convoy next day!

Whatever the cause, the first attack proved singularly ineffective, and the story of it is soon told. At 9:15 twenty-four Junkers approached the convoy out of the sun. While still some way from the screen they were intercepted by the *Indomitable*'s Martlets and Hurricanes. Eight were shot down; five jettisoned their bombs and fled; and only eleven broke through to the screen. These attacked halfheartedly and without effect; two more were shot down by the destroyers' ack-ack, and within twenty minutes the attack had been beaten off, the convoy suffering neither damage nor casualties.

The second assault, which started at midday, was far more serious and had obviously been planned with the greatest care. How much care, we now know from Italian Naval

Intelligence Documents. According to these documents, it was intended that the attack should consist of five carefully synchronized waves, launched by some seventy bombers and sixty long-range fighters. First, ten Italian torpedo bombers were to drop their *"motobombas F.F."* (experimental parachute mines) a little ahead of the convoy; next, eight Italian fighter-bombers were to machine-gun the outer screen—the objective of these two attacks being to dislocate the convoy's formation and leave the merchantmen vulnerable to the principal torpedo attack, which was timed to commence five minutes after the last of the fighter-bombers had turned for home. These torpedo bombers—forty-two Savoias, heavily escorted—had been told to penetrate the screen and attack the columns of merchantmen simultaneously from either bow. As soon as this attack was completed, twenty-four Junkers were to finish off the merchantmen by shallow dive bombing; while two Reggiane fighters were to deliver a specially planned attack on the aircraft carrier *Victorious*.

It was an ambitious plan. On the whole, it was carried out according to schedule—although the torpedo planes arrived somewhat late—but it was carried out without quite the expected *élan:* the result perhaps of *"notte di veglia."*

At a few minutes to midday the convoy's Hurricanes and Martlets were vectored out to a group of aircraft approaching from the south. These turned out to be the Italian mine layers. They were heavily escorted, but one was shot down and the others forced to drop their mines hurriedly, inaccurately, and at long range. As soon as Syfret saw the parachutes he ordered an emergency 90-degree turn, and a few minutes later the *motobombas* were heard exploding harmlessly along the convoy's flank. The fighter-bombers meanwhile, approaching the convoy's bow, had met with a warm reception; they ran into the *Indomitable*'s Martlets head on, and only three penetrated as far as the screen. These did little damage; and soon the first and second attacks had been decisively repulsed.

There was now a welcome lull of some twenty minutes before the Savoias were spotted, coming in low from the starboard bow and the port beam. Meeting a heavy concentration of fire—including sixteen-inch salvos from *Rodney*—they dropped their torpedoes outside the screen from an excessively hopeful range. The convoy swung 45 degrees to port, then 90 degrees to starboard, and the torpedoes were all avoided. By

12:30 this attack, too, had petered out. Then came the Germans' and Italians' one success. The ack-ack barrage was still concentrating on the torpedo planes when a group of dive bombers came steeply out of the sun. Of the original twenty-four, only eleven were left—for they, too, had met the *Indomitable*'s fighters. But these eleven pressed their attack home. They came screaming down on the *Deucalion*, the merchantman leading the port-wing column; and the *Deucalion* vanished in a flurry of bomb splashes. Four near misses, two of them within less than six feet, lifted her clean out of the water. Then she was hit flush amidships on the hatchway of No. 5 hold. She heeled over, her engines shuddered to a stop, and she started to settle by the stern. Of the fourteen merchantmen, it seemed that only thirteen would continue to hold course for Malta.

But the *Deucalion*'s master, Captain Ramsay Brown, had other ideas. Within twenty minutes he had restarted his engines and was making eight knots. Obviously, at this speed the *Deucalion* couldn't stay with the convoy; but Ramsay Brown was a determined man; he headed his damaged vessel south for the Tunisian coast, hoping to make his way alone and undetected through the inshore shoals. It was a brave venture, but it didn't meet with success. For as she limped away to the southward the *Deucalion* was attacked again and again. The first, second, and third attacks, she beat off—although more near misses increased her list; then, in the gathering darkness, when she was less than six miles from the Cani Rocks, a pair of Italian torpedo planes gave her her deathblow. Two torpedoes thudded into her port quarter; a twin pyramid of flame shot mast-high; her canned spirit ignited; the flames spread; and Ramsay Brown had no alternative. He ordered "Abandon ship." The crew had barely pulled to safety when, with a vast explosion, the *Deucalion* blew up: first of the many merchantmen in Operation "Pedestal" whose wrecks were soon to bear witness to the danger of the run to Malta.

The convoy meanwhile had proceeded steadily east. By one-thirty the last of the dive bombers had been driven away; and Admiral Syfret was beginning to think that they had—as far as the Sardinian airdromes were concerned—weathered the storm when there occurred one of those audacious indi-

H.M.S. Indomitable

vidual tours de force at which the Italians, every now and then, excelled.

With the attacks apparently over, the aircraft carrier *Victorious* was landing her Hurricanes on. Two planes had touched down already, and another three, it seemed, were circling the carrier with their wheels down, awaiting their turn to land. Quite suddenly two of these broke circle and came sweeping low over the flight deck. Before the astonished gun crews realized they were being attacked, two 1000-lb. bombs came screaming down. A pair of specially camouflaged Reggiane

2001s (aircraft whose silhouette is very like a Hurricane's) had joined the carrier's landing circuit and delivered a brilliantly conceived and executed attack. The first bomb burst fine on the carrier's bow, showering the gun crews with splinters and spray. The second bomb fell flush on the center of the flight deck. The carrier should, according to the odds of war, have been crippled, if not sunk. But she was lucky. The bomb broke up without exploding; its fragments skidded over the side, and the *Victorious*, undamaged, steamed steadily on. Before her gun crews had time to open fire, the Reggianes were out of sight.

The assault from the Sardinian airfields was over.

The honors up to now had been with the convoy. For the loss of an aircraft carrier and a merchantman, they had fought their way as far as Longitude 10° E, a distance from Gibraltar of over 800 miles, and Malta was now only 300 miles ahead. They had inflicted heavy losses on the enemy: two submarines and twenty-six aircraft. And they were well up to schedule.

Yet there was no room for complacency; for the greatest dangers still lay ahead: the danger of the Sicilian-based bombers (who were expected to attack that evening) and the danger of the Narrows (where U-boats and E-boats were beginning to concentrate). And already, at four o'clock that afternoon, there were indications that both these dangers were likely to materialize in no uncertain fashion. For the radar screens were reporting a great concentration of aircraft forming up some forty miles ahead of the convoy; while the destroyers scouting ahead were already picking up asdic contacts at the mouth of the Skerki Channel.

The Sicilian bombers made their attack a little after six o'clock. It was a heavy attack, perfectly timed and pressed home with great determination. The planes—consisting of forty-two Junkers, forty Savoias, and thirty-eight fighters—spent over an hour circling the convoy, waiting until every aircraft was in the right place at the right time; then they came in, one formation after another, in wave after wave. For twenty minutes the sky was dark with flak; the air vibrated with the thud of gun, machine gun, and cannon; while fighters and bombers wheeled and cartwheeled among and over the ships.

Then quite suddenly the sky cleared; the bombers were heading for home; and in the moment of calm after the storm Syfret was able to assess his damage.

The thirteen merchantmen were still with him, all undamaged. But the destroyer *Foresight* was heeling over, her engines stopped. And far astern the great aircraft carrier *Indomitable* was moving slowly, erratically; smoke and flame were pouring out of her after-lift well. The dive bombers had singled her out; had concentrated on her as eighteen months earlier Fliegerkorps X had concentrated on the *Illustrious;* and they had come very close to sinking her. For the *Indomitable* had suffered two near misses and three direct hits; her flight deck had been buckled up and twisted out of alignment; and the great ship was now reduced to a useless liability, unable to operate her planes, which were forced to land on the already overcrowded *Victorious.* Of the hundred and twenty German and Italian planes taking part in this attack, eleven were destroyed and a further eleven damaged.

By seven o'clock it was clear that the main attack from the Sicilian airfields was over. The warships had suffered two more casualties; but of the original fourteen merchantmen, thirteen were still unscathed. And the whole force was now approaching the Skerki Channel, less than 250 miles from Malta. Another twenty-four hours, thought Syfret, and, God willing, the merchantmen will be there.

But much was to happen in the next twenty-four hours.

The mouth of the Skerki Channel was the familiar parting of the ways; and here, a little after seven o'clock, Admiral Syfret turned back. He took with him the heavy units, which couldn't be risked in the Narrows—the two battleships, the two carriers, three cruisers, and a screen of eleven destroyers. With the merchantmen he left the customary lighter forces— four cruisers and twelve destroyers—a dangerously small screen to guard over a dozen merchantmen, but all, under the circumstances, that could be spared. These light forces were commanded by Admiral Burrough, an officer who had already rendered distinguished service on the run to Malta; and at seven-thirty that evening they stood boldly into the mouth of the Channel.

Fortune up to now had favored the convoy. On board both warships and merchantmen hopes were high. Already they had covered 900 out of their 1150 miles; and it seemed as if, with the disappearance of the Sicilian aircraft, their greatest danger had passed.

Yet within an hour the convoy had been shattered beyond all hope of recovery; the warships had been rendered impotent, and the merchantmen had been turned into a defenseless and disorderly gaggle, stripped of their cohesion, deprived of their interdependability, bereft of all protection.

The transformation was swift as it was unexpected; complete as it was unprepared for.

The Skerki Channel runs roughly northwest by southeast: a strip of deep water between irregular underwater sand bars. It is a difficult place in which to maneuver. Early that afternoon five U-boats had come cautiously into the Channel; they had taken up position a little inside its mouth, and here, hour after hour, they had lain waiting, screened from the destroyers' asdic by the distorting echoes of the sand bars. At 7:30 their hydrophones picked up the sound of the advancing convoy.

It was 7:45 when the first of Admiral Burrough's ships came nosing into the mouth of the Channel. The convoy was in the process of changing formation: in the middle of maneuvering from four columns into two. They were, therefore, momentarily disorganized: vulnerable at the very moment of crisis. And the U-boats made the most of their opportunity.

First in through the mouth of the Channel was the port-column leader, the *Nigeria*, Admiral Burrough's flagship. A torpedo hit her amidships. Blowing off like a harpooned whale, she shuddered to a startled halt. Less than a minute later the starboard-column leader, the *Cairo*, came nosing in. Two torpedoes thudded into her stern, blowing away her screws; almost at once she began to sink. And two minutes later, at 7:55, the *Ohio* was torpedoed amidships, level with her pump room. She, too, ground to a halt.

Three ships had been disabled in as many minutes; and, what was more, the three most vital ships of the convoy.

For the *Ohio* was the convoy's only tanker. The *Nigeria* and *Cairo*, besides being column leaders, were the only ships equipped with fighter-direction apparatus; and, in addition, the *Nigeria* was Admiral Burrough's flagship.

The convoy was in difficulties now; the destroyers having to divide their attention between hunting the U-boats, standing by the damaged cruisers, and getting the merchantmen away from the danger area. A further complication arose from the fact that the *Nigeria* was so badly damaged that she was forced to turn back for Gibraltar, and Admiral Burrough was obliged to transfer his flag to a destroyer; it was some time before he regained effective command.

In the confusion that followed it wasn't immediately clear whether the disabled ships had been the victims of U-boats or mines. But one fact stood out clearly; all three had been hit to port; the danger, whatever it was, came from there. The convoy therefore swung away to starboard. But the Skerki Channel—as already pointed out—is a difficult place in which to maneuver; and in the process of simultaneously altering course and formation, the merchantmen, lacking column leaders and with too few destroyers to guide them, became scrummed up in a heterogeneous mass along the sand bars lining the southern edge of the Channel.

Here, in the gathering darkness, the torpedo bombers found them.

The sun had set now, but the sea still retained a sheen of light, and against this the silhouettes of the merchantmen stood out clearly. Admiral Syfret's carrier-borne fighters had been struck down for the last half hour; and the long-range Beaufighters from Malta, which had put in a brief appearance over the Channel, had been forced through lack of fighter-direction guidance to return to Luqa and Hal Far. The merchantmen were therefore easy targets. Within half an hour two had been sunk and two damaged.

These losses were bad enough; but infinitely worse was the ensuing separation of merchantmen and warships. For within forty-five minutes of entering the Channel, seven ships had been sunk or disabled; and the destroyers were too much occupied in dealing with these vessels to spare time to round up and protect the rest of the merchantmen. Thus, after about nine o'clock that evening the convoy, as such, simply ceased to exist; it degenerated into a rabble of individual vessels, strung out at intervals along the southern edge of the Narrows. And before the vessels could reform, the E-boats were among them; and the E-boats finished off what the submarines and torpedo bombers had begun. In the middle watch, in the darkest hours of the night, the straggling merchantmen were picked off, one by one. By dawn only six were left.

First victim of the torpedo bombers was the *Empire Hope*. She was following close behind the *Ohio* when the latter was hit, and she had to reverse her engines to stop herself from ramming the disabled tanker. She had barely got back under way when two Savoias came low out of the west. The *Empire Hope* avoided the first torpedo but the second hit her amidships, level with No. 4 hold. The merchantman, her rudder jammed hard over, slewed around to starboard; her engines stopped; flames started to pour out of the damaged hold. There was no pressure in the fire hoses, and the flames spread: spread to the coal bunkers. Soon the heart of the *Empire Hope* was turned into a glowing, banked-down furnace. She was abandoned a little after nine o'clock, her crew being picked up by the destroyer *Penn*.

Next victim was the *Clan Ferguson*. She was an ammunition ship, peculiarly vulnerable. At 9:15 two torpedoes smacked into her starboard quarter. For perhaps half a minute she continued under way, apparently undamaged. Then with a shattering roar she blew up: disintegrated into a mushroom cloud of smoke and a haze of acrid, gently falling dust.

The same plane which had torpedoed the *Clan Ferguson* also hit the *Brisbane Star*. Its second torpedo smacked into the merchantman's bow, blowing out her stem piece and shattering her for'ard bulkheads. The *Brisbane Star* shuddered to a halt; water flooded into her hold.

There now began a minor epic of the sea.

The *Brisbane Star*'s bow had been blown clean away; she was down by the head and taking water, and her engines were stopped. Many masters would have abandoned ship. But not Captain Riley, who was determined, somehow, to get his vessel to Malta. The damaged bulkheads were shored up, the engines were restarted, and within twenty minutes of being hit the *Brisbane Star* was again under way and making five knots. Captain Riley headed south. In his own words:

I decided that as we could only make 5–8 kts. we had better leave the convoy (to whom we would only be a lame duck) and make our way alone down the Tunisian inshore channel. . . . As we headed south we could see the rest of the convoy, including to our surprise the tanker *Ohio*, going away at a tangent to the southeast. They were being continuously attacked from the air. Soon they were out of sight, and we were on our own. . . .

All that night the *Brisbane Star* limped slowly through the Tunisian shallows. A little after they had rounded Kélibia Point they saw the silhouette of a warship, motionless, dead ahead. As they were well inside French territorial waters, they thought it was probably a *Léopard*-class destroyer; but not being sure, they gave it a wide berth. Dawn found them with ten feet of water in No. 1 hold and with their bows dipping under the larger waves, but still making eight knots. As they crossed the Gulf of Hammamet they were spotted, a little after sunrise, by an Italian torpedo bomber.

Inside territorial waters neither had the right to open fire, unless they were attacked.

The torpedo bomber circled the *Brisbane Star* three times at close range; then it came sweeping down. At mast height it passed straight over the top of them. But Captain Riley held his fire. And so did the torpedo bomber. Three times the plane made dummy attacks, trying to provoke the merchantman to open fire. But the *Brisbane Star*'s oerlikons remained peacefully fore and aft; and at last the torpedo bomber, disappointed, flew away. As Captain Riley put it, "He was a gentleman and observed the rules of war." The merchantman continued slowly across the bay.

At ten o'clock the French signal station on the shore of Hammamet started to take an interest in them, which was hardly surprising, since the *Brisbane Star*—13,000 tons and with her bow blown off—could scarcely have looked less like a small French coaster. There followed a classic exchange of signals.

HAMMAMET:	You should hoist your signal letters.
BRISBANE STAR:	Please excuse me.
HAMMAMET:	You should anchor.
BRISBANE STAR:	My anchors are fouled. I cannot anchor.
HAMMAMET:	You appear to be dragging your bow and stern anchors.
BRISBANE STAR:	I have no stern anchor.
HAMMAMET:	Do you require salvage?
BRISBANE STAR:	No.

There followed a slight pause, then the cryptic signal from Hammamet: "It is not safe to go too fast."

On receiving this, Captain Riley ordered a jumbled series of flags (with several furled and knotted) to be hoisted, and increasing speed to nine knots, headed out of the bay. Rather to his surprise, the French made no effort to stop him.

But a few minutes later he realized that he had jumped out of the frying pan into the fire, for he spotted a U-boat, obviously trailing them from the edge of territorial waters.

All that afternoon the *Brisbane Star* and the U-boat played hide-and-seek among the Tunisian shallows. The U-boat didn't dare to come inshore, to attack inside territorial waters; and the *Brisbane Star* didn't dare head out to sea. For the time being, both were content to wait; but time, as Captain Riley knew, was on the side of the U-boat; for the merchantman couldn't hug the shore forever; sometime she would have to stand seaward for the final dash to Malta.

At five o'clock there came a further complication. A French patrol boat put out from Monastir Bay and started to follow the merchantman. After a while she signaled her to heave to. Captain Riley altered course and speed, flashed indecipherable signals, and prevaricated as long as he could. For half an hour the pantomime continued; then the patrol boat lost patience, and a warning shot fell less than ten yards from the merchantman's bow. The *Brisbane Star* came to a reluctant stop. A few minutes later two French officers clambered on board; very formally and correctly they requested Captain Riley to follow them back to the nearest French port, where, they said, the *Brisbane Star* and her crew would have to be interned. It was a delicate situation. But Scotch whisky and Irish charm rose to the occasion; and, in the words of the official report, "Captain Riley refused the request very diplomatically, and in due course the French officers left, giving the captain their very best wishes and taking with them a member of the crew who had been seriously injured in the torpedo attack. The patrol boat returned to harbour alone. . . ."

Having circumnavigated the French, Captain Riley next proceeded to outwit the U-boat. Steering a carefully deceptive series of courses among the offshore shallows, he lost her in the gathering darkness, and that night cut across to Malta. Next morning the *Brisbane Star* was met by mine sweepers and Beaufighters and escorted into Grand Harbour. Her bow, by this time, was almost continuously awash and her holds were badly flooded. But her vital cargo was safe.

For this "initiative, tact, clear thinking, and determination" Captain Riley was awarded the O.B.E. Certainly few other masters could have survived such a series of impasses with such delightful *sang-froid* and dexterity.

But the *Brisbane Star* was one of the few ships that were lucky. For, while Captain Riley was limping undetected through the shallows, the rest of the convoy was being increasingly heavily attacked.

The next ship to succumb was the *Santa Eliza*.

At nine-thirty it was almost completely dark. Most of the bombers had turned for home by now, but one apparently still hadn't found a target. Then, at the last fragment of daylight, its bomb aimer spotted the *Santa Eliza*, and the plane came sweeping down. Four bombs straddled the merchantman with mathematical precision, two on either beam. Though not directly hit, the *Santa Eliza* was lifted bodily out of the water, and her engines were badly shaken. At reduced speed she went limping on through the Narrows. Soon the E-boats found her: a lone straggler, plowing a solitary wake in the rear of the undamaged merchantmen.

It was very dark in the middle watch. The crew of the *Santa Eliza* could hear the E-boats' engines echoing all around them; but the craft themselves remained invisible. Suddenly a lookout on the merchantman's poop gave a cry of warning. Less than a cable astern gleamed the phosphorescence of a wake. The *Santa Eliza* spun around, almost on her axis, and simultaneously both vessels opened fire. Tracer tore gold ribbons out of the night; gun crew on both E-boat and merchantman slumped to the deck like string-jerked marionettes. Then, quite suddenly, all was quiet. The crew of the *Santa Eliza* peered anxiously into the night, but for several minutes nothing was heard or seen. Then came the stuttering throb of engines being restarted on the opposite side of the ship, and a second later, before the *Santa Eliza* could turn, two torpedoes struck her starboard bow. There was a heavy explosion, and almost at once flames came pouring out of the for'ard holds. The for'ard holds were stowed with grain and ammunition. Both caught fire; and exploding crates of cannon shell and .303 were tossed like squibs out of the blown-off hatchways. Soon the deck of the *Santa Eliza* was a mosaic of smoke and flame. She was abandoned. Her crew were being picked up by the destroyers *Penn* and *Bramham* when she blew up, broke her back, and sank.

The *Rochester Castle* was also hit in the middle watch; but only by one torpedo. For two hours her master, Captain Richard Wren, had been twisting and turning to avoid the attacking E-boats. In all, he made that night eleven emergency turns; and eleven times the torpedo tracks ran wide. But at last—inevitably—the *Rochester Castle* was hit; and through a hole ten feet by twelve feet the water came welling into her for'ard holds. The merchantman had, however, been swinging away at the moment of impact; and this perhaps lessened the effect of the explosion. For Captain Wren discovered, much to his astonishment, that the *Rochester Castle* could still make good speed and steer with reasonable accuracy; and so he kept on course, "merrily making a good thirteen knots."

But his troubles were not yet over.

Dawn found the *Rochester Castle* in the van of the convoy, which was at last sorting itself out into some kind of order. By seven o'clock twelve ships were in company—two cruisers, seven destroyers, and the merchantmen *Rochester Castle*, *Waimarama*, and *Melbourne Star*. While astern, the merchantmen *Ohio* and *Port Chalmers*, escorted by the *Penn* and *Bramham*, were struggling to close up with the main body.

Dawn, of course, brought the bombers.

They found the convoy reduced in strength, without its fighter-direction ships, and with only spasmodic air cover from Malta. They attacked relentlessly, hour after hour; and the handful of merchantmen that had survived the night found the hours of daylight as grim, exhausting, and perilous as the hours of darkness. Several more were sunk.

The *Rochester Castle* was damaged again at 8:30, but she managed to struggle on. At ten o'clock she was damaged yet again, three bombs exploding immediately beneath her bow. She was lifted bodily out of the water; her engines vibrated to a stop; and fires broke out for'ard and amidships. The fires spread. But after ten minutes her engines were restarted; and the fire parties, with pressure in their hoses, tackled the flames with renewed hope. Eventually they brought them under control. But in the process of extinguishing the fires, the small-arms magazine had had to be flooded, and this damaged the steering. The *Rochester Castle* had also shipped some 4000 tons of water and was lying dangerously low; this added to the difficulties of keeping course. But Captain Wren never gave up. Somehow he coaxed his vessel on, creeping gradually closer to Malta. At last they came within radius of the island's short-range Spitfires, and the air attacks mercifully slackened off.

Finally, at six o'clock that evening, their efforts were rewarded, and the *Rochester Castle* limped slowly into Grand Harbour. When she berthed, her gunwale lay under the quay; for she had shipped so much water that her freeboard was less than six feet.

Not many vessels were as lucky. The accompanying table shows how, one by one, they were whittled away, first by torpedo bombers, then by E-boats, and finally, on the morning of August 13, by the Sicilian dive bombers.

Of the fourteen merchantmen which had left the Clyde, only five—all of them damaged—got through to Grand Harbour. It was not a large proportion, but it was enough to save Malta. For the five ships, among them, unloaded over 60,000 tons of vitally needed supplies (oil, ammunition, kerosene, naval stores, aviation fuel, coal, grain, meat, and flour): enough to meet the island's needs for a good two months. And by the time these stocks were starting to run low, the task of reprovisioning Malta had become comparatively easy. For Montgomery's victory at El Alamein brought under Allied control vast reaches of the North African shore; and the Narrows, in consequence, lost much of their former peril. Malta, that August, had survived her darkest hour.

But it had been a near thing: far too near for comfort or complacency. For had the five merchantmen failed to fight their way through, Malta would have fallen, and the course of the war would have been substantially altered—for with Malta under Axis control, Rommel's Afrika Korps could have been easily and heavily reinforced, and El Alamein, "the turning point in the war," could easily have turned the opposite way. As in the case of the Battle of Britain, seldom had so much depended on the courage of so few.

Admiral Syfret realized this. In his battle report he wrote:

Tribute has often been paid to the personnel of His Majesty's ships; but both officers and men (who served in

DAMAGE SUSTAINED BY THE MALTA CONVOY OF AUGUST 1942

SHIP	Time of First Hit	Cause of First Hit	Position of First Hit	Subsequent History
Deucalion	12:30/12	Dive bombers	West of the Narrows	Damaged 12:30/12 and 16:00/12. Finally sunk by torpedo bombers off Cani Rocks 19:30/12.
Ohio	19:55/12	Submarine	Mouth of Skerki Channel	Damaged 19:55/12 and 09:05/13. Ju 88 crashed on deck 09:10/13. Damaged 10:00/13. Ju 87 crashed on deck 10:04/13. In tow: damaged 18:35/13 and 09:00/14. Arrived Malta 09:30/15.
Empire Hope	20:15/12	Torpedo bomber	Mouth of Skerki Channel	Set on fire 20:20/12. Abandoned 21:00/12. Sunk 21:30/12.
Clan Ferguson	21:15/12	Torpedo bomber	Mouth of Skerki Channel	Exploded instantly and sank without survivors.
Brisbane Star	21:15/12	Torpedo bomber	Mouth of Skerki Channel	Damaged: speed reduced; headed south through Tunisian shallows. Arrived Malta 12:00/14.
Santa Eliza	21:30/12	Torpedo bomber	Mouth of Skerki Channel	Damaged: speed reduced; finally sunk by E-boat in Narrows 05:00/13.

SHIP	Time of First Hit	Cause of First Hit	Position of First Hit	Subsequent History
Rochester Castle	03:30/13	E-boat	Narrows	Damage 03:30/13. Damaged by dive bombers 06:30/13 and 10:00/13. Arrived Malta 18:00/13.
Glenorchy	04:00/13	E-boat	Narrows	Sunk. No survivors.
Almeria Lykes	04:15/13	E-boat	Narrows	Abandoned by her crew.
Wairangi	05:00/13	E-boat	Narrows	Sunk.
Melbourne Star	08:00/13	Dive bomber	South of Pantelleria	Damaged. Arrived Malta 18:00/13.
Waimarama	08:30/13	Dive bomber	South of Pantelleria	Exploded and sunk.
Dorset	10:45/13	Dive bomber	South of Pantelleria	Damaged and disabled. Damaged 19:00/13. Sunk 20:00/13.
Port Chalmers	11:25/13	Torpedo bomber	South of Pantelleria	Slightly damaged. Arrived Malta 18:00/13.

Operation "Pedestal") will desire to give first place to the
conduct, courage and determination of the Masters, officers and men of the merchant ships. The steadfast manner
in which these vessels pressed on their way to Malta
through all attacks, answering every manoeuvring order
like a well-trained fleet, was most inspiring. Many of these
fine men and their ships were lost. But the memory of
their conduct will remain an inspiration to all who were
privileged to sail with them.

PART II

Out of so many examples of courage and endurance it may
seem invidious to pick on one for special attention. Yet the
story of the *Ohio* illustrates Syfret's comment so aptly that it
merits detailed telling. The *Ohio*, too, has a rather special
claim to fame; for she was continually singled out for the
enemy's most determined attacks, and, because of her peculiarly
vulnerable cargo, her survival was little short of miraculous.

She entered the mouth of the Skerki Channel at 7:55 P.M.
on August 12, 1942, and at the very moment she passed into
the Channel the torpedo thudded into her bow.
In Captain Mason's words:

> . . . there was a bright flash and a column of water was
> thrown up to mast height; this was followed a second later
> by flames equally high. The deck on the port side was torn
> up and laid right back to the centre line. The Samson
> derrick post canted over, damaging the flying bridge. The
> pump room became a shambles and was laid open to the
> sea. The main steering-gear telemotor pipes were carried
> away, plus the electric cables and steam pipes; and the lids
> of the kerosene tanks were blown off and buckled. Within
> a dozen seconds the pump room was ablaze and flames
> were pouring out of the deck. I rang for "finish with
> engines" and got the men out of the engine room. We
> then started to fight the fire. I thought it was a forlorn
> hope, but we set to with foam extinguishers.

* * *

One thing saved the *Ohio*. When the torpedo hit her it blasted a hole in her side twenty-four feet high and twenty-seven feet long; and through this hole the sea water came pouring in, in a great swirling flood. And the water helped to extinguish the flames. Soon, under the combined assault of sea and foamite, the fires weakened and died; and the buckled lids of the kerosene tanks could be hammered down.

By 8:15 the fires were under control, the damaged keel had been temporarily shored up, and Captain Mason ordered his chief engineer to get under way. Since the *Ohio* was equipped with a diesel generator, this took less than ten minutes. As soon as the engines had been tested and found to be still in working order, Captain Mason ordered them to be stopped; for the ship, when under way, could move only in lurching erratic circles and was a danger to the rest of the convoy—especially to the disabled *Nigeria* and *Cairo*. With the telemotor pipes blown away, there was no hope of returning to normal steering; but after much improvisation the emergency (or hand) steering gear was rigged up aft—no easy task with the ship in darkness and under continual attack from marauding torpedo bombers. But eventually, a little after 8:30, the *Ohio* got slowly under way. Her compasses and gyros were shattered beyond repair, she was difficult to hold on course, and she could make no more than seven knots; but Captain Mason headed her after the rest of the convoy—which he could see far ahead, the vessels under heavy attack as they moved slowly through the Narrows.

After a while they were hailed by a destroyer coming up from astern; it was the *Ashanti*, carrying the admiral's flag; she asked if they needed help. With his compasses and gyros out of commission, Captain Mason had no means of steering a course; he therefore requested a guide ship to see them through the Narrows; and soon another destroyer, the *Ledbury*, came nosing out of the darkness and took up station a little ahead of the tanker. The *Ledbury*'s captain rigged up a blue signal lamp on his sternpost, and this, Captain Mason did his best to follow. But it was impossible, from the tanker's after-steering position, to keep the lamp in view; so the first officer had to take the wheel while Captain Mason directed him from the bridge. Luckily both telephone and helm recorders were in working order; but even so, keeping station astern of the destroyer was a nightmare, with the damaged tanker continually trying to yaw off course. Their passage that night through the Narrows was nerve-racking and exhausting; it was also, in the words of Vice-Admiral, Malta, "a remarkable feat of seamanship and tenacity." But other and far greater perils were soon to come.

Soon after midnight they passed the remains of the *Clan Ferguson*, gutted and burning fiercely to the water's edge. Some of the *Ohio*'s kerosene tanks were still partially open; and they gave the burning vessel a wide berth.

By 3 A.M. they had been able to work up a fair turn of speed—nearly thirteen knots—and the *Ohio* now started to overhaul the rest of the convoy, which reduced speed to enable her to close. She caught up with them at dawn.

There were four merchantmen in convoy now: the *Rochester Castle*, followed by the *Waimarama* and *Melbourne Star*, with the *Ohio* bringing up the rear; while around them were ten warships forming a defensive screen. But none of the warships was equipped for fighter direction; and so, that morning, the Malta Beaufighters failed to find the convoy, and the air cover which was so desperately needed never materialized. From eight o'clock until midday the Savoias and Junkers came flooding in; wave after successive wave, in a crescendo of devastating attacks.

At 8 A.M. the first of the dive bombers was spotted high in the northern sky. Others quickly followed. And in every attack their chief target was the already damaged *Ohio*. In less than an hour she suffered six near misses.

At 8:30, when the four merchantmen were in single column, two cables apart, the *Waimarama* received a direct hit. With a shattering roar she blew up. Wreckage and pools of blazing oil fanned out across the sea. The *Melbourne Star*, close behind, couldn't turn quickly enough to avoid the flames; she passed straight through them, and in the deafening confusion of battle thirty-four of her crew, thinking their own vessel had been hit, leaped overboard into the burning sea. The *Ohio*, close behind the *Melbourne Star*, heeled violently to port and managed to avoid the center of the flames; but sparks and burning wreckage showered her deck and one of her kerosene tanks was again set ablaze. The destroyer *Ledbury*, by magnificent seamanship, rescued over thirty men from the blazing sea.

The convoy had barely got back into station when another wave of Junkers came screaming in. A 500-pounder burst flush under the *Ohio*'s bow, shaking her violently, buckling her for'ard plating and flooding her forepeak tanks. Her engines began to grate uneasily.

A few minutes later, a Junkers 88, hit by the combined fire of the *Ohio* and *Ashanti*, was shot flaming into the sea. The plane hit the water obliquely less than fifty feet from the *Ohio*, bounced off the crest of a swell, and landed flush on the tanker's foredeck. There was a deafening roar. Debris was flung high into the air. But—mercifully—the plane had already dropped its bombs, and it didn't penetrate the deck. The *Ohio* struggled on. Malta was still a hundred miles to the east.

At ten o'clock the tanker was damaged again. Two sticks of bombs straddled her with mathematical precision, three 500-pounders falling amidships on either beam. The *Ohio* was lifted clean out of the water. She shook and vibrated and quivered; but she didn't give up; she still kept on.

A couple of minutes later, a Junkers 87, damaged by the *Ohio*'s oerlikons, failed to pull out of its dive; it hit the sea, bounced high into the air, and it, too, came crashing on deck, flush on the tanker's poop. The *Ohio* staggered and lurched and reeled; but—like a punch-drunk boxer refusing to take the count—she still kept moving forward. Wreathed in smoke and cordite fumes and flame, listing to 5 degrees, with the wreckage of two crashed aircraft littering her deck, and with her engines vibrating unevenly, she still held course, still kept up to the convoy's eleven knots.

But at 10:30 her engine beat weakened and died. Captain Mason rang through to the engine room.

"What's the trouble, Mr. Wyld?"

"The electric fuel pumps, sir. They've packed up."

"How about the steam pumps?"

"They're O.K. But we can't get a vacuum on the condensers."

While they were speaking, the No. 1 boiler blew out, extinguishing several of the fires. Repairs were improvised, and for a few minutes the *Ohio* juddered along at less than fourteen to sixteen revolutions. Then a second boiler exploded, extinguishing the rest of the fires. The *Ohio* lost way. She came to a reluctant halt. The rest of the convoy passed her by.

There was nothing to be done. And inspection only confirmed what the captain already knew. The *Ohio*'s engines would never start again.

Only one hope remained: a tow.

As soon as Admiral Burrough saw that the *Ohio* wasn't getting under way, he sent back three destroyers to screen and help her. These came alongside. They were in the process of passing lines across to the tanker when an urgent message reached them. Off Kélibia Point, the cruiser *Manchester* was sinking: the destroyers were needed to go back and rescue her crew.

The lines were reeled in. The destroyers headed westward. The *Ohio* was left alone.

The Sicilian dive bombers were still out in force. Sometimes now the long-range Spitfires from Malta managed to keep them at bay; but sometimes, too, they broke through. The assault on the tanker never slackened. Twice again in the next couple of hours she suffered from near misses.

At 11:30 the destroyer *Penn*—detached from the convoy— came alongside. She passed the *Ohio* a ten-inch manila line and tried to take her in tow. But the *Ohio* by now weighed 30,000 tons; she was drawing thirty-seven feet; her damaged bow increased her water resistance, and her list continually yawed her off course. The *Penn* could move her only very slowly, and always in circles. Around and around they went; whenever the *Penn* tried to haul her straight, the towline parted.

Captain Mason knew it was hopeless. Their only chance, he told the *Penn*, was to have two destroyers on the towlines: one ahead and one astern. But two destroyers couldn't be spared. For two and a half hours *Penn* struggled with the unwieldy tanker. But she moved her less than a hundred yards. At last she gave up, and the *Ohio* drifted helplessly away, spiraling sluggishly around in the random underwater currents.

There was no point now in her crew's remaining on board; for until other vessels arrived to tow her, the *Ohio* was beyond help. Accordingly, at 2:15 her boats were lowered and pulled across to the *Penn*, and her crew clambered aboard the already over-crowded destroyer. They were filthy, wet, and exhausted: but they were not disheartened. Captain Mason, now in his third day without sleep, went from man to man asking for volunteers to reboard the *Ohio* if and when more vessels arrived to tow her. Without exception the whole crew volunteered to return.

All that afternoon *Penn* circled the drifting tanker while her crew slept; until at 5:30 they were joined by a solitary mine sweeper and two small motor launches—all that could be spared for the moment to help with the tow.

The *Ohio* was still afloat. She had been near-missed again during the afternoon, but Malta's Spitfires had kept most of the bombers at bay. Captain Mason and his crew returned on board. They found their ship lower in the water now, drawing all of thirty-eight feet. She was down by the bows, too, and listing increasingly steeply. She had no light, no water, no power; and her steering was smashed beyond repair. Even with three destroyers it wouldn't have been easy to tow her; with one destroyer and a solitary mine sweeper it seemed so hopeless as to be hardly worth the trying. But they set to work.

There followed fifteen hours of alternate hope and disillusion, success and failure, progress and frustration, as the tanker would move slowly forward, only, after a couple of hundred yards, to override or break her towlines. In fifteen hours she covered less than twenty miles.

And she hadn't yet seen the last of the dive bombers.

The events of the next few hours are recorded factually in the mine sweeper's log; and the facts need no embellishment.

17:45   *Penn* passes tow to *Ohio*. Commences towing.
18:35   *Ohio* overruns tow. *Rye* (mine sweeper) passes sweep wires to *Penn* to keep her steady.
18:40   Dive bombing starts. Heavy attacks.
18:45   *Ohio* hit for'ard extremity of boat deck. (Bomb exploded on boiler tops, blowing crew out on deck.) Fires started, but brought under control. Towlines cast off at start of bombing.
20:25   Tow recommenced.
20:35   Twelve bombs within 20 yds. of *Rye*.
20:40   *Penn* casts off *Ohio*'s tow, as she is being dragged stern first under the tanker's bow.
20:45   *Rye*'s sweep wires damaged. 250 fathoms cut off and replaced with 3½-inch hawser.
22:20   *Rye* passes *Ohio* strengthened chain cable, and tow

recommences, *Penn* acting as stern tug. Good progress at 4 kts.

01:05　*Ohio* sheers badly. Both hawsers part.

01:10–04:00　*Penn* attempts to tow from alongside. Little success.

04:15　*Rye* takes both ships in tow, using 10-inch manila aboard *Ohio*, and a sweep wire attached to *Penn's* cable. 1½ kts.

05:05　*Ohio* sheers. Both wires part.

07:45　Joined by *Ledbury*.

08:00　*Ledbury* tries to act as stern tug, but *Ohio* gets out of control and parts hawsers.

So they went on, hour after hour, with the tanker slowly settling by the bow, and the odds on their survival lengthening with every parted tow. At dawn on August 14, Malta was still some seventy miles to the east; and it seemed as though the vital oil fuel would never reach Grand Harbour.

But at 8:30 that morning fresh life was brought to the towing operations by the arrival of Commander Jerome in the mine sweeper *Speedy;* for Jerome brought with him not only the *Speedy* but also three motor launches and the destroyer *Bramham*. For over thirty-six hours Captain Mason had been fighting to save the *Ohio* with quite inadequate resources; now at last he had a force sufficiently powerful to meet his needs, a force of three destroyers, two mine sweepers, and several launches. He made a complete and thorough inspection of the damaged tanker. He found that water was filtering into the kerosene tanks, forcing the kerosene to overflow; he found that the engine room was flooding—in spite of the efforts of two ships' pumps—at the rate of six inches an hour; he found that the *Ohio's* freeboard was less than three feet and that she was settling slowly by the head. "But," he reported to Commander Jerome, "I think that with luck we'll last twelve hours; and that should be enough for you to get us to Malta."

A few minutes after he made his report, the Junkers began their last assault.

It was as if they had been watching the crippled tanker's progress and had suddenly realized that the prey they had been so sure of was slipping away. They came in now in a last desperate effort to finish her off. But this time they were met by Malta's short-range Spitfires, which formed a protective circle around the slowly advancing ships. Out of some two dozen dive bombers, only three broke through, and of these, only one pressed its attack home.

But this one attack came close to giving the *Ohio* her *coup de grâce;* for a 100-pound bomb landed flush in the tanker's wake. The *Ohio* was flung violently forward; her screws were twisted out of alignment; her rudder was carried away; and through a great hole in her stern the water came gushing in. Her deck plates—already damaged and overstrained—began to buckle. It seemed to Captain Mason that she was liable, at any moment, to break in half.

Many masters would have abandoned ship, but Captain Mason simply reported to Commander Jerome: "There is a strong possibility of our breaking in half; but even if this happens, I estimate that our for'ard portion—which contains seventy-five per cent of our oil fuel—could still be saved."

As soon as the last of the bombers had disappeared, the tanker was again taken in tow. The *Penn* and the *Bramham* secured on either side of her, the *Rye* secured to her bow, and the *Ledbury* circled her watchfully. Soon the macabre procession was under way and making a steady couple of knots.

The tow was never easy. For the *Ohio* was heavy, waterlogged, and unpredictable, tending to sheer and bludgeon aside the destroyers with every fractional change of course. But they kept her moving, hour after hour, while her pumps struggled to stem the rising flood and her deck plates gradually buckled and folded back. Soon she was so low in the water that a man could lean over the side and trail his fingers in the sea.

All that day the snail-like procession kept under way, watched over by an umbrella of Spitfires; and a little before sunset they sighted their goal. Malta. The island for whose salvation they had endured so much.

The danger from the air had passed now; but one last danger remained: the U-boats, known to be congregating at the entrance of the searched channel. In the words of Vice-Admiral, Malta, "The night passage through the channel was a most anxious operation." The *Ohio* was very unmanageable and settling fast; the night was pitch black, and two awkward corners had to be negotiated. As the vessels were proceeding at a snail's pace up the channel, a plot, obviously a submarine's, was picked up south of the Comino Channel. Coastal 9.2-inch guns fired a blind barrage at the plot and it turned away. Then to the north more submarine plots appeared; a searchlight swept and a barrage of 9.2-inch gunfire kept them at bay. At 2:30, August 15, *Pilditch* and three tugs put out from Grand Harbour; they met the *Ohio* at dawn.

The last word in the drama belongs, by right, to Captain Mason. His report is brief and to the point.

06:00   In Malta Channel. Tugs fore and aft. Destroyers alongside.
08:00   In Grand Harbour.
09:30   Berthed beside *Plumleaf*, thanks to magnificent seamanship of the destroyers.
11:30   All crew ashore. Ship in hands of Naval Fuelling authorities. My thanks are due to the Royal Navy and to the Royal Air Force for the protection and assistance given, also to all those connected with the salvage operations.

It was, of course, fitting that Captain Mason should express appreciation of the part played by others in saving his ship. But, in fact, most of the credit belongs to him. For it was his courage, his seamanship, and, above all, his tenacity which inspired his crew to fight with such unswerving singleness of purpose. In the course of sixty hours his vessel suffered seven direct hits and some twenty near misses. Any one of these could—quite easily—have touched off the fuel in the *Ohio*'s tanks and turned her in a couple of minutes into a blazing funeral pyre. This, Captain Mason and his crew knew. Yet—and here is the measure of their courage—they stayed on board the *Ohio* hour after hour, day after day, even when it seemed inevitable that their ship was doomed.

Their services did not pass unrewarded. That autumn the following notice appeared in the London *Gazette*. "His Majesty the King has been pleased to award the George Cross to Captain D. W. Mason, in recognition of the gallantry displayed by him and his crew, as a result of which the major part of the *Ohio*'s cargo, so vital to the defence of Malta, reached its destination."

Never was a decoration more richly deserved; for in all the history of the sea there is no more inspiring epic than the passage of the *Ohio* to Malta.

18

Be pleased to inform Their Lordships that the Italian battle fleet now lies at anchor under the guns of the fortress of Malta.

—ADMIRAL CUNNINGHAM

In addition to saving Malta from the specter of imminent starvation, the August convoy also provided the island with the means of launching a renewed offensive on Rommel's supply lines. Aircraft stores and naval ordnance were unloaded by the thousand ton—bombs, cannon shells, mines, and torpedoes—grist to the mill of Malta's revenge. And that September, on the eve of the great land battle which was to decide the fate of North Africa, aircraft from Luqa, Takali, and Hal Far were able to resume their offensive on Axis shipping. Swordfish, Albacores, Wellingtons, and Beauforts flew that month no fewer than 124 antishipping strikes and sent to the bottom over 100,000 tons of Rommel's much needed supplies, including two 12,000-ton tankers. As a result the Germans were forced, at this critical moment, to shift their supply lines east; to send their Africa-bound merchantmen via the Corinth Canal—a route which took far longer and was far more exposed to attack by Allied submarines. In addition, the cruisers and destroyers of Malta's famous Force K, now replenished with ammunition and oil fuel, took on a fresh lease of life, harrying the Axis supply routes with renewed determination. Thus, the eve of El Alamein found Rommel before the battle had even started, desperately short of supplies.

On the island itself the results of the convoy were equally beneficial. Rations were increased—not to normal, for reserves of food were wisely stockpiled against another emergency, but at least to a level which afforded adequate nourishment.

AA ammunition was de-restricted, and the guns were able, for the first time in four months, to fire at will. The Spitfires were reserviced with new engines, improved-type cannons, and a host of small but vital modifications; they had plenty of ammunition now and plenty of 100-octane fuel; and by the end of October daylight raiding had been brought to a virtual end. The cost to the Axis was too high. Between June 1940 and October 1942 their assault on Malta had cost them 1378 aircraft, with a further 420 damaged. They couldn't afford to keep their offensive up; and it was clear, that autumn, that Malta had weathered the storm. After two years of ordeal by bomb and terror and near starvation, her people were able at last to look into the future and see the promise of better things to come.

The siege of the island was finally raised by a convoy from the east; by a great armada which left Alexandria on November 16 and reached the island four days later. This convoy was virtually unopposed. For the Axis had too many other commitments now to launch an all-out attack; and they had, too, blunted their claws too often on the Malta convoys to want to try again. The island whose destruction had seemed at first so easy a task had proved too much for them. On November 20 the relieving merchantmen were met at the approaches to Grand Harbour by an umbrella of Beaufighters and Spitfires. Watched over by the patrolling planes, they formed into line ahead and stood into harbor. On the decks of the escorting warships bands were playing as though at the climax of a summer cruise; while on the bastions of Valletta, the Baraccas, and the Three Cities, the people and garrison of Malta stood in their thousands, cheering and waving flags as ship after ship unloaded its lifesaving cargo. At dusk the Germans sent over a small force of Junkers 88s to try and disrupt the unloading. But the Junkers did no damage, and every one of them was shot down. The tide had turned, and in no uncertain fashion.

Next month no fewer than four convoys reached the island without opposition, and more than 200,000 tons of stores were unloaded at Grand Harbour and Marsaxlokk. The siege was over. The task of transforming the island into a springboard for the invasion of southern Europe had begun.

It was a task in which the Maltese reveled. Their years of endurance were over, their years of victory were about to begin: years in which they repaid in full the blows that the Axis had been raining on them with such sustained ferocity for the last thirty months. From then on, events in Malta marched forward, smoothly and inexorably, to a triumphant climax.

There were in those years of victory three milestones which marked significant stages in the island's road to recovery. First was the visit of His Majesty King George VI.

Less than a year before, Malta had been on the brink of capitulation, but in June 1943 its fortunes had so greatly improved that a visit by His Majesty was deemed practicable and not unduly dangerous. That in itself is a yardstick by which conditions on the island can be judged.

It is fitting that the King's visit to Malta should be described by the man who did most to make it a practical possibility: Admiral Cunningham, formerly Commander in Chief, and now back in the Mediterranean as Allied Naval Commander (of the North African) Expeditionary Force.

On the evening of June 19th [he writes] we embarked in the battletried *Aurora* for passage to Malta. The *Aurora* was escorted by the destroyers *Eskimo, Jervis, Nubian* and *Lookout,* and the 200-mile voyage passed off without incident. At dawn a large fighter escort was roaring overhead, and soon afterwards we met the sweepers who had been making certain that no mines existed in the approaches to the Grand Harbour. For obvious reasons the visit had been kept a dead secret, but at 5 A.M. the Maltese were informed of His Majesty's impending arrival. It was time enough. The Baraccas and all other vantage points were thick with cheering people as the *Aurora,* flying the Royal Standard, passed through the breakwater at 8 A.M. and moved to her buoys. The King stood on a special platform built in front of the bridge so that all could see him. I have witnessed many memorable spectacles; but this was the most impressive of them all. The dense throngs of loyal Maltese, men, women and children, were wild with enthusiasm. I have never heard such cheering, and all the bells in the many churches started ringing when he landed.

The King made an extensive tour of the island... and lunched with the Governor, Field-Marshal Viscount Gort, at Verdala Palace. It was the first time a Sovereign had

H.M.S. Aurora

landed in Malta since 1911, and the effect on the inhabitants was tremendous. The visit produced one of the most spontaneous and genuine demonstrations of loyalty and affection I have ever seen.

It was a far cry now back to the bad old days of continuous bombing, near starvation, and the imminent threat of glider-borne invasion.

The next milestone was the setting up in Malta of Allied headquarters for the invasion of Sicily. The fact that Malta

was chosen as the site for this headquarters marked a significant and long overdue change of heart: the Army at last had
come to recognize the island's strategic importance. That
summer Generals Eisenhower, Alexander, and Montgomery
arrived to conduct the final stages of the Sicilian landings; and
from the moment of their arrival Malta became the hub from
which air-borne and sea-borne assaults were launched
unremittingly against the "soft underbelly" of the Axis. In
this crescendo of warlike activity—the planning, assembling,
launching, victualing, supplying, and repairing of the assault

forces—the people of Malta rejoiced, regarding the retribution which the Allies were soon carrying to the shores of Italy as their own just vengeance: compensation for the years of their ordeal.

But for the Maltese the greatest moment of all was still to come. On September 8 armistice negotiations with Italy were finally concluded; and late that evening the Italian fleet set course for Malta. They were coming to the island to surrender.

The main body of the fleet—three battleships, six cruisers, and thirteen destroyers—left Spezia according to instructions; but en route for Malta they were tricked by the Germans into altering course toward the Sardinian shore. Here they were attacked by a formation of Junkers with radio-controlled glider bombs. Their flagship, the *Roma*, was sunk, and several other vessels were damaged. The remainder, however, made good their escape. Next morning they were joined by other units from Taranto and Naples, and by dawn on September 10 the combined fleet was within sight of Malta. They were met at the approaches to Grand Harbour by the *Warspite*, the *Valiant*, and a screen of destroyers; and soon the *Warspite*, watched by General Eisenhower and Admiral Cunningham, was leading her erstwhile adversaries into captivity. It was, especially for Admiral Cunningham, a moving moment. That afternoon he broadcast the following signal to his command.

I have today informed the Board of Admiralty that the Italian fleet now lies at anchor under the guns of the fortress of Malta. So ends a chapter in the war. For just over three years the Royal and Merchant Navies, in close contact with their sister Services, have fought the Battle of the Mediterranean, so that our object has now been achieved and the Mediterranean is once more fully under our control. The way has been long. We have had our great moments and our bad times, when the horizon looked black. During this time, except for a short break, it has been my privilege and my pride to command the main forces at sea in the Mediterranean. At this moment, when all for which we have worked has at length come to pass, I send to every officer and man of the Royal and Merchant Navies who has contributed to this achievement my thanks and admiration for the resource and resolution and courage which have made these things possible.

It was fitting that this message should have been sent from Malta, from the very heart of the Mediterranean: from the tiny but vitally important island for the sake of whose survival such stirring battles had, in the last three years, been fought on land, by sea, and in the air.

The story of the defense of Malta is a proud one. It is a story of courage and of fortitude and, above all else, of partnership: of working together in a common cause. For the efforts of Malta's defenders were, to an unusual degree, complementary; and the island might be likened to a precious jewel held firm by three clasps: Navy, Air Force, and civilians. If any one of these clasps had given way, the others would have been powerless to hold the jewel, and Malta would have fallen. It is to the undying credit of all concerned that each of the clasps, though battered almost beyond endurance, held.

In one respect the civilians—the Maltese themselves—played the noblest role. For they were a people, if not unwarlike, then at heart unaccustomed to war—not for one hundred and fifty years had they heard a shot fired in anger. Yet when they found themselves pitchforked overnight into the front line of a struggle whose origins they couldn't even guess at, they accepted the struggle as their own. And when things got bad, they didn't give up. They kept faith. They kept faith not for a few days or weeks or months, but for over two years. In those two years there was terror and death, near starvation, unparalleled destruction, and unspeakable weariness; there was disease and all the cumulative effects of undernourishment. But the Maltese stood up to them all; until, in the end, they had their reward and could listen to the thunder of bombers and know that overhead were not Savoias and Junkers, but Wellingtons, Mosquitoes, and Beaufighters, carrying the vengeance which their own fortitude had made possible, to the "soft shores of the Axis underbelly."

The role of the Royal Air Force was equally proud. From insignificant beginnings (four borrowed and obsolete planes) they built up an impregnable air base, defended by over two hundred fast modern fighters and with a striking potential of some three hundred bombers. In two years of bitter air fighting against fantastic odds they had accounted for 1378 enemy planes and more than 80 enemy supply ships. By the winter of 1942, Luqa, Takali, and Hal Far were crowded with planes and operating at peak efficiency. It was a far cry from the days of *Faith, Hope,* and *Charity*.

Last but not least was the Navy, without whose efforts Malta would have been starved and pounded to surrender within a matter of weeks. One day some naval historian may attempt a detailed analysis of the strategic and tactical lessons to be learned from the success or otherwise of the various convoys to Malta. Such an analysis is beyond the scope of this book, but certain conclusions of general interest can be drawn.

In the first place, the fact that Malta was able to survive at all is evidence of the resilience of sea power in the face of apparently overwhelming difficulties. For it is hard to imagine a more hazardous task than the continual reprovisioning of an island which is hemmed in by narrow approaches and dominated by enemy aircraft operating within easy range of their bases. Yet somehow—by subterfuge or deception, by skill or courage or sacrifice—the supplies were somehow brought through. Those who doubt the effective value of sea power under modern conditions should consider the implications of Malta's survival.

In the second place, the convoys demonstrated the vital importance of the Navy's Air Arm and in particular of the armor-decked aircraft carrier. A convoy might not seem the most effective form of operation in which a carrier could operate; but the fact remains that whenever the *Illustrious* or the *Indomitable* escorted the merchantmen to Malta the convoy invariably got through with trifling losses, while when no armor-decked carrier was available the merchantmen either failed entirely or suffered heavy losses. The Air Arm may often have lacked modern planes, but through the skill and devotion to duty of their pilots they never failed to provide the merchantmen with adequate protection.

A third point to be proved was the importance of a flexible and on-the-spot system of command. Certain Russian and Malta convoys both demonstrated with tragic clarity the evil that can spring from an operation being conducted by remote control; by a Commander in Chief maneuvering his ships from some headquarters in London or Alexandria which is far removed from the actual scene of operations. As the tempo of war increases, so the need for quick and on-the-spot decisions increases also. This is generally recognized now; and it seems likely that P.Q.17 and Operation "Vigorous" were the last convoys to suffer from the old-fashioned system of remote and inflexible control.

The final point proved by the Malta convoys is one so obvious that it is sometimes overlooked: the remarkably high standard of seamanship of the men of the Royal and Merchant Navies. This is something it is all too easy to take for granted. Good seamanship, however, is not a quality that is acquired easily or overnight; it is acquired only by years of hard work and by a continual adherence to the very highest of standards—standards which, in the case of both Royal and Merchant Navies, have become both a heritage and a tradition.

The Malta convoys, indeed, could not have been fought through by any other navy. The Royal and Merchant Navies alone possessed the resources, both physical and spiritual, to endure so much, so frequently, and for so long; and the annals of British achievement at sea can boast of nothing finer than the story of the men who sailed on the many and hazardous convoys which brought Malta her vitally needed supplies.

APPENDIX

A chronological table of the principal convoys to Malta, their composition, losses, and the cargoes they landed, from July 1940 to December 1942

Date	Code name	Composition	Losses	Cargoes landed
August 1940	Hats*	4 merchantmen 4 destroyers: close escort 3 battleships: distant escort 1 aircraft carrier 4 cruisers 13 destroyers	1 merchantman damaged	Approx. 40,000 tons
November 1940	Collar	3 merchantmen 1 battle cruiser 4 cruisers 10 destroyers 4 corvettes	Nil	Approx. 20,000 tons
January 1941	Excess†	3 merchantmen‡ 3 battleships 1 aircraft carrier 9 cruisers 23 destroyers	1 cruiser sunk 1 aircraft carrier severely damaged 1 cruiser damaged 1 destroyer damaged	Approx. 10,000 tons

*This operation included the reinforcing of the Mediterranean Fleet.
†Included in this operation was the passage of a convoy to the Piraeus.
‡Two bound for Malta, one through to Alexandria.

Date	Code Name	Composition	Losses	Cargoes landed
March 1941	M.C.9	4 merchantmen 3 battleships 1 aircraft carrier 6 cruisers 13 destroyers	2 merchantmen damaged (in harbor) 1 cruiser damaged (in harbor)	Approx. 45,000 tons
July 1941	Substance	6 merchantmen 1 battleship 1 battle cruiser 1 aircraft carrier 4 cruisers 1 mine layer 17 destroyers	1 merchantman damaged 1 cruiser damaged 1 destroyer sunk 1 destroyer damaged	Approx. 65,000 tons
September 1941	Halberd	9 merchantmen 3 battleships 1 aircraft carrier 5 cruisers 18 destroyers	1 merchantman sunk 1 battleship damaged	Approx. 85,000 tons
March 1942	M.G.1	4 merchantmen 5 cruisers 17 destroyers	1 merchantman sunk 1 merchantman beached and capsized 2 merchantmen sunk in harbor 1 destroyer sunk 2 destroyers damaged	Less than 1,000 tons

Date	Code Name	Composition	Losses	Cargoes landed
June 1942	Harpoon	6 merchantmen 1 battleship 2 aircraft carriers 4 cruisers 1 mine layer 17 destroyers 4 mine sweepers	4 merchantmen sunk 1 merchantman damaged 2 cruisers damaged 1 destroyer sunk 1 destoyer damaged	Approx. 25,000 tons
June 1942	Vigorous	11 merchantmen 1 special-service vessel (*Centurion*) 8 cruisers 26 destroyers 4 corvettes 2 mine sweepers 2 reserve ships 4 motor torpedo boats	2 merchantmen sunk 2 merchantmen damaged; remainder of merchantmen turned back 3 cruisers damaged 3 destroyers sunk 2 corvettes damaged 1 torpedo boat sunk	Nil
August 1942	Pedestal	14 merchantmen 2 battleships 4 aircraft carriers 7 cruisers 33 destroyers 2 tugs 4 corvettes	9 merchantmen sunk 3 merchantmen damaged 1 aircraft carrier sunk 1 aircraft carrier damaged 2 cruisers sunk 1 cruiser damaged 1 destroyer sunk	Approx 55,000 tons

Date	Code Name	Composition	Losses	Cargoes landed
		4 mine sweepers§ 7 motor launches§	4 destroyers damaged	
November 1942	Stonehenge	4 merchantmen 5 cruisers 17 destroyers	1 cruiser damaged	Approx. 35,000 tons
December 1942	Portcullis	5 merchantmen 1 cruiser 1 mine layer 14 destroyers	Nil	Approx. 55,000 tons
December 1942	(Quadrangle A) (Quadrangle B)	14 merchantmen light (destroyer) escort only	Nil	Approx. 12,000 tons

§From Malta.